Jennifer, Where Are You?

Jennifer, Where Are You?

Katherine Ann Longo

iUniverse, Inc.
Bloomington

Jennifer, Where Are You?

iUniverse books may be ordered through booksellers or by contacting:

iUniverse
1663 Liberty Drive
Bloomington, IN 47403
www.iuniverse.com
1-800-Authors (1-800-288-4677)

ISBN: 978-1-4620-2842-9 (sc)
ISBN: 978-1-4620-2844-3 (hc)
ISBN: 978-1-4620-2843-6 (ebk)

Printed in the United States of America

iUniverse rev. date:08/19/2011

ABOUT THE AUTHOR

Kathy Longo tells her story as no one else can. It's riveting, compelling and it's a true life story of her struggle in the search for her missing daughter, Jennifer Marteliz. She is a mother who has continued her search for twenty eight years after Jennifer was abducted. Kathy bares her soul to the reader.

Kathy has appeared on numerous national and local talk shows and newscasts.

Kathy was born and raised in Tampa, Florida where she still resides with her daughter, Toni Lisa, and four grand-children.

To Jennifer
and the memories
of the short seven years we loved,
laughed, and cried together.

With an enduring hope that
by some miracle of God, Jennifer
reads this written portrait
of her life with me,
and finds her way home.

ACKNOWLEDGMENTS

The greatest gift through this tragedy has been the unending support of my family. I thank God that we have maintained the closeness and love our parents bestowed on us. Dad was my hero. He inspired independence and taught dignity. Mom was my shelter in the rain, my island in the sunshine during a very dark period, and my best friend.

To Laurie: What would I have done without you? You made my story shine. Your patience with me can't be measured except to say it was a true labor of love and compassion that you showed me. Thank you for the countless hours of hard work to make my dream of telling Jennifer's story a reality. I am so blessed you are in my life.

Toni Lisa, thank you for supporting me while I searched for your sister. I know your childhood wasn't what anyone would wish for, but you have been the most loving daughter a mother could ask for. I cherish you more than you will ever know.

Nancy, my only sister, thank you for all the time, energy and giving part of your life to help me find Jennifer. I love you and appreciate everything you do to help me and our family.

My brother, Frank and his wife, Julie: Thank you for all your support yesterday and today. When Jennifer disappeared you were both right by my side no matter what. I don't know what I would have done without you two.

My youngest brother, George: You were too young when our parents died. My heart is heavy that they have not known you as the admirable and wonderful husband, father and brother that you are today.

"Nelson, Mom would have been so proud of you. Thanks for being you."

Sherry, you are more than a cousin to me. Thank you for always being my sounding board and for always being so supportive now and when Jennifer disappeared.

Anthony, Alexis, Danny Boy and Dyneka; you four have given me so much love and joy, I couldn't have personally chosen better grandchildren. You keep me young at heart, I love you.

Aaron: Thank you for all the undying support and a shoulder to cry on as I relived every moment while writing Jennifer's story. My life has been enriched since you came into it.

To Bruce: Thank you for being you and for all you do for me and your family. You are a true gem.

To my extended family and friends – thank you and you know I love you too.

Last but not least to the Tampa Bay area residents, you're the best. I firmly believe that without you I would never have made it during our search for Jennifer. Your dedication in helping when I needed you the most has endeared you all to me. I give you each a big hug.

They said time heals all wounds,
I do not agree, the wounds remain,
in time,
Your mind protecting your sanity,
covers them up with scar tissue,
and the pain lessens,
but it's never gone.

ROSE KENNEDY

CONTENTS

PREFACE

After paying the locksmith with shaking hands, I pushed on the newly installed door handle, slowly shutting it, and turning the lock. After enduring a year of abuse, I was determined to be strong, today would be different . . . I had a plan.

I listened by the door as his car pulled in the driveway. The engine went silent; the car door slammed and with each step he took, in those steel toed boots, brought him closer to the front door.

Barely breathing, I leaned against the door as if my body weight would strengthen it. Too scared to move, I felt the tears squeezing from between closed eyelids. I kept telling myself, "follow the plan—keep the door locked and don't let him in!"

I could hear him trying to open the door with his key. In frustration he started hammering on the door, demanding I open it. I yelled at him:

"Go away, Carlos leave us alone!"

I felt the door give a little as he leaned his weight into it with his entire body. By the sound of his muffled words, I could tell his lips were pressed against the door as he growled.

"Kathy, let me in . . . NOW!"
I tried to breathe normally. I needed to concentrate, find a way out of this nightmare. I could hear him shouting my name. Fear

took over. Tears were familiar for me, but these tears were caused by growing hysterics. Carlos began pounding on the door demanding:

"Kathy, what's going on?"

Then it was absolutely still, I couldn't even hear him breathing. He changed his tactics, trying to fool me by acting nice, but I could hear the anger in every word he spoke.

"Kathy, please let me in."

I could see no option. My hands were still shaking even worse than before as I grabbed the doorknob. It twisted and I let the door fall open. I took a step back, my whole body froze I knew it was mistake! All hell broke loose.

CHAPTER ONE—THE BOMB

When I met Carlos in the spring of 1968, I was thirteen years old. Carlos was a seventeen-year-old James Dean wanna be, not in looks, but attitude. You know the cocky kind, with a chip on his shoulder, just waiting for someone to knock it off. To a thirteen-year-old girl with the same attitude, he was the catch of the season. Even if he wasn't very good looking, he had a car! He treated me like a princess, my own Prince Charming.

I felt like a big shot when Carlos picked me up from school in his car, buying me presents and telling me how pretty I was. My Mother, Frances, was extremely unhappy about me dating Carlos, which, of course, made me want to date him even more. After three years, I became pregnant. At 16, I thought I was old enough, I could handle anything, including raising a child. I knew I had to tell my parents, but I was scared to death. Carlos wanted us to run away and get married. We even started looking at places out of town. But the thought of never seeing my Mother and Father again changed my mind. To this day, I'm still not sure what I was more afraid of, my parents killing me or the news killing my parents.

I walked into my Mother's bedroom; she was in her closet hanging up clothes.

This is a bad idea . . . I'm so dead; she is so going to kill me . . . . Maybe I should just make a run for it . . .

My thoughts ran a race with the beating of my heart. I held my breath, trying to figure out what to say, when Mom looked at me with those piercing eyes. For a second, I felt certain she already knew my secret.

"Kathy is everything Okay?"

I blurted out my guilty secret before I even thought.

"Mom, I'm pregnant!"

Oh my God, did I just say that?

Her eyes rolled up into her head and she fell flat on the floor! I started screaming. I knew for sure she was having a heart attack.

"I killed Mom!"

I ran to my mom, in a total panic saying:

"Mom, please Mom, please don't die!"

I screamed at the top of my lungs, demanding that someone call for help, not knowing Mom and I were alone in the house. At that moment, I realized how much I loved my mother. All I cared about was that Mom was okay. She opened her eyes, her face was very pale, but she looked like she was okay! I helped her up, and we sat on the bed. Looking at me with very sad eyes, she grabbed me and hugged me. She kept saying:

"My poor baby, my poor baby"

Mom and Dad

Let me tell you a little about my mother. She was a beautiful women and I am not just saying that because she was my mother. Wherever Mom went, men would always do a double take. Her long jet-black hair hung below her shoulders. Mom could have been a model if only she had been taller than 4'11". Her personality lit up any room she entered, with her bright smile and caring attitude toward everyone. She was well known, loved and respected. Mom felt each and every person was special and deserved respect. She especially loved children, and was more than willing to organize benefits that would raise money for their needs.

Mom volunteered a lot at the school, and I believe she did that so she could be close to us. Now I am not saying she did not yell or spank us because she did. But if someone were to hurt us, watch out! She would be right there to protect us, whether we were right or wrong. If we were wrong though, we had better watch out when we got home.

These qualities didn't even include her fabulous parties. I can see her now dancing and singing, making so many people laugh and just having a good time. I was very proud to say she was my Mom.

Now I had let her down, but she wasn't yelling at me, she just hugged me and rocked me in her arms saying:

"Everything will be okay my baby, don't you worry! I need to call your Dad though, okay?"

Her voice was soft as she talked to me. I knew my Dad would not be mad, probably hurt, but not mad. He was always so calm and easy going and I was his precious little princess. I could hear Mom's voice as she called him at work.

"Tony, I need you to come home. It's very important. No, I need you here now!"

I could tell by the way she spoke, he would be right home. It felt like my mother had just gotten off the phone when Dad walked through the front door. The sound of his boots walking through the kitchen drew me into a state of fear, much like a horror movie. The sounds were getting closer and closer. I kept telling myself to calm down, everything would be okay, but my heart was racing. Dad started calling: "Franny, where are you?"

As Dad walked into the room, I glanced up to see his face. I felt so ashamed; it was hard for me to look at him!

Now you need to understand a little about the reputation I had at school. It seemed as though I was constantly getting into trouble. Once I caught a couple lizards before going into class. I let them bite into my earlobes and wore them into class like earrings. Of course, they eventually got tired and dropped off. The other girls (not me) disrupted class, screaming and climbing on top of their desks, just because those lizards were running around on the floor. Basically, Mom made a trip each week, to the principal's office regarding my bad behavior. I was the black sheep of my siblings, always in trouble at school, which was probably Dad's first thought upon getting Mom's call. She had tears pouring down her face as she ran over to him, hugging him around his waist. Her words rang out,

"Tony, Kathy is pregnant." Let me tell you, there wasn't a hole deep enough to swallow me at that moment! My eyes never left the floor as he walked over to me, keeping an arm around Mom at the same time. Not really knowing what would come next, yet never in a lifetime would I have expected to see the tears silently streaking down his cheeks. He folded me into his strong arms, between Mom and him, hugging both of us. In a sad, yet strong voice he said:

"It will be okay Princess; I will make arrangements for an abortion."

The hole that wasn't deep enough to swallow me wasn't deep enough to hold me either. I stepped away from them and put my hands over my abdomen in a protective manner. I could hear my own shocked voice saying through the tears running down my face:

"NO! Dad, I am going to get married and have my baby!"

Mom blurted out: "But you are only sixteen years old."

Putting his arm back around me, Dad gently led Mom and me into the living room, motioning for us all to have a seat. He tried to explain:

"Honey, you are too young, you have only just finished the ninth grade. We can't let this happen to you. You have your whole life ahead of you! Kathy, please just think it over, we can discuss this again in the morning, after you have had a chance to think this through."

Looking at their tear streaked, pale faces, I told him:

"Okay!"

But I already knew what my answer would be in the morning. I felt as though a weight had been lifted from my shoulders and asked them if I could call Carlos. My mind was on the discussion I was planning to have with him, not the turmoil I had created for them. After a rather tense evening meal, we were all excused from the table earlier than normal. Mom and Dad retreated to their bedroom.

I shared a bedroom with my sister Nancy. We would spend hours talking about our day each night before sleeping. This night was no different. As we were getting ready for bed, she wanted to know what was going on. Had I done something at school to upset Mom and Dad? Relieved I could finally share my secret, I pulled her down to sit on the bed. As I sat there explaining everything to her, I felt a sense of dread sitting on my shoulders again. I thought about never sleeping in my bed, or having Nancy to talk to each night. Not to be able to roughhouse with my brothers. The emotions of the entire day just flooded in, overwhelming me. They paraded through my brain; fear, despair, pain, sorrow, relief, excitement, and loss. I began shaking, the tears rolling down my face. Nancy put her arms around me, and hugged me tight.

"I will always be here for you Kathy. We will always be best friends; we have each other no matter what happens."

Slowly her words sank in, and I hugged her back.

"Thank you. I love you Nancy, I couldn't have asked for a better sister."

We were in the room together for several hours discussing everything: baby names, if giving birth would hurt; anything we could think of that had to do with babies. We were finally talked out, on the verge of sleep when Dad walked into our room. His eyes were red from crying. Nancy pretended she was asleep, but I knew she wasn't, not yet anyway. Dad walked over to the rocking chair he and Mom used when reading us bedtime stories years ago. Picking it up, he moved it in front of my bed facing towards my pillow. I watched wide-eyed, finally asking:

"What are you doing Dad?"

I could tell by the sound of his voice, he was still extremely emotional, but he stood tall. He was my hero no matter what was thrown at him. We could always lean on him for strength. Slowly he sat down and said:

"I am going to stay here until you wake up and give me your decision. I love you Kathy, and your Mother and I will be beside you. Whatever, you decide to do!"

His voice was shaking as he spoke. I didn't want to hurt my parents any more than I already had, but I wanted this baby, I loved this baby, I NEEDED this baby. I couldn't explain it! I just thanked him, jumping out of bed to give him a big hug and kiss. I felt so loved, so lucky to have such a great Dad. I fell asleep that night as the silent tears streamed down my face.

I crawled out of bed the next morning and saw Dad still sitting in that chair. His face was wet from the tears he couldn't seem to stop. Before I was all the way out of bed, he said:

"I—I'm so sorry Kathy, I just can't leave until I hear your answer."

He was watching me with knowing eyes. He already knew what I was going to say before I even said it. In a reasoning voice, I said:

"Dad, can you understand how I feel? I don't want to hurt you or Mom, but Carlos loves me. I want us to become a family like you and Mom."

Dad stood up, cupping his hands around my intent face saying:

"You are my little Princess, Kathy. Your Mother and I love you very much. I can't say I agree with your decision, but we will honor it!"

I hugged him as relief washed over me! I said:

"Please Dad, don't worry about me, I will be fine."

After hugging me back tightly for a minute, he left the room.

Believing I was doing the right thing gave me the strength I needed to fight for my baby. I already decided I was old enough. I was ready to get married, and take care of my baby. Suddenly I realized I was going to be late for school. After frantically dressing, I drove to school. Even after talking to Carlos on the phone, I had to make sure everything I had told my parents was what he also wanted. Carlos was waiting for me at school, running up to my car as I parked. He didn't even wait for me to get out of the car before poking his head in my window, kissing me hard. Breathlessly, I began telling him what . . . but he stopped me by pressing one finger to my lips saying:

"Let's talk later; you are going to be late for class."

Getting through classes that day was a real chore. All I could think about was my parents, Carlos and the baby I was carrying. When the final school bell rang, I ran out to my car where Carlos was waiting for me. He grabbed me around the waist, swinging us in a small circle.

"How's my girl?"

After a small hesitation, I replied:

"Carlos, I told my parents everything, they are okay with us getting married; if that is what you really want?"

He slowly set me back on my feet while smiling the entire time.

"I love you Kathy, I promise we will have a great life together".

CHAPTER TWO—WHITE PICKET FENCE

September 27, 1970. My name changed that day. Kathy Marteliz, no Mrs. Kathy Marteliz. WOW! A roller coaster of thoughts zoomed through my mind as I lay there looking at everything around me. I thought of all I would miss after I moved out. My emotions were riding that roller coaster; and they changed from the happiness I first felt upon waking to a profound sadness. Excitement replaced that sadness, as I visualized owning my own home, with a white picket fence. A beautiful baby cradled in my arms as I sat swinging on the front porch. No matter, boy or girl, I would name the baby after Dad, showing him how much I loved and respected him. I wanted the type of marriage and family life my parents' lived. My emotions were high and I didn't know how to turn them off. Anxiety crept back in, fear of what the future would hold. I shook my head as I jumped out of bed; today was going to be a very long day. We had a small wedding planned, just the family!

I dressed in a rush when I heard a lot of noise coming from Mom's kitchen. I hurried to open my door only to find Mom standing there.

"Kathy, close your eyes."

She covered my eyes with her hand, and then helped me walk into the family room. As she took her hands away from my eyes everyone greeted me with a loud chorus of

"SURPRISE!"

As I looked with amazement the ceiling was covered in white and pink balloons. Dozens of crystal bowls filled with hundreds of white roses. The tables were draped with white lace tablecloths and pink candles everywhere. On one of the tables was a wedding cake with roses all around it and mom's good china plates. It was a hundred times more beautiful than I could have imagined. They had done all of this for me. Tears of excitement and love cascaded down my face; I just couldn't believe my parents did this for me! Handing me some tissue from her own pocket, Mom said:

"Okay, Kathy, you're going to make your face blotchy. I want you to go back to your room and get ready. Your dad and I will be taking you to the church for your ceremony shortly."

I had already seen Mom's red eyes and knew the tissue had been hers. She looked tired and had been crying.

"Mom, can I talk to you for a second?"

She guided me back toward my room away from everyone, saying:

"Sure, what is it honey?"

I turned and gave her a big hug, telling her:

"Thank you for everything you have done for me Mom. I know this has to be hard for you and Dad. I love you both so much and I won't ever forget all you have done."

Mom didn't say anything, just hugged me back that much tighter. Suddenly, she let me go, giving me a little shove in the direction of my room.

"It's hard letting go Kathy, but I will work on it. I love you too."

Shadows filled the chapel. The only light came from the flickering candles in the windows. Carlos stood there by the sculpture of the Blessed Mother. Mom and Dad were seated in the front pew. It could never be fixed, never. I can't undo what I had done and I just hoped they would forgive me in time. I walked down that lonely aisle, but as I walked, hope that something good would come of all this pain gave me strength. As I stood at the altar Carlos looked at me with such warmth and caring in his eyes, smiling from ear to ear. He whispered to me how much he loved me, but all I could hear was the crying behind me.

Shockingly, at that very moment of sadness, the baby moved. I felt the baby move! Wonder filled my mind. God let me know then and there that I was doing the right thing. Mom and Dad I hope one day you can forgive me!

After the wedding, my parents offered for us to stay with them until we found a place of our own. I was very happy about their offer; on one hand, I couldn't wait to get married and be on my own, yet now that it was a reality, I didn't want to leave my safe haven. I wanted to stay with my parents.

Carlos was working full time in construction, with his family, making ten dollars an hour. He didn't like living at my parent's home and forced me into looking for a home of our own. We eventually found a new government unit. The home wasn't ready to move into yet, so Carlos agreed we could stay with my parents' until the baby was born.

CHAPTER THREE—NEW LIFE

Toni Lisa Marteliz was born January 21, 1971. When I woke from the anesthesia, my heart stopped beating for a second, then began racing. I heard my baby's strong little voice for the first time! My Doctor leaned down to tell me:

"Kathy, it's a beautiful baby girl."

Excitement made me speechless. My thoughts raced into the future; we were going to do everything together. I would never let her out of my sight! All the pain I had felt disappeared when I heard her cry. It became apparent as that little cry developed into a full-blown wail; she had a strong opinion regarding her own self-defense. I could hardly wait to hold her. When the nurse brought her to me, I just couldn't stop looking at her. I loved every inch of her tiny little body. I very carefully touched her and she felt so soft. Her coloring was such a pretty pink. She had big black eyes and so much hair. There were little curls all around her face. I just couldn't believe she was mine. She was just so beautiful! Suddenly a smile broke over her tiny face, just for me. She was God's personal gift to me. How could I possibly love anyone more than I loved her?

Carlos never moved a muscle, just stood there with this funny smirk on his face, never taking his eyes off the baby. "Carlos, I want to name her after my Dad, it's important to me."

He began shaking his head back and forth.

"Kathy, the baby's name is going to be Lisa."

The nurses had finished. The room was ready for visitors, but the only ones I wanted to see were Mom and Dad. As they both walked into the room, they each carefully leaned over to kiss me. They saw the baby bundled up in my arms. Mom just started to cry with joy, and Dad ran a finger down the side of her tiny face in awe. Their happiness at seeing their new granddaughter pushed the sadness away. I decided then and there what my baby's name would be and I said:

"Mom, Dad, meet Toni Lisa, named after my hero—Dad!"

I had made up my mind. I didn't even bother looking at Carlos after making that little announcement. Never had I seen a bigger smile on Dad's face.

"Toni Lisa. Wow Kathy, what a beautiful name!"

Mom stood there, hugging Dad's arm, smiling through her tears. Finally, Mom said:

"She is my favorite grandbaby!"

Laughing, I said:

"Mom, Toni Lisa is your only grandbaby."

We all laughed. Suddenly there was a nurse standing in the doorway.

"Young lady, you have about fifty people out here waiting to see you and your daughter!"

My sister was so cute, she hid in the closet until everyone left, just to stay and help me.

I stayed in the hospital for a week due to health complications (the Doctors said it was because I was so young), and then it was time to go home. Toni Lisa was dressed in a beautiful pink and purple outfit. I was so proud I was her mother; love for her made my heart dance!

I won't lie. I remember feeling nervous, having to be responsible for this little person. I wanted everything to be perfect for her. She was my little girl, my princess, she was everything to me. I walked through the hospital doors and down the hall where I could see my Mother's beautiful smile; I reached for her, and hugged her. I know now how much she loved me, having Toni Lisa made me understand that feeling. I didn't have to say anything to her: I loved her and I know today that she did everything she did because of her love for me. She was my Mother, yes, but she was also my best friend! For a moment, neither of us said anything. Then she told me:

"Honey, I moved all your clothes, and everything is ready for you in your new home."

I could hear the sadness she felt in her voice. She did not want me to leave, we had become very close. Her daughter was a new wife and Mother at 16 and she was reluctant to let me go. Her eyes filled with tears and it ended up with us both crying.

"Please, mom, I promise I will be there to see you every day, please do not cry."

"I am sorry, you are my baby and sometimes it is hard to let go. However, I am proud of you. You are a mother and I know you will cherish your baby girl. I love you."

"I love you too Mom and will miss you very much."

CHAPTER FOUR–EXPECTATIONS

When we arrived at our new home, it was like a fairy tale. I just sat in the car for a moment looking and imagining what a great life I was going to have. The furniture Carlos and I picked out was contemporary, but Mom had my old piano delivered and set up. Everything was perfect. Toni Lisa's room looked like a room for a princess; painted all pink and purple, with butterflies hanging from the ceiling.

After Mom left, I laid Toni Lisa in her brand new bed and just walked around looking at everything. I walked outside, then walked back in and very nicely sat down on my new couch. Then I laid on it. Before I could help myself, I started jumping on the couch. Adult, what adult?

Wow, this was all mine. I walked into the kitchen; all the dishes I had gotten for wedding presents were already put away in the cabinets. I was very excited; I wished Carlos were here to see this with me. I know! I would make tonight a romantic evening. In a rush, I hurried to get out our good dishes, so I could set the table. I wanted Carlos to feel as excited as I did about our new home and life. Not really knowing how to cook was a bit of a disappointment, but I pulled out two frozen dinners, and the table was gorgeous. Our new dishes and silverware sparkled in the candlelight. I folded the cloth napkins perfect, just like Mom had taught me. I was excited, anticipating Carlos' pleasure when he came home and saw how everything was so beautiful! It was almost five, I hurried to freshen up my makeup and got Toni Lisa dressed in one of her new outfits. As five o'clock hit, I was out of breath, but everything was done. Five came and went, six dragged by, still no Carlos. This was not the way I had imagined our first night. I sat there by that window, holding Toni Lisa, still dressed in her beautiful outfit, looking out each time I heard a car. I thought he must have forgotten and went to my parents' house. Then around seven, he pulled into the driveway. He walked into the house as if it was the same thing he did every day. Carlos had a beer in his hand.

What was his problem? This is what he wanted, us away from my parents, he should have been happy!

Not speaking, he hurried past me to the bathroom and started throwing up. No one in my family drank, so this was all new to me. Carlos never even spoke to me that evening! In fact, he never left the bathroom that night; he fell asleep on the floor. As I blew out the candles and prepared for bed, my dreams for our new life were tarnished. Not enough to burst the bubble, not yet anyway.

Three months passed and things did not get any better. I felt like I was trapped in a nightmare, and I wasn't ever going to wake up. Finally, I decided we were going to talk it out and I promised myself I wouldn't accept any excuses. I had to do something. I waited there in the doorway for him to come home and it wasn't long before he drove into the driveway, drunk as usual. He pushed past me but I followed right behind him, trying to maintain control over my anger. I wasn't very successful because I demanded:

"Carlos, what is wrong? Why are you drinking all the time? Did I do something wrong? We have everything we could ask for! Just tell me if I have done something wrong."

His silence was unbearable. I had hoped he would tell me what was bothering him. I felt if we talked about it, we could fix it so everything would be okay. I just wanted the nightmare to be over, but he refused to say anything and ignored me. I pushed a little more when I said:

"Okay Carlos, if you continue coming home drunk like this, I'm going to move back to my parents'."

His dark green eyes glared out at me in a sinister way, as though he wanted to kill me. I had never seen this side of him and it scared me. He was quiet for a long moment, and then this dark deep voice says to me:

"I am tired of being harassed at work. They say I am a Longo. I should have changed my name, not yours. They continually ask me, 'Who wears the pants in your family anyway?' I am tired of it! I didn't want to get married or have a kid this young. You forced me into this marriage!"

I listened, speechless. I knew he was waiting for my reaction, but I was so hurt I couldn't speak. Tears welled up and as I reached up to wipe them away, I told him that it was the beer talking, not him. I felt a crushing blow to my face, my head jerked to the side. Then as if someone switched my life to slow motion, I felt myself falling to the floor as the blood gushed out over my lips.

Hate and anger coursed through my mind. I had always been considered tough in school, and I had been in my share of fights. He was not going to hit me! How dare he hit me! I lunged up from the floor and I got right back in his face screaming:

"How dare you!"

I was no match for Carlos, and he let me know it. I felt myself flying backwards, hitting the kitchen table, crumbling onto the floor. I mumbled around a mouthful of blood and shook my head in disbelief as I scrambled on my hands and knees to Toni Lisa's basinet. I used the table next to her to pull myself off the floor, grabbed her, my keys, and fled out the door like the young scared girl I was. I remember how difficult it was to focus as I drove through those dark, lonely streets; I sobbed so hard, not knowing what to do or where to go. I didn't want to go to my parents' house, they would go crazy if they saw the blood on both Toni Lisa and I.

I wrestled with the despair that tried to overwhelm me. Not wanting to think about what had happened, or what he had said to me. Somehow, this was my fault and I needed to fix it without involving Mom and Dad. I wanted my marriage to work; I didn't want to be a failure. I realized, as I crossed another road, that I was headed back home. Toni Lisa was crying so I stopped the car to comfort her. She actually comforted me; and while I sat there holding her tight, my thoughts turned in Carlos' direction. If he ever hurt Toni Lisa, I would kill him! After a while Toni Lisa and I had both calmed down. I got back behind the wheel, but was still not sure where I was headed. I tried to reason through all the events. I succeeded in convincing myself all that had happened wasn't Carlos' fault, it was the beer. Carlos loved me; he would not have hurt me if he hadn't been drinking. How could he possibly not want our perfect little girl?

I stood at the front door, not remembering getting out of the car. I placed my hand on the doorknob with hesitation. Before I could make a decision, Carlos opened the door! He asked softly:

"Please forgive me! Are you alright?"

He reached out slowly and touched the bruised and swollen cut on my lip. I couldn't help myself I flinched back, hugging Toni Lisa a little tighter. He waited but I couldn't speak. This wasn't the same man I had run from two hours earlier. Finally, he said:

"Please don't be afraid of me Kathy, I love you and Toni Lisa more than anything else in this world. I don't know what happened to me."

His eyes were red and watery. They met mine across the doorstep, begging me to forgive him.

"Kathy, I couldn't live my life without you."

Not yet sure of anything, I asked:

"But Carlos, why did you hit me."

He looked down ashamed. He walked over to his recliner where he sat down and started to cry. He looked up with tears streaming down his cheeks and said he was so sorry, that he loved me and would never lose his temper again. Still standing outside our front door I demanded:

"Swear it Carlos, swear it!"

Carlos swore to never hit me again. A slow smile drove away my fears. I love him and I know he loves me, he just had to stop drinking. I felt it was going to be ok, we could work it out!

CHAPTER FIVE—BURSTING BUBBLE

Two weeks was all it lasted before Carlos was back to his old routine. Why had this happened? Was God mad at me? What had I done wrong? I tried very hard to have everything perfect when he got home, but Carlos was an over-achiever when it came to finding fault with me. In fact, at that time in my life, he easily made me believe our problems were my fault.

The only good thing I can say about our family relationship was Carlos never became abusive to Toni Lisa. I think he knew that would push me over the edge. Being strong for Toni Lisa was easy; but when it came to me, there wasn't any strength left. My self-worth, well I didn't have any. I was not able to be strong for myself.

Toni Lisa and I made daily visits to my parents' home, but I never said anything to them. I did not want to burden them with my problems. I felt I had caused them enough grief. I needed to stand on my own two feet and handle this myself. Truth is, I was scared of Carlos and he had broken my spirit. It wasn't just the physical abuse; it was also the daily verbal and mental abuse. I knew it was getting worse. I was going to have to do something but just didn't know what. It didn't seem like my prayers were being answered, my hope was gone and my will was broken. I was just a shell of the girl I had been just a short year ago. After paying the locksmith with shaking hands, I pushed on the newly installed door handle, slowly shutting it, and turning the lock. After enduring a year of abuse, I was determined to be strong, today would be different . . . I had a plan.

I listened at the door as his car pulled in the driveway. The engine went silent; the car door slammed and with each step he took, in those steel toed boots, brought him closer to the front door.

Barely breathing, I leaned against the door as if my body weight would strengthen it. Too scared to move, I felt the tears squeezing from between closed eyelids. I kept telling myself, "follow the plan—keep the door locked and don't let him in!"
I could hear him trying to open the door with his key. In frustration he started hammering on the door, demanding I open it. I yelled at him:

"Go away, Carlos leave us alone!"

I felt the door give a little as he leaned his weight into it with his entire body. By the sound of his muffled words, I could tell his lips were pressed against the door as he growled.

"Kathy, let me in . . . NOW!"

I tried to breathe normally. I needed to concentrate, find a way out of this nightmare. I could hear him shouting my name. Fear took over. Tears were familiar for me, but these tears were caused by growing hysterics. Carlos began pounding on the door demanding:

"Kathy, what's going on?"

Then it was absolutely still, I couldn't even hear him breathing. He changed his tactics, trying to fool me by acting nice, but I could hear the anger in every word he spoke. "Kathy, please let me in." I could see no option. My hands were still shaking even worse than before as I grabbed the doorknob. It twisted and I let the door fall open.

I took a step back, my whole body froze I knew it was mistake! All hell broke loose.

Carlos stepped over the threshold, forced the door to close, all the while staring down at me with fury in his eyes, they were no longer green, but black. Backing away from him, I lost my balance. Grabbing my arms, he jerked me to a wobbly stance in front of him. His grip on my arms was hard and cruel.

"Damn you! What have you been doing all day? At your Mothers' house again? Are they putting thoughts in your head to leave me! You are mine, do you hear me?"

Fear gave me strength to jerk my arm from his grasp. I knew there wasn't anywhere to escape, but I ran to the kitchen just to put a little space between us. It didn't work, he followed, ranting and raving, swinging his arms around like a wild man! He closed the distance between us and put his face within an inch from mine. The smell of beer on his breath gagged me. He shouted repeatedly that he was the boss, he was in control and that I needed to listen to him. He grabbed a hand full of my hair jerking my face to his, screaming:

"Do you hear me bitch, you're mine to do with as I want? Your name is changed now, you're mine!"

He swung me in a circle by my hair throwing me to the kitchen floor. I wanted badly to run, but I lay there frozen, not able to move. I knew he could see my fear as I stared up at him. I felt repulsed and hatred for him and I think he saw that too. He threw himself on top of me and started kissing me. I remember praying to God to help me. I hated this man. I felt like death would be a gift. I believed Carlos relished the idea that I was afraid of him. He could manhandle me anyway he wanted, including rape. After proving he was stronger and all powerful, he found the one fear I held in a very secret place. Fear that something would happen to my parents because of me.

His face contorted as he looked down at me and said:

"You tell your parents and I will kill your Father. I will go to their home and when he answers the door, I will blow his brains out. Kathy it will be your fault because you couldn't keep your mouth shut, your actions will kill your Dad, not mine, yours!"

He struggled to a standing position and emphasized his words with a bruising kick to my hip, then stumbled away into the bedroom. When I finally got myself back together and on my feet, I found him passed out across the bed. I realized Carlos had succeeded in closing the trap door on my life. What a mess I had made. Helplessness robs a person of hope; Hope motivates a persons' spirit. No hope—no spirit.

Emotions took their toll as I tried to shower away the mental and physical filth of him. Grief, anger, and depression each took their turn.

CHAPTER SIX–MOTIVATED

We were always broke! There wasn't money for food much less to pay bills. I had to go to my parents for money. I was embarrassed and ashamed. I hated what I had become, the weight I had gained, the depression I felt, and my failure. I felt ugly and worthless. Carlos had succeeded in manipulating me into believing everything wrong in our marriage was my fault! The mental and physical beatings just got worse. I attempted to stay out of his way, rarely succeeding.

I was lying to myself thinking this was not hurting Toni Lisa. She was getting older, three years old now. She could see and hear what was going on. Carlos always ranted about how I was nothing. I remember him coming home one evening, drunk again, and the door hadn't closed all the way before he started in on me. What a shock, one minute Toni Lisa and I were watching *I Love Lucy* on TV, the next minute this crazy, drunk, maniac was screaming at me from the door way:

"You have been a pain in my ass, your parents too. It took me beating you to tame you."

The anger in his face made him uglier than usual. The insults didn't satisfy his need to dominate and he lunged at me grabbing my hair, jerking me off the couch. It is shameful to admit, but this didn't shock me anymore, I just didn't care. It angered him further when I refused to fight back; guess it wasn't satisfying to beat on a rag doll anymore. His rage escalated.

"You think you're so tough huh? I will show you."

He dragged me by my hair into the kitchen where he jerked me to my feet. He pushed me into the stove, holding me there with his body. Waiting for the burner to reach maximum heat before proving his point, giving him a little time to think about what he was doing to me. I could hear Toni Lisa starting to cry. The burner became red. He shoved my face toward it while I pushed away from that stove with all my strength. My face just kept getting closer and closer. I screeched, kicked and squirmed, all while he yelled:

"Now, I have your attention! You are finally smart enough to be afraid of me aren't you? Try to leave me and I will burn that pretty face of yours so badly, no one will want you."

Poor Toni Lisa, hitting at her Dad, screaming:

"Stop it, stop hurting mommy."

Carlos finally jerked his hand out of my hair and shoved me against the sink. He was so out of control, spit flew from his lips as he screamed:

"Don't you ever think you can leave me! If you do, I will kill your Dad and you will regret it the rest of your life."

He grabbed my face in his hand to emphasize his words and shoved my head back with a snap. He stomped out of the kitchen and I remember my hand was shaking so much it was difficult to turn the burner off before collapsing to the floor. Toni Lisa ran over to me crying:

"Mommy, Daddy scares me."

What was I to do, the beatings had escalated! My Daughter was afraid of her father. I believe Toni Lisa's words that evening, motivated me,

I began dreaming and scheming about how I was going to get away from this monster. I hated him more and more every day. I was terrified of him and I believed him when he told me he would kill my father.

CHAPTER SEVEN—HAPPY TIMES

My happy times were when Carlos left in the mornings. I never knew if he was going to work or out drinking with the guys. It didn't matter, I was just happy he was gone so I could spend time with my princess. Toni Lisa was my shining star. I hated what Toni Lisa was witness to, watching her father beat me all the time. I wanted the world to be perfect for her. I figured when he wasn't home during the day, she and I could make it a special time together. I knew she was too young for many things, but I just wanted to show her there was fun in life too. I would run to her room after Carlos left. What a beautiful little face she had, so sweet and innocent, it was hard for me to wake her up, but I did it with a song:

"*Time to get up this morning, this morning, this morning*
Time to get up this morning, right, right now."

The smile on her face when she got up was worth a million dollars. We would take a bubble bath and then watch cartoons while we had breakfast together. Toni Lisa would sit on my lap as I put on my makeup.

"Mommy, mommy I want some."

Anything for my little princess. Then she would run to my closet to pick out what we were wearing that day. As I dressed her, we would play this game where I asked her:

"Who is the most beautiful girl in the world?"

She would say:

"Toni Lisa, Toni Lisa!"

"Who is my little princess?"

She would say: "Toni Lisa, Toni Lisa!"

Then I would start tickling her all over.

"I am mommy, I am!"

Toni Lisa would scream, giggling and squirming.

"Ok my princess we are off to see Grandma."

Toni Lisa loved it there; Mom had lots of games, toys and a swimming pool. She never wanted to leave Mom's. I loved spending time with Toni Lisa, she was pure joy.

She never cried, as I remember!

CHAPTER EIGHT—NEW BEGINNING

My Dad had started a new business called American Aluminum, and he did great. His business was booming. He turned the aluminum to gold, becoming a self-made millionaire.

He and Mom began going on trips to England, France, and Italy, but their favorite destination was Las Vegas. My dad loved it there. If he could have moved there, I think he would have. They started going at least once a month. It was November 1974 and I had just turned twenty years old. That is when my parents invited me to go with them. I was so excited. Nancy offered to take care of Toni Lisa, which was the only way I would have left her. When Friday came, I packed up and left without saying a word to Carlos. I knew Carlos would never have let me go and I was willing to pay the consequences when I came home.

The plane we flew was filled with my parent's friends. You could tell they were all very rich; the diamonds sparkled all over that plane. The flight was over eight hours, but I did not care. Everyone taught me how to throw dice and play blackjack.

A limo was waiting for us when our plane landed. I had never seen anything as beautiful as the drive up Las Vegas Blvd; each hotel was bigger and better than the last. The lights alone were amazing; it was like daytime even at two in the morning. What a sight! When we reached our hotel, it was something you could only dream about.

Two men opened the car doors for us and they treated Dad like a celebrity.

"Mr. Longo, everything is ready for you sir. You have your same suite as always, and we put your daughter in the suite beside you."

I felt like royalty. When I entered my own private suite, it just took my breath away. Finally becoming a Princess in my own castle, something I had dreamed about as a little girl. The bed was round, covered by a red velvet bedspread and big gold pillows. The pillows were so big I could sit on them. The curtains were red velvet and the molding on the walls was painted in gold leaf. The floor was white marble, and there were red roses all over the room. The bathroom had a Jacuzzi bath with gold columns at each corner.

Having never seen anything so amazing, I didn't know what I wanted to do first, jump on the bed, order room service, or take a bath! I put on the music and just danced all over the room singing loudly. Then the phone rang, it was my Dad.

"Princess, do you like your room, it's great, isn't it? Hurry and come down, we're playing craps and I want you to be here with me."

I didn't want to leave the room I was having too much fun, but he insisted.

"You will have more fun down here, now hurry."

"Okay dad, I will be right down."

Once I got downstairs, I could see all the people around one table and Dad was in the middle of them, screaming.

"Come on SEVEN!" He noticed me standing there just looking at everything in awe. He pulled me to his side and introduced me. "This is MY daughter Kathy; she's here to bring me luck."

He acted so proud that I was his daughter; it made me feel good about myself. He took a twenty-five dollar chip and placed it on the line for me, holding the dice in front of my face saying:

"Ok honey blow on them for luck, and a seven will come out."

When he threw those dice, everyone around the table screamed: "SEVEN!"

I won FIFTY dollars on that one roll! I couldn't believe it. We played for hours. I could tell Dad was getting tired, but we were winning so much money. I had arranged all my chips, neatly along the table.

Dad had been playing this game long enough to realize our luck was due to run out. He felt it best to stop while we were ahead. I was very excited and he finally had to gently touch my hand to get my attention. I saw him putting his chips away and felt he meant it was time to go. He said:

"Let's get ready for dinner; I have another surprise waiting for you tonight, grab your chips so we can cash them in."

I was a little disappointed but, actually my stomach had been growling for an hour. As usual, Dad was right; it had been time to stop.

You know the whole time we stood at that table, I didn't realize until the cashier started counting the chips just how much money I had actually won! *Ten Thousand Dollars!*

I had no idea how much money Dad won. My mind was busy calculating over-due bills, shopping with Toni Lisa and even thinking about a new TV. Once I got to my room, I joyously tossed that money on that big round bed and rolled around in it, throwing the cash in the air. The phone rang. Again, it was my Dad.

"Kathy, come to our room, I want to give you that surprise I mentioned downstairs."

I wondered what could be any better than ten thousand dollars. Dad and Mom met me at their door with huge smiles. Dad handed me an envelope to open. I could have fainted right then and there, not just a shocked faint. I truly felt lightheaded and dizzy. Can you guess what was in that envelope? Front row tickets to see Elvis Presley. Yeah! He was staying in the same hotel.

After dinner, I retired to my room; I was not feeling very well. Dad was worried, so he requested a Doctor to visit my suite. Dad wanted to make sure there wasn't anything seriously wrong with me.

After asking me several questions the doctor couldn't be positive, without a test, but informed me he thought I was pregnant. Pregnant? NO WAY! He assured me that indeed, he believed I was pregnant. In a panic, I requested he not inform my parents, I wanted to find out for sure first. He agreed. After the Doctor left, I called Dad; I told him I was doing fine, just a touch of the flu. I could not understand how God would allow this to happen knowing how unhappy I was. I didn't want to bring another child into the hell Toni Lisa and I had been living! Fear and questions bombarded me that night but I knew the doctor was correct. I refused to allow this news to ruin my great weekend. I put it aside and decided to deal with it when I got home!

That night I cried myself to sleep in that big round bed. The weekend went by so very fast and I silently wished I could stay there and forget the life I had in Florida. I realized if that wish were granted, I would no longer have Toni Lisa or my Mom and Dad. That just wasn't worth it. I had to get back home and decide what I was going to do.

Even though I was excited to see Toni Lisa, I knew Carlos and I needed to talk first. Mom and Dad dropped me off at home, and as I walked up to the door, I stopped to take several deep breaths for courage. Carlos pulled the door open from inside the house, his other arm behind his back. I could tell something was different. Before I could say anything about being pregnant or the money I had won, Carlos pulled a vase full of roses from behind his back, holding them out for me.

"Kathy I am going to change, I want to be a family again. I missed you so much when you were gone. I can't live my life without you and Toni Lisa."

He assured me there would be no more drinking, no more hitting, he wanted this to work. He kept telling me how much he missed me while I was gone. I was suspicious of what he had to say, but I was pregnant. If he could change, I would give it a chance, for our family. I was silent for so long he said: "I know you don't love me anymore. But I will win that love back, you loved me once, you will love me again."

He felt certain but I knew I could never love him like in the beginning. I thought it was as good time as any to tell him about being pregnant.

"Carlos, I am pregnant!"

The look on his face was one of excitement. He knew he had trapped me again.

"This is a sign Kathy, for us to make this time a whole new start for us."

He wanted to come with me to tell my parents. The image of my first pregnancy announcement flashed through my mind; I knew this time was different. As we drove to my parent's, I told Carlos about winning ten grand in Las Vegas. He just considered that icing on his cake.

As we drove up the driveway, I could see Toni Lisa's beautiful face pressed against the window, watching for me. The car hadn't even come to a complete stop when I got out and ran to the door. Hugging Toni Lisa was better than all that money I had won, no comparison. I prayed she would be excited about the new baby, not feel as though I was trying to replace her. My sister Nancy, was all smiles and excited to hear about my trip and how much money I had won. What she didn't realize was there wouldn't have been a trip had it not been for her. She treated Toni Lisa as if she were her own child. I wouldn't have left her with anyone else!

My immediate family had gathered at Mom and Dad's to welcome us home. That night we informed my family.

"Everyone, Carlos and I have some news to share with you! Mom, Dad, you are going to be grandparents again."

Everyone was extremely happy for us. That's when my Dad made a very generous offer.

"Carlos, it is time you came to work for me as Plant Manager. What do you think?"

If Dad had known how Carlos had been treating me and the threats made toward him, Dad would never have offered Carlos the job. But I knew Dad made the offer to help us financially.

CHAPTER NINE–BETRAYAL

In May 1975, Carlos had been working for Dad as Plant Manager going on six months. At around eight in the morning, I got a call from Dad.

"Honey, would you be able to come down to the office, I need to talk to you in person?"

"Sure, Dad, is everything okay?"

I should have been weary of his response.

"Honey, I just need to talk to you. Come on down to the office and drop Toni Lisa off with your Mother."

In my mind, during the trip to the office, I rolled every possible reason I could think of for this surprising request. Little did I know, I wasn't even close. I arrived at the office and said:

"Hi Dad, is everything okay?"

Gently touching my arm, he said:

"I just want you to listen, don't say a word, okay?"

I was a little puzzled by his request.

"Okay Dad."

I knew something was up, but the serenity in his voice calmed me. Dad picked up the phone and called Carlos into his office. When Carlos walked in, I knew it was something bad. Dad came right to the point.

"Carlos have you been stealing from me?"

Carlos didn't answer Dad right away but you could tell he was debating with himself about his answer. In embarrassment, I looked at Carlos then Dad. Carlos started screaming:

"Of all the f . . . ing nerve, I quit!"

He stormed out of the room. I felt sick to my stomach, after Dad gave Carlos a good job, he blew it. I hugged Dad, telling him how sorry I was. Dad told me it was okay and that it wasn't my fault; he just wanted me to be present when he confronted Carlos. He didn't want Carlos to come home telling me a different story. He said Carlos had been stealing the aluminum and selling it for scrap to make extra money.

I drove home on autopilot that day. It overwhelmed me that Carlos had thrown away not only our future, but also the future of Toni Lisa and our unborn child for a little extra money. It was just unthinkable. When I got home Carlos was at the house.

"Your Dad is full of shit, I never stole from him. I didn't like that job anyway I am going back to what I know, Construction."

I knew in my heart he would go back to drinking. I prayed that night like I've never prayed before. God please help me keep my babies safe.

CHAPTER TEN–JENNIFER

On June 8, 1975, I gave birth to a beautiful baby girl. When the nurse brought her to me and put her in my arms I never wanted to let go. She was so tiny. I found myself watching her as she slept. I felt myself welling up with such love for her that my heart was going to burst. Looking at her tiny face, so innocent and pure I could just melt. As she opened her eyes, a tiny smile came across her face for me. I whispered to her, "I am your mommy and love you with all my heart. I promise to protect you and give you everything I can. I promise to always be there for you. Her big beautiful black eyes just stared at me like she understood. She reminded me of a beautiful doll, perfect pink skin with big black eyes, long eyelashes and lots of black hair. She was just so perfectly beautiful.

Everything bad that has happened in my life didn't matter, just having this precious baby was everything I could ever want.

Then my thoughts went to Toni Lisa I didn't want her to feel left out, we had been through so much together.

That is when I decided Toni Lisa could name her sister. But, I didn't know Mom was hoping I would name her Sophia, after her Mother. I decided that would be the baby's middle name, a great solution to that little problem. We all agreed that it was a beautiful name for the baby, Jennifer Sophia Marteliz. For once, I was happy Carlos was out drinking it allowed me to name her.

While in the hospital, recovering, I decided things at home were going to change. Carlos wasn't going to change so I had to make the change. It was time I became strong for my two beautiful, helpless, daughters!

I was packed and ready to take Jennifer home. I waited for hours on Carlos, but he never showed up. I finally called my Mom and asked if she would take us home.

When we arrived, Carlos was standing outside with a beer in his hand. When I looked at him, I could feel the rage burning away at that little parcel of hope still alive in my heart. Carlos ran up to the car door as if nothing was wrong.

"Let me help you, I was just coming to get you."

I knew Mom was as angry as I was, if not more, and her silence spoke volumes. She could feel the tension between Carlos and me. Just before driving away she told me:

"I love you honey, call me if you need me."

"Thanks Mom, I love you too."

I took Jennifer to her room and was lured into a false sense of well-being. Jennifer's room looked beautiful. Nancy had spent days painting her room in the Flintstones theme. Above her dresser drawer she had painted a tree with Bam Bam hanging from it. The wall where her crib had pebbles riding on Dino's back. There was green shag carpeting on the floor to look like grass. What a great room for my little girl. What a great sister!

After putting Jennifer in her crib, and hugging Toni Lisa who was still doting on Jennifer, I walked back out to the living room.

The look on Carlos face was frightening, I should have been warned, but the last six months had been 'beatings free'. Suddenly, Carlos grabbed me around the neck. He caught me off guard, lifting me off the floor and slammed my back against the wall, knocking the air from my lungs. He stared into my eyes as I dangled there with him choking me. Carlos strong hands circling my throat stopped the blood flow to my brain. It felt as though my head was going to explode. He held me there, unable to move, his breath reeked of beer. He screamed at me:

"How dare you look at me like that, you owe me respect. Do you hear me Kathy, I WANT RESPECT?"

I was desperate for him to release me but all I could do was move my head in agreement, just a fraction. Even though my eyes were open, the room around me was foggy and getting dark. When he let me go, I dropped to the floor like a rock. I rubbed my neck. Just trying to gasp in air took all my concentration. I didn't even feel his foot connect with my leg, I just saw him kick me from the fog in front of my eyes. He stormed away into the kitchen, proud that he had once again proved who was boss. Awkwardly I pulled myself up with the doorframe. It took me a couple attempts before finally succeeding. My fear of Carlos pushed me into a frantic wobbling run into Jennifer's room. I closed her door anxiously, putting that small barrier between that thoughtless drunk and us. I grabbed Jennifer and Toni Lisa then cowered in the corner, praying he would leave us alone. God answered my prayer. When all had been quiet for a long time, I snuck out of the room and found him passed out on the couch.

Realization hit! I had failed in this marriage! Nothing I could do would make it any better. I hated the man I married, and somehow I had to free us from him. He was just a drunken loser!

CHAPTER ELEVEN–HOPE

Every day was different for Carlos. One day he would work then two days he would be off. We hadn't made a house payment in two months. There wasn't any food or formula in the house. All our money was going toward liquor. I felt ashamed, but with no options left I went to Mom for help. Mom was there for us, whatever we needed. I knew in my heart she wanted to see me with a good man. One who could support and take care of us in a manner like my Father. I hated to think what would have happened if they ever found out Carlos had been beating me up for years. Mom looked at me lovingly and said:

"Kathy, I think you need to get a job, it doesn't look like your husband is going to support you, much less your girls."

With a total lack of confidence I said:

"Who would want me Mom, I barely finished the 9th grade, I don't have any skills?"

Mom was prepared.

"Kathy, you know how you love doing hair and makeup? Wouldn't it be great to have a job as a Beautician? We will pay for your schooling and care for the girls while you are at classes. What do you think?"

God answered my prayers. Mom called and made the arrangements. I began classes in two weeks. I dreaded the thought of leaving the girls but knew this was our way out. I would finally become self-sufficient, never having to ask my parents for money again.

Needless to say, Carlos didn't like my parent's interference in his personal business, his control over me. I paid dearly for the decision to begin a career. (Mentally, physically and emotionally)

My first day of class was extremely difficult. I got up at five o'clock in the morning scared to death but determined to follow through. I walked back to my closet after showering and while deciding on what to wear, I heard Carlos' heavy breathing from the bed. Slowly I turned around to find him staring at me.

"What the hell are you doing?"

Cautiously and quietly I turned back to the closet making my selection.

"I'm getting ready for school."

I didn't look at him. I just continued getting the girls and myself ready as fast as I could, which amused him even more. He thought it was funny that I was in such a tizzy. I was extremely nervous and didn't know whether he was going to blow a fuse or not. He flipped over with his back to me and remained silent. That silence itself scared me more than his screaming abuse. This was new for Carlos, and I didn't know what to expect, so I hurried. I wanted out of there. I don't think I really took a deep breath until the girls and I were on our way to Grandma's house.

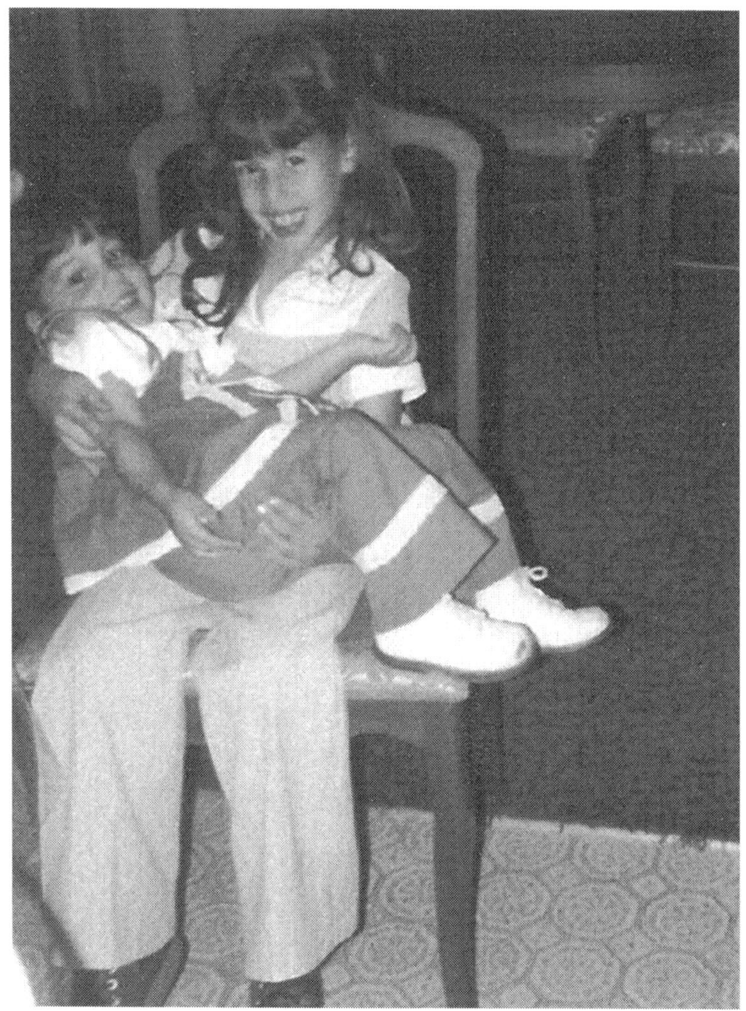

Toni Lisa Holding Jennifer

Hillsborough Beauty College, Wow! It was my first day of school. There were about fifty students, all around my age. I hadn't really been around anyone my own age for several years.

Being out of that house brought a whole new perspective to the way I thought. I enjoyed school a lot, but I also loved getting back to my girls. Having them run to me, giving me huge hugs and telling me about their day. At my parent's house we were like a normal family.

Wishing didn't work! I promised myself, one day I would leave him.

After a hard day at school, the girls and I arrived home to find a variety of empty bottles sitting all over the coffee table. The room reeked of liquor. Carlos wasn't sleeping; he was hammered into unconsciousness on the living room floor!

With him passed out, I was able to get the girls ready for bed and read them a bedtime story. I very quietly went to bed hoping to get a good night's sleep. It was hard sleeping, I never knew if he would wake up in a rage yelling, or be interested in me for something else. My school attendance gave him a new daily argument. He hated every aspect of the independence I was gaining.

Each morning as I opened my eyes I realized I had lived through another night with him. I thanked God for that. School became my only escape from my personal prison. I just had so much fun doing hair and talking to everyone about their lives.

I became close friends with one girl in particular. A special bond existed between Vicky and I; we did everything together. I became comfortable enough with our friendship to tell her about my relationship with Carlos. The only reason I told her my secret was that I didn't have anyone else I felt comfortable telling. I wasn't looking for her pity but for her to understand. I had a goal to achieve in attending these classes. I wanted to make a future for my babies and give them a good life. Gradually I changed, I began losing the baby weight from both children and I was getting my confidence back. Not just in my ability as a hairdresser but also in my personal appearance. I began believing I could actually become the breadwinner for the girls and me.

Vicky listened to my horror stories, progressively becoming upset with the sordid details of my home life. Eventually she didn't want to talk about anything other than what was going on in my home. One day she told me:

"Carlos is a very weak man Kathy, why do you think he beats up on you. His nickname should be 'Wimp'. I would like to go over there and punch his lights out. Someone just needs to stand up to him. How about if I come over and do that for you?"

I truly believed she could do it! Vicky was an Italian woman you automatically realized you shouldn't mess with. That night Vicky called me at home. She wanted to talk to Carlos! In shock, I handed the phone to Carlos and realized too late what I had done. I knew I was in for it, as his eyes opened wide and I saw the rage building. I started backing away, only to have him throw the phone at me. As I picked the phone up from the floor, Carlos stormed into our bedroom. I could hear Vicky yelling at me through the phone.

"Kathy, Kathy, you there, good, stay on the phone and don't say anything."

I thought to myself, what am I going to say—my prayers? But I did as she instructed, watching in amazement as Carlos packed his things. The look on his face was priceless. Carlos never looked at me; he just packed up and walked out the door. He didn't even slam the door! Flabbergasted I asked:

"Vicky what did you say to Carlos, he just walked out the front door?"

She said:

"I introduced myself and told him to pack his stuff. He could move out or I would come over with my shotgun and blow his f . . . ing head off."

Vicky was my hero. She must have been related to someone very powerful for Carlos to believe if he didn't get out alive, he would get out dead.

FREE, WE WERE FREE! God sent a special Angel to answer my prayers. Maybe it is the number of times each prayer is prayed before an answer is forthcoming? I don't think so; it just had to be in God's time, not mine!

It was time to explain everything to the girls and my parents. The girls and I sat there on the floor in Jennifer's room. Gently I explained:

"Your Daddy won't be living with us anymore but you can still see him when you want."

Toni Lisa was so excited.

"I don't ever want to visit him, I hate him. It will be so nice here without him yelling and hitting you all the time."

I felt the same relief as Toni Lisa, but Jennifer was having a hard time understanding why her daddy left. She was too young to understand.

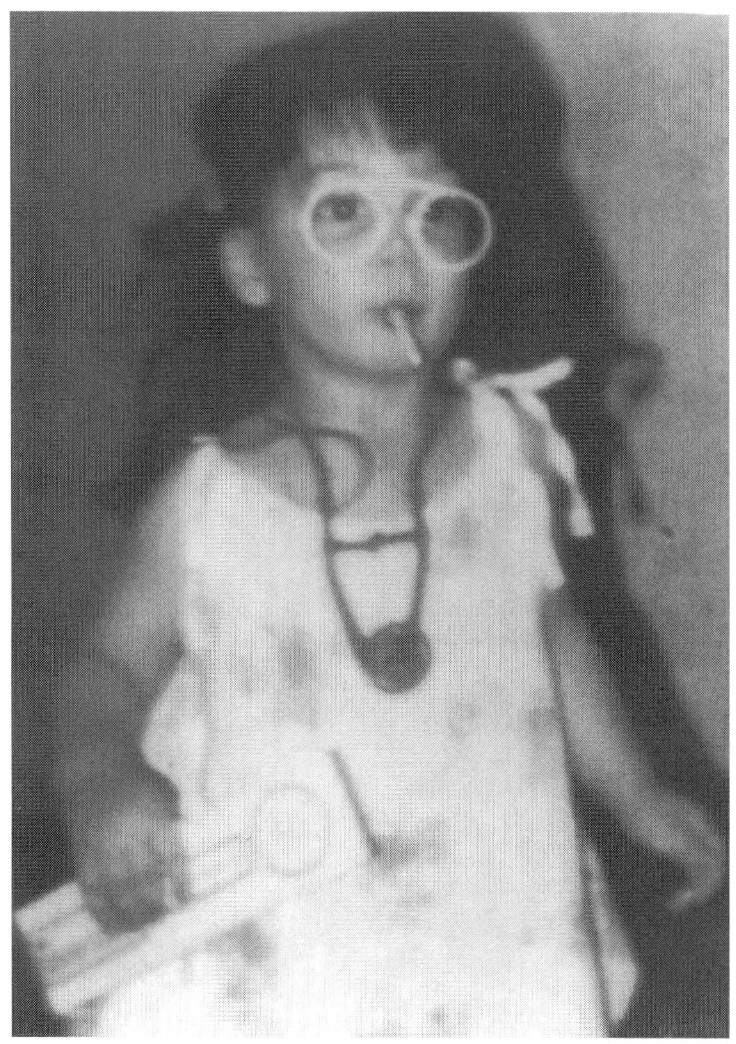

Jennifer

We packed some clothes and headed to Grandma and Papa's house. They asked me a million questions, non-stop. Why, why, why . . . When we arrived, the girls went running and announced:

"Papa, Grandma, Daddy left! He is not going to be living at home anymore."

Well, guess I didn't have to think about how I was going to tell them. The girls took care of that for me. Mom yelled for me:

"Kathy, what are the girls telling us, is it true?"

With a little spring to my step, I sang my answer back to her.

"It's true, Carlos has moved out. We are free girls now!"

Mom wrapped me in her arms tight and just as tightly I hugged her back!

CHAPTER TWELVE—FAMILY

"Dad I want to sell the house and move in with you and mom for a while, if that's okay?"

Dad answered, smiling from ear to ear.

"Sure Honey, I think that's a great idea! You'll be right here under my watching eyes again."

Laughing, I said:

"That's okay by me."

I still felt a little jittery that Carlos might change his mind and move his stuff back home. The girls and I never spent another night in that house. The house was nice but I was so happy to be out of there; so many bad memories. That night in my old bedroom, I got down on my hands and knees and thanked God for everything I had and for helping me.

Toni Lisa and I each changed after moving in with my parents. Fear of Carlos gradually dissolved little by little.

Jennifer Learning To Swim With Her Cousins Mark & Chris

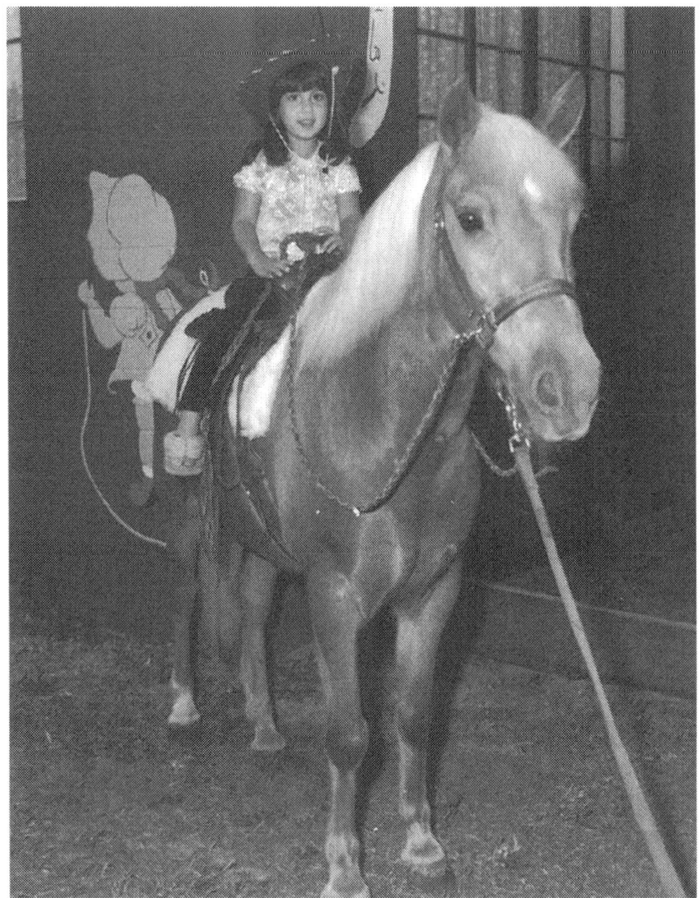

Jennifer

Living under Mom and Dad's safe, protective roof became the cure for our battered spirits. But Jennifer was unscathed by his vile nature. She became a spirited, independent young lady we nicknamed 'Firecracker.' She loved to dance around the house singing.

"Firecracker, firecracker, boom, boom, boom!"

Swinging her hips sweet and sassy, Jennifer was a ray of sunshine. The girls were very close, except when it came to their Dad. Toni

Lisa hated him, pure and simple. Just as simply Jennifer loved him. Youth had protected her. That was okay with me. I didn't want them to hate him. He never touched them, only me. My Dad became the perfect 'father figure' for the girls. They watched how he treated his family on a daily basis and it gave them an idea of how a loving family should be. It was very difficult for me to express how I felt living there with so much love and acceptance in their home.

Our Family All Together At Church

Things were moving pretty fast. In twelve months I was almost finished with school; my divorce became final and I sold my house.

Vicky finished school before I did. She opened her own salon close to her home. I missed her very much but at the same time I was happy for her. I felt full of life, on top of the world, energetic and more vibrant than ever. That simple thank you never seemed sufficient to me. To this day, I really don't believe she realized what she did for my daughters and me.

Moving in with my parents allowed the rebirth of my abused soul. After graduation, I accepted a position at Maas Brother Beauty Salon located in the most prestigious department store in the mall. My first job!

My station had its own style; it reflected a Japanese style whereas my neighbor's station had a Hawaiian motif. Being a hairdresser is almost like being a psychologist. The client's share their lives with you while in your chair. Being in that relaxed environment, sometimes they shared more than they should have. That was a favorite part of being a hair stylist for me. I loved meeting people and hearing about their lives.

My life with my children was everything to me. I tried to work my schedule around their school hours. I would schedule my appointments early so I was finished in time to pick them up from school. Mom offered to pick them up and sometimes that was necessary, but usually I was there for them. We would always sing in the car together:

> "Toni Toni bo woni, banana fanana for oni.
> Jen Jen bo bin banana fanana fo fin fee fi mo."
> You get the idea . . . . . .

They never wanted the songs to end. I believe they enjoyed that special time together. They were both getting so big and beautiful.

Jennifer At The Park

Toni Lisa and Jennifer

Toni Lisa had long brown curly hair, big dark brown eyes, with the cutest little shape. She looked like an adult with a little tiny body. Jennifer had long, straight, black hair with huge black eyes, and a little belly. You couldn't help but want to hug them. Jennifer's clothes had to have rhinestones and she loved wearing boots. Personally, I liked them in dresses with the pretty matching socks, but they had opinions of their own. We would compromise. One day they wore what I wanted and the next day they would get to choose. Joint decision-making was our way of handling our day-to-day activities. I felt the best way to be their Mother was by being their friend, thereby, enabling them to share anything and everything with me. I hoped they would never feel as I had . . . desperate to run away.

My tips from work helped make memories. We spent time at their favorite place, the Pizza Plaza. Let us not forget Disney World, we went there at least once a month. In fact, we did everything together; we even shared the same room at night. The girls had their own rooms, but we always ended up in my bed at night. We took turns reading to each other. There were even times the girls would put me to sleep!

Jennifer was very good about going to bed at night, Toni Lisa on the other hand, never wanted to go to sleep. My Aunt tried to help me, she told me to let Toni Lisa stay up if she wanted that she would eventually fall asleep. To her dismay, this technique didn't work with Toni Lisa. At four o'clock in the morning, I finally insisted she go to bed. No way would I try that again. To this day, I don't know if she just didn't require a lot of sleep or if she was afraid to go to sleep. Maybe she thought these happy times were a dream and she wasn't about to lose them.

My job at the salon was wonderful. Not only had I become friends with those working there, I had a great relationship with the customers as well. If I didn't have anyone in my chair, I would take the customers awaiting their hairdresser and do their makeup for them.

Representatives from the New York salon visited to congratulate me on being our salon's number one makeup sales person. They decided to use my picture outside the salon as an advertisement for facials and makeup.

Until Ms. Ladman began managing the salon, I was very happy. She was a mean person to say the least; none of the girls liked her very much. She reassigned me to the manicure station where I was never very good. In fact, it took me so long to take care of a client, my facial and makeup sales declined rapidly. The boss from New York phoned me personally, wanting to know what had happened. Upon learning the reason for my decline in sales, he told me not to worry; he would put things back to the way they had been. When I went to work the next day, I was over taken with joy. The roads weren't packed, it was a beautiful spring day, the flowers were blooming, and I couldn't wait to get to work. Entering the salon front door, I said:

"Good morning everyone, I'll make some coffee!"

Ms. Ladman came up to me saying:

"Kathy, after lunch it shows you don't have any appointments, schedule me there."

Happily, I said:

"Sure thing Ms. Ladman."

She had that sharp bossy tone to her voice and she didn't look very happy. Naturally, my thought was, I wouldn't be doing nails anymore. Lunch went by so fast; I was almost late for my appointment with Ms. Ladman. She was a very large woman, between the ages of 40 to 45, red hair and bright red lipstick. And I hated her voice.

"Kathy where were you yesterday?"

Not understanding her question, I said,

"I called in; my sister had her baby yesterday. I was at the hospital all day, with my entire family!"

Snottily, she replied:

"I see you come from a rich family Kathy. I want employees on my payroll that will show up when they have appointments, not rich socialites who think they don't need to show up for work."

Hurt at her implication, I tried to explain to Ms. Ladman that my job was very important and necessary to me. I had called my appointments the night before, explained my reason for not coming to work yesterday, and rescheduled them. None of them seemed to have an issue with the rescheduling. Appeasement wasn't what Ms. Ladman was looking for.

"Kathy I have on my desk a report I'm filling out for New York, explaining my need for loyal employees who don't sit around doing nothing all day. Whom do you think they are going to believe, you or me?"

I was enraged at the injustice of her attack and embarrassed that everyone in the shop could hear her reprimand me. I lashed back at her.

"You know what Ms. Ladman; you've had it out for me since your arrival here. You win! You can take this job and stuff it up your fat ass, I quit."

I stomped out of that office feeling extremely erratic. First off, I needed that job. Secondly, I loved the people I worked with and for, except Ms. Ladman of course. I know I should have remained calm; accepted her abuse and lies, but my relationship with Carlos was still too fresh. I lashed out at Ms. Ladman, as I should have done to Carlos years ago. The more I thought about it, she had already decided to fire me. No matter what my side of the story was her side was already trumped up with her lies. Since she was a Supervisor, who was going to believe me? What was I going to do; I had to find a job as soon as possible. I knew it couldn't last! It was just too good to be true.

CHAPTER THIRTEEN–OPPORTUNITY

After our divorce Carlos got visitation rights mandated by the court, not that I liked the arrangement much. On Carlos weekends, he was always late or would forget the girls entirely. There was always some reason he did not show up as scheduled. When he did manage to have the girls, I called those weekends my grown up time.

One weekend my Mom and Dad took me to a Lebanese convention. Mom was hoping I would meet a nice guy.

Mom is of Lebanese descent, whereas Dad is Italian. I had so much fun. I never sat down I had a line of guys waiting to dance with me. As the convention ended, one of the waiters brought me a note from a stranger. The note said, '*I request the most beautiful girl in the room to give me the honor of coming to my home for dinner.*' At the same time I finished reading my note Mom arrived at my side waving her note at me. She and Dad had been invited as my chaperones. I didn't know at that time the note was from a Prince of Saudi Arabia. I went over to his table and accepted his invitation. We ended up spending what was left of the evening together. We laughed a lot and just had a great time together. I think we were the last ones to leave the dance. He invited me to his home the following weekend. My parents were unable to attend instead, Mom had her best friend Yoli, escort me as my chaperone. When we arrived, courtesy of the Prince's personal limo (talk about plush), his home consisted of the entire top floor of a hotel on Bay Shore. When I got off the elevator he was standing there waiting for me. It was amazing. He smiled at me and said;

"Welcome to my home."

When I walked through the doors everyone greeted me. I felt like it was my birthday.

"I hope you don't mind but I invited my family to meet you"

He says to me in a very soft whisper.

How could I be upset I felt honored. I was seated across from him at the dinner table. After a wonderful meal, he told me:

"Kathy, what would you like to do? Anything just name it."

Not thinking I said;

"I would love to go dancing!"

He smiled and clapped his hands; a man came running.

"Yes Prince Syan, what is it you wish?"

My handsome prince grandly said:

"We are going dancing!"

Pushing his chair back, he held his hand out to me and we walked to the elevator. When that elevator landed on the ground floor the limo was there waiting for us along with several bodyguards and family members. Surprised, I asked:

"Are they all coming with us?"

"But of course, I have twelve brothers. All of whom desire my death, which would put them each closer to becoming Prince."

He lifted his shirt, showing me a four-inch long scar on his abdomen.

"One brother has already attempted the deed!"

Dancing in a nightclub with the Prince, bodyguards, and Yoli didn't work out very well. We decided to return to his home and relax with his family. After several dates, the Prince and his bodyguards appeared at my door with the keys to a Porsche. He told me he purchased the car for me. He wanted a commitment of affection from me. Before I was to answer his proposal, he had an additional surprise to show me. Taking me to a huge estate, he grasped my arm and hurried me up the stairs. The home was beautiful and took my breath away! So did the stairs he practically dragged me up. He stopped at a beautiful wooden door.

"Kathy your favorite color is purple, right?"

After I nodded yes, he opened the door to this most amazing room decorated in purple velvet and gold with crystal chandeliers and stained glass windows everywhere. He said:

"Kathy, I wish to spend my life with you, the car, the room, it's all yours, you just have to be mine. You would not be allowed to see anyone else!"

Flabbergasted, I responded:

"Prince Syan, I have two daughters whom I would never give up for anyone."

Nodding his head, he said:

"Yes, I know of these children, they shall live here also. Do you accept?"

Prince Syan and his entire court treated me like royalty. I didn't want anyone controlling me ever again. I wanted the freedom to make my own choices. Nothing was worth giving that up again. I explained my feelings to the Prince. We dated off and on for a year or so after that. I remained uncommitted about the relationship.

After being married to Carlos, it was hard for me to feel close to anyone much less trust another man with my well-being or that of my daughters. Just hearing Carlos' voice would still make me sick to my stomach.

Even with all the excitement of being escorted around Florida by the Prince, his bodyguards, and a chaperone, I still considered myself a working woman, and diligently looked for another job. Shortly after walking away from my job at the Salon, I came across an ad that read:

WANTED; a trustworthy person to manage clothing store.

This sounded like a fun job and they hadn't requested any certain amount of education in the advertisement.

"Hi, I am calling about the job in the paper for a clothing store manager."

With a very deep voice, the man answered:

"I am seeing applicants tomorrow between nine and three come anytime between those hours."

Excitedly, I said: "Thank you very much; I will see you bright and early tomorrow."

After getting the location I hung up the phone. I felt things were looking up for me.

The interviewer was a very good looking older gentleman. With gray hair dressed in a very sharp looking suit, cowboy hat and boots. I felt we clicked immediately. He showed me the clothing store I was destined to manage. I loved the place. He did ask me however what schooling I had and with my fingers crossed behind my back, I responded with a big fat lie:

"Two years at HCC Junior College."

He then asked how much I was looking to be paid. I told him minimum wage with a catch. I would work for him for two weeks at minimum wage, and upon his evaluation of my work, we could discuss my worth at that time. He hired me on the spot, telling me to report for work Monday at 10:00am. I hated lying to Mr. Burns, but I really wanted that job.

CHAPTER FOURTEEN—MANAGEMENT

My new job required many personal hours at the library. If I didn't understand something, I would talk with accountants at my Dad's office, making sure I understood all the ins and outs.

Dad and Mom couldn't believe how seriously I had applied myself in my new position. I felt I had a lot to prove to them, Mr. Burns, and myself.

Mr. Burns promoted me twice in six months. I now took care of all his businesses, real estate, car lots, mortgages and the clothing store. Everything I did consisted of accounting work. Thankfully, I loved all aspects of math, my one good subject in school.

While working with the fifty or so mortgages Mr. Burns paid, I created a schedule for payments. The spread sheet showed the banks holding the mortgages had made errors in their calculations. I could hardly wait to show Mr. Burns what I had discovered. I arrived to work early and was so involved in my work I didn't notice him standing over me. He always greeted me with a big cowboy smile.

"Good morning Kathy, you're here early, how is everything going?"

I was so excited about my news, I just blurted it out: "Oh, Mr. Burns, I did all new adjustment schedules and the bank owes you lots of money."

All he did was ask me if I had proof to back up my statement. Assuring him I had checked all my figures several times, he said:

"Let's go confront the bank then."

Suddenly, I wasn't so sure anymore. As scared as I was, as embarrassed as it would have been if I had miscalculated, I still wanted the bank to check their figures. We contacted a woman named Valerie, who handled Mr. Burns' accounts. She asked me for copies of my calculations and requested a few days for review. She told us she would get back to us in a week. I think at that point, Mr. Burns was more excited than I was about finding the errors in the accountants' calculations. He decided in the way of celebration, he would take me to a fancy restaurant for lunch. During lunch he told me if I won against the bank, he would be sending me and my family, on a weeklong all expenses paid vacation. Anywhere I wanted to go! The week slid by quickly. An appointment was arranged with Valerie who had checked my work and wanted a consultation. Upon arrival, my stomach was churning. I thought; what if I had just succeeded in embarrassing Mr. Burns and myself?

Not to worry. Valerie apologized to him for their mistakes and handed him a check for $3,162.00. WOW! I couldn't wait to dig into the other banks holding mortgages for Mr. Burns.

My hourly wage had increased to the point I felt the girls and I could start looking for a home of our own. Not that we didn't love living with my parents but it was time for us to make our own way.

We eventually found our dream home in Northdale. A two story, four bedroom, three bath that included a loft upstairs. I wanted the girls to have their own rooms. Toni Lisa was ten now and loved talking on the phone. The master bedroom located on the ground floor, had a large walk-in closet and my own personal bathroom. In addition to all that comfort, the living room had a fireplace.

There was enough money in my savings account to cover the down payment. Only one problem it was fourteen miles from my parent's home. I hated the thought of leaving them, not to mention moving that far away. The house was everything I ever dreamed and it was our new start. We moved in December 1980.

The girls decided they didn't want their own rooms, and insisted on sleeping in the same room. Life was great. I had a great job, great home, wonderful children and a loving family.

"I, thank you God, for giving me the strength to persevere and for always watching over us."

CHAPTER FIFTEEN–DEVASTATION

I can truthfully say my journey has been guided by my love for my children, and what I thought would be right for them.

On the weekends after Carlos had the girls, I started to see a pattern in their discussions. One particular weekend after visiting their Father, the girls came home arguing. When they walked through the door they both looked disgusted. It looked like they were upset about something but I tried to play it off saying:

"Where are my kisses girls, I missed you?"

Jennifer came up to me with a serious face.

"Mom, I want you to take Dad back. He promised he would be good to us. He wants to be a family again and he still loves you."

Toni Lisa became extremely upset! I didn't even have a chance to say anything.

"Are you crazy? Jennifer I hate him, he used to hit mom all the time! I don't want him back!"

Toni Lisa was upset but I was shocked and hard pressed not to let Jennifer know right then what I thought of her idea. How could I ever go back with that man? I hated him! Jennifer wouldn't stop rambling on about how great it would be for us all to be back in one house again. She upset Toni Lisa so badly they got into a fight. As calmly as I could, I told Jennifer:

"Jennifer, I know your Father put you up to this. He knows we are living in our own home now, not with Papa and Grandma anymore. He is trying to slip back into our lives by telling you lies. I will not allow your Father into our home ever again. He was very abusive to me before and after you were born. I'm just now getting our lives back in line and promise you this is the right way. You can love and see your Father whenever you like. I don't like him! I don't want to ever be with him again. Nor do I care to discuss this any further. Can you understand that Honey?"

Jennifer stood there with her hands on her hips and said:

"Fine, I want to live with Daddy, he needs me!"

I stared at her and felt the very first hint of a new kind of fear. The fear, that he would use my daughter against me. I wasn't entirely sure what to do. Desperate to understand I asked:

"Jennifer, how does he need you?"

Logically, she answers:

"Mom, you have Toni Lisa, Grandma, Papa and all your family. Dad has no one, his Mom and Dad are both gone. He only has me. Toni Lisa hates him."

The entire argument had to have come from Carlos' own mouth. How would she have known that? He knew how much my children meant to me. He was going to use whatever he could to ruin the peace I had worked so hard to achieve.

My heart was shattered! Carlos had reached me through Jennifer! He slammed that well remembered fist into my heart once again!

I realized it was the compassion in Jennifer's heart speaking. I reminded myself that it was her Father we were discussing. Not the abusive man Toni Lisa and I were familiar with, just the Father she loved.

"Jennifer, can we think about this please?"

I decided I needed help. I looked in the phone book under family counseling and made an appointment with Dr. Edwards for three o'clock the next day.

Dr. Edwards was a tall man in his sixties with a gentle, caring face. After introducing himself, he says:

"Kathy, I would like to speak to your daughters alone, prior to visiting with you, if that is okay?"

Half an hour later, they walked out of his office. The girls were both smiling leaving me to wonder. He asked the girls to please wait while he and I went to the office to talk. Before the door had finished closing, I anxiously asked him:

"What did they say? I don't want my girls to hate me; I just want to do what is right for them."

Dr. Edwards looked at me with his soft dark eyes, and told me what I already knew.

"Jennifer has strong feelings for her father. She has been fighting with you and Toni Lisa because she feels he needs her. I sincerely believe it would be in Jennifer's best interest if you were to allow her to live with her father. In doing so, she will see the disciplinarian side of him and decide that isn't what she wants after all. When she realizes she isn't happy living with him, she will want to move back with you. Kathy, if you don't let her, she will hate you and continue causing problems."

His words were like a death sentence, sending shivers down my spine. Just thinking about Jennifer living with Carlos made me feel faint. I felt the blood drain from my face and I couldn't stop the criticism as it poured from my heart. Built up anger and fear forced the words from my mouth:

"No way, he is a drunken loser! He used to beat me. I can't believe this! I've tried so hard to be her friend, yet she still wants to leave me. I refuse to release custody of Jennifer to Carlos, "NO WAY!"

By this time, I was practically screaming. I went silent and started to cry. He handed me some tissues and said:

"Kathy, I know this is a very difficult decision and I want to remind you that you don't have to make it this minute. Discuss this with your family, let them help you. I also want to assure you, you do not have to release custody of Jennifer to your ex-husband for her to live with him. Just let her stay with him a while; let her decide. I've worked with many cases just like yours. Trust me, you can get her back anytime you like. Just give her the choice. She will love you all the more for it in the long run."

The girls chattered all the way home, but my heart and mind were being strangled. I hid my hurt and anger from the girls but it was hard. I never gave Dr. Edwards an answer. I decided I needed to talk to my parents. When we got to my parents home no one was there. The girls ran to play in their old room as I paced the floor. Bright lights flashed across the living room windows as their car drove up. I ran and opened the door for them, they hadn't even removed their jackets when I started in:

"I went to a counselor today and he recommends I allow Jennifer to live with Carlos."

Dad knew how much the thought of Jennifer living with Carlos hurt me, yet he said:

"Kathy, give Jennifer a chance to find out on her own how her father really is. You have custody and can get her back anytime you choose. I think you should let Jennifer have the choice." I did not believe my ears! I never thought Dad would agree with Dr. Edwards.

"But Dad, I don't want her to live with him. Carlos' living conditions aren't what I want for her. I'm her Mother, she should live with me!"

Then Mom sided with Dad and Doctor Edwards, voicing her opinion:

"Honey, Jennifer has become uncontrollable and head strong, just like you were at that age. She loves her Dad, the same way you have always loved your Dad. When you were young, you would have wanted to live with him, not me!"

Mom was right, I knew it. Then Dad suggested:

"Sweetheart, I know you're not happy about this, but you need to call Carlos. Give him some guidelines. If he doesn't want to follow them, Jennifer returns home with you."

By now I was crying again! Mom relented a little, telling Dad:

"I don't know Tony, Jennifer is just a little girl, she doesn't know what is best for her."

Accepting defeat, I miserably said:

"I'll do as Dad says Mom; I'll call Carlos, and tell him, just to see what he says."

So I wouldn't lose my courage or changed my mind, I called Carlos right then and there. When he answered the phone, I tried so very hard to remain calm, cool, and collected. It didn't last.

"Carlos, why do you keep telling Jennifer we can be a family again? You know that's not true."

I would never go back to him and he knew it. I loved Jennifer with all my heart, but I hated her father! I would never ever let him touch me again!

"You put all these ideas in her head and she believes them. If you love Jennifer, don't put her in the middle of us."

I knew immediately with the first word he said, he was drunk.

"Kathy, I still love you. I want us to be a family again. We can do it."

"Not, if your life depended on it Carlos! Are you drunk?"

Slurring his words, he said:

"No, I am just tired but I promise I will quit drinking. I will do better if I have her with me. Just give me a chance. Toni Lisa hates me, I only have Jennifer she will help me change."

In disgust, just wanting to get off the phone with the pathetic, whining drunk, I said:

"Ok Carlos, I know this is what Jennifer thinks she wants. Just please don't hurt her heart. She does love you very much."

I was not ready for the next request! I stood there for a full minute in total shock, what nerve . . .

"Kathy can you give me a little money just to help me out so I can get her a bedroom set?"

The words that came out of my mouth were not what I was thinking at all:

"Sure I can help, but if it gets to be too much, just call me. I want Jennifer happy, whatever it takes. Let's make something else perfectly clear, Carlos, no drinking when you're with Jennifer. If you must drink, bring her home. I don't want her seeing that part of your life."

He was getting his money he wasn't interested in anything else.
"Okay Kathy, I promise!"

Demanding his attention a little longer, I said:

"Carlos, I am doing this for Jennifer, not you! Are you going to be responsible enough to get her to school on time, and make sure she eats?"

With a sigh in his voice:

"Yes Kathy, I am!"

Still not giving up on this last chance I said:

"Carlos, if you can't do this let me know now?"

"Okay Kathy, okay! When can I pick up the money?"

I felt less in control of Jennifer's future than ever before. I hung up the phone. To this day, I have no idea why I helped Carlos take Jennifer from me. I sank into the chair behind me. I felt exhausted and defeated.

Adult decisions are not all easy, or necessarily based on personal desires. Adult decisions don't always reflect what they want. If this was what becoming an adult consisted of, it sucked!

Now I needed to let Jennifer know. I walked down the hall to the playroom with a very heavy heart. Jennifer saw me and said:

"Hi Mom, do you want to color with us?"

The thought of her leaving was just so hard on me. I didn't want Jennifer to know how hard her moving in with her father was for me. I had to accept that my children's way of looking at the world would not always coincide with my own.

"Sure Princess, but first I need to talk to you." I sat down on the floor and pulled Jennifer into my lap. I combed her hair with my fingers and said:

"Jennifer, I know how much you love your Dad, I love my Dad just like you do. You have been telling me how much you want to live with him. Well I just talked to your dad and I am going to let you. He is going to get his own place, a place for just the two of you."

Her excited voice pulled at my heart and I had a hard time keeping from bursting into tears.

"Really? What about Toni Lisa, Mom?"

I looked up at Toni Lisa and she was standing there looking down at me in disbelief. Then she looked at Jennifer with disgust and asked:

"Are you crazy or something, I would never leave Mom. I hate it when I have to go Dads'! I hate him! I love you Mom! I want to stay with you! Jennifer I can't believe you want to leave us!"
I could see the hurt in Jennifer's eyes but I knew she felt like she couldn't let her Dad down.

"I don't want to leave I love you both, but Dad hasn't got anyone! He needs me! I don't hate him, I love him!"

She looked like the six year old she was, but sounded like an adult. She was so beautiful inside and out. Her love is for everyone, not just herself. I loved her so much for that.

"Jennifer, I want you to know that even though you're going to be living with your Dad, all you have to do is call me and I'll come get you okay?"

"Okay Mom"

I was trying to keep myself from crying, so I changed the subject. For me it was easier to forget about a problem if I thought about something better. That is just what I did. I hugged my girls and just kissed them all over.

"Mom!"

They started screaming as I just kept saying:

"I love you, I love you, I love you!"

As I hugged them tight, I said:

"Okay, anywhere you would like to go, name it!"

Jennifer yells:

"Can we go to the pizza place again?"

"Sure my little princesses let's go."

Forcing a smile, plastering that mask of happiness to my face, I lived the lie! Thank God Toni Lisa hadn't wanted to leave me too. The hell I put my parents through, it was coming back to haunt me! Jennifer didn't waste any time and decided to move her things the very next weekend. It was very hard for us packing up Jennifer's clothes. At one point, all three of us were crying.

CHAPTER SIXTEEN–MOVING

Jennifer was as positive about the move to Carlos's house, as I was unshakably negative. The thought of being under Carlos control again made the hair on my neck stand on end. I just could never go back to that man. I know I must sound stupid, that I even considered it, but that's just how much I loved my children. I knew in my heart she would be back soon. She would see the real Carlos. We packed most of her clothes, along with a few of her stuffed animals and dolls. Why couldn't I say 'NO, you have to stay home, like it or not!'

I wanted her to be happy. I wanted her to want to come home. It had to be her choice.

CHAPTER SEVENTEEN–STEPMOTHER

Jennifer had been living with Carlos for a year. I can say it never became any easier. Fears continually plagued me. The crying, each time Jennifer left to go back to Carlos had finally stopped. Being busy at work had a lot to do with my acceptance. She would come stay with Toni Lisa and I, every other weekend, so I tried to make those weekends special.

Mom and Jennifer signed up for swimming lessons at the YMCA. It was cute watching them learn how to swim together. After classes we would all head back to my parent's pool. Those were such good times.

One weekend in particular, my sister joined us to give the girls each a very special gift. The paper flew everywhere as they opened their boxes. Nancy had made them each a belly dancing costume. They were beautiful made from aqua colored silk, with gold detailing. She worked for hours on those costumes.

The girls were of an age to join in our family custom.
As young girls, our female family members were all taught to belly dance. Tradition, we would gather in a circle the men played the drums, and the women dance. We would all have a great time.

Both girls screeched with excitement. They showed their appreciation by mauling Nancy; hugging and kissing her. Our plans for the day included a restaurant. Naturally, the girls wanted to wear their new costumes. My explanation that the costumes were only for family gatherings put a little damper on their spirits. Their spirits lifted when I told them their Uncle Frank would play the drums for them when we got home and they could dance all night if they wanted.

The next morning we left the house at seven am, headed for Disney World. It was a beautiful day, the weather was perfect not a cloud in the sky. It was a two-hour ride, so we played games and sang all the way.

Nothing was better than seeing my girls so happy! As we drove into Disney World, Jennifer saw Mickey Mouse. She jumped up and down in her seat screaming. I couldn't park the car fast enough. We jumped out of the car, running over to see Mickey Mouse. I must admit, I was probably as much of a kid as they were. Their excitement was contagious. Next, they wanted to go to the haunted house. Eventually we went on every ride. We were exhausted, but the girls begged to stay for the parade and fireworks show at midnight.

I was glad we did, it was beautiful! The three of us sat on a truck filled with hay and watched the entire show. Usually I liked to leave a little early so we would miss everyone else leaving. This time was different, we stayed for everything. To this day I am so happy we did.

Carlos was supposed to pick Jennifer up Sunday afternoon. He did, but he wasn't alone. He introduced his companion as Amber Cohen, and made a shocking announcement:

"We are getting married, so I wanted you two to meet!"

I invited them into my parents' house, more out of curiosity, than from a desire to become acquainted with her. Amber's eyes looked up at the soaring ceilings that were decorated with molding and gold leaf. Her eyes continued to roam looking at the Italian marble fireplace then the black slate floors with oriental rugs as she walked into the living room.

"Wow, your parent's home is beautiful!"

As Amber sat down she continued to say;

"I just wanted you to know my father is a very rich man and I attended all private schools. I'll be an excellent mother to Jennifer."

With a mind of its own, my body became very rigid as I spoke:

"Amber, I happen to be Jennifer's Mother!"

It felt like she was applying for a job. Who did she think she was? She immediately apologized.

"I'm sorry, I meant step-mother. I'm pregnant and we're getting married. {Wow, another bombshell} We have been taking Jennifer to and from school, but we only have one car. It has become hard for me to drop Carlos off at work, and still get Jennifer to school. As my pregnancy progresses, it will become even harder."

Now comes the real reason they were here, besides picking up Jennifer of course. I jumped on that statement.

"Then Jennifer needs to move back home with me. I will not have Jennifer walking to and from school; she is only six years old."

She started to explain.

"That isn't what I meant! I was just trying to tell you that I'm not working, and Carlos can't afford another vehicle. If I had another vehicle, I would be able to take Jennifer to and from school."
Can you believe it? She was actually asking me to buy a car for her. She proceeded to tell me she would like a Toyota four-door. Of all

the nerve! Shocked and not knowing what to say, I told them that my boss owned a car lot and I would check it out. That isn't what I really wanted to say at all. My mind was screaming 'you're not supposed to be taking my daughter anywhere, that is her father's job. Who the hell do you think you are?

My hope was that maybe after Jennifer got to know this woman, she would willingly want to come back home. It would be different now that she had to share him with this new wife and baby. While these thoughts ran through my mind, I heard her say:

"We would like the title in our names."

I started to really steam but simply said:

"No problem! I don't want the responsibility of the car in my name anyway. But you must take Jennifer to school and pick her up."

Carlos finally manned up and joined the conversation, saying:

"That will be fine, we can do that."

I hated seeing Jennifer go. The girls and I had such a great weekend. I hoped now that Carlos had a girlfriend, Jennifer would come back home where she belonged.

CHAPTER EIGHTEEN–PRAYER

Sitting at my desk, I was amazed it was May 1982. Where had the last two years gone? I had been employed with Mr. Burns for two years, and I still loved my job. He promoted me to Office Manager. His daughter Susan worked with me and we had become best friends. We laughed a lot and just generally had a great time while we worked.

Mr. Burns' business was growing. After recovering all that money from the banks, I felt like I needed to check out all the mortgages he held, including the ones with the FDIC. We were so busy at the office I was bringing my work home with me. I went back as far as fifteen years. That is when I discovered some major mistakes in the bank calculations. I called to make an appointment with a representative of FDIC, but they couldn't schedule it for six months. I told Mr. Burns and he took it an extra step. He started bragging to everyone that I was going after the FDIC and they were going down. That was all he talked about for the next six months. In fact, he started betting with people that I would win. Talk about pressure, I couldn't let him down.

It was Friday, November 12, 1982; just three more days before the big meeting. I could hardly believe the past six months had gone by so fast. I was nervous but my presentation was ready.
My little sweetheart Toni Lisa was going to her Dad's this weekend. It had started to get a little chilly outside, I thought I better help her pack. Toni Lisa wasn't having any of that.

"Please Mom; I know what I want to wear."

I just put my arms around her and we started play fighting.

"Okay, Okay, you win just bring a sweater. That will make me feel better."

"Okay, Mom."

I loved spending time with her, hearing all her stories from school. She told me everything. I hoped she did anyway. The shrill ring of the doorbell made us both jump.

"It must be your dad. I will go downstairs and let him know you're almost ready."

"Thanks Mom."

I walked to the door and my thoughts turned very dark. How I hated the man at my door. I had to hide my hatred, he was the father of my children; one in particular who loved him very much. As I opened the door, he said:

"Hi Kathy, how are you?"

"Fine, Carlos. Toni Lisa is just about ready. I had her pack a sweater; it looks like it's getting chilly."

"Chilly would be nice; it has been a hot summer. It feels great, except when you have to work outside in that sun."

"How's Jennifer doing? I didn't hear from her yesterday."
"She had a lot of homework last night; she was up late getting it finished. I'll have her call you tonight."

"That would be great Carlos."

I was extremely relieved when Toni Lisa came to the door. I was becoming uncomfortable with this pretend small talk.

"Hi Dad, I am ready. Bye Mom, love you!"

"Ok princess girl, I love you too. Have a good time and don't forget to call me."

Carlos tired of our chitchat, turned and walked toward his car.

"I will Mom. Are you going to be okay by yourself?"

"Yes, I am going to Grandma's for the weekend. Call me there!"

Toni Lisa went running off to the car.

"I love you, Mom!"

Saturday, Mom and I spent all day shopping for a new outfit for my meeting. I wanted everything to be perfect. By the time we were done shopping and getting everything organized, the day was over. We shared hot chocolate and toast as we sat in front of the fireplace just enjoying some one-on-one time. When I went to my old room that night, it was like going back in time. Mom hadn't changed anything! The stress I felt evaporated as soon as I walked through the door. It was the first, no best night's sleep I'd had since Jennifer moved to her Dad's home. I woke up to birds singing outside my window. I loved it here. Waking up in my old bedroom brought back good memories, of when the girls and I had lived here. Our lives here had been the best, we were a family! Darkness edged its way into my mind as I began feeling sorry for myself. Mom's knock on my door saved me. Oh, how nice it felt to hear Mom singing, 'time to get up my beautiful daughter'. Mom was always so chipper, it was contagious. You just couldn't help but smile when you were around her!

"It's Sunday, Mass is in two hours."

As I walked into the kitchen, it was plain Mom had already been up for hours preparing the food for dinner. Our entire family met at Mom's house after Mass to eat dinner and visit every Sunday.

"Honey, can you set the table please? I am running a little late."

How did she even know I was in the room? She had to teach me that one.

"Sure Mom."

Like always, I set the table with her white china, only the best for her family. She always treated us with so much love and respect. Mom always went the extra mile when it came to the people she loved. I heard her calling Dad from the kitchen.

"Tony, we need to go or we will be late."

Dad was mischievously walking ever so slowly, teasing Mom.

"Okay Franny, I'm walking as fast as these ole legs will move. Don't yell at me, yell at them!"

He looked over the top of Mom's head and gave me a wink, grinning from ear to ear.

When we got into the car, she handed him a breakfast sandwich and then slapped his leg playfully.

"I don't want you going to church hungry, although your legs can starve for all I care."

Dad laughed and Mom started giggling.

"Thank you, honey."

Their love for each other was refreshing.

We arrived at Church just in time to rush to Mom's favorite seats up front. I had a special prayer I prayed each week:

"Please dear Lord, I would love to have a family life like my parents; both of my children living with me, and a good husband who loves me and my girls."

Visiting the nuns each week after Church was another ritual. Mom loved them and they loved her. Dad opened the trunk to retrieve the six bags full of goodies and groceries Mom collected through the week for them. Mom was a firm believer in the work they performed for the community, and wasn't afraid to show them her appreciation.

After visiting with the nuns we rushed home to change clothes and finish making dinner before everyone arrived. Everyone helped clear the table after eating a scrumptious meal, and then we retired to the family room to watch the Buccaneers.

CHAPTER NINETEEN—BEATING HEART

Around five that evening I heard the doors slam to Carlos' 78 Mustang. The muffler backfired as he drove away. I ran to open the door for Toni Lisa and realized she was already inside, tears streaming down her beautiful little face.

"What's wrong my princess?"

"Mom it's' Jennifer! She wants to come home. She told me to tell you and Grandma to come and get her."

Just as she finished, Mom walked towards me wide eyed. I knew she had heard Toni Lisa's outburst. Mom wanted Jennifer back home as much as I did. I put my arms around Toni Lisa and led her over to sit on the couch. Mom sat on the other side of her.

"Okay Toni Lisa, start from the beginning. Tell us what happened."

Toni Lisa sat on my lap. She relaxed a bit, but as she tried to explain what went on at Carlos she became more agitated.

"Mom, it was horrible. Poor Jennifer, she was punished the whole weekend. Amber said I was not allowed to talk to her, but I snuck into her room and we talked anyway. Jennifer told me Amber had been yelling at her to clean the house, but Jennifer told her to get off her lazy butt and clean it herself, she wasn't her slave."

Mom and I both started laughing at that one. Amber had met her match with Jennifer.

"But Mom, Jennifer told me Amber hit her and told her to go to her room. When Jennifer slammed her door, Amber told her she was to remain in her room, even while I was there!"

"What?" I screeched?

The hair stood up on the back of my neck; there were goose bumps all up and down my arms. Those were fighting words to me! No one touched my daughter, much less, some bimbo who thinks she would make a good stepmother! I was raging and crying at the same time. I looked at Mom and could see the reflection of my rage. Her eyes were on fire. I took a deep breath and tried to calm myself down so I wouldn't scare Toni Lisa.

"Did Amber allow you to spend any time with Jennifer?"

"No, Mom, Amber even took her food to her room. She wasn't allowed to eat with us. But I did sneak into her room; I saw the bowl of food that Amber gave her. Mom, it had bugs in it! I asked Jennifer if she ate it, she said she picked out as many as she could but she was hungry. Jennifer thinks Amber is trying to kill her. Jennifer told me to tell you and Grandma, that she wants to come home. She doesn't want to live there anymore. She said Dad isn't ever home, and she has to stay there with Amber all the time."

My heart skipped; these were the words I had been waiting to hear for a year and a half! The rage I felt, knowing my youngest daughter was being abused by her stepmother increased. My mind was racing. Toni Lisa had watched her being punished. Their pain became my pain. All the suffering I had known while I was married to Carlos resurfaced and it pushed my control to a breaking point. I was furious beyond imagination, and yelled:

"Mom can you believe this? That's okay, because she is coming home no more games it is over."

Mom was just as upset as I was, and said:

"Honey, I'm going to get my keys, we are going to go get Jennifer back now!"

The entire family had been in the family room watching the football game, but I knew they heard everything going on in the foyer. Dad had the remote in his hand, and he lowered the volume to the TV. Dad called to Mom:

"Franny, what's going on, why are you two so upset?"

Mom replied with a sharp tone.

"Tony, they punished Jennifer the entire week-end; we are going to bring her home."

Still trying to be reasonable Dad said:

"Franny, call Carlos first, see what happened. It won't hurt to call him."

That did it for Mom. I had never heard her speak to Dad in that tone of voice.

"NO, Tony we are leaving now!"

Turning to me, Dad said:

"Kathy, please call Carlos first. Your mother is not listening to reason."

Dad is the calm, cool, collected leader of our family, and rarely did I disobey him. I told Mom it would just take a minute to make the phone call. I should have had Dad make that phone call. I dialed but my hands were shaking so bad I had to hang up and re-dial to get the right number. I was so angry I couldn't see straight. The phone rang only once before Amber picked up.

"Can I speak to Carlos?"

"Hold on."

Carlos answered the phone, but instead of asking him what had happened, I just laid into him. All the built up anger I had shoved to the back of my mind just exploded from my mouth:

"How dare you punish Jennifer all weekend? Who do you think you are? Who does Amber think she is, treating my daughter like that?"

I called him every name I could think of, and the way I was spitting out words, I probably made up a few more no one had ever heard before.

"Jennifer is coming home Carlos! I am not playing this game anymore. I'm not giving you any more money; in fact, I am going to get you for child support. You owe me over seven thousand dollars! Carlos, I'll see you in court!"

So many things came out of my mouth I can't even remember everything. Top that off with Mom grabbing the phone to yell at him; we were out of control.

After listening to this tirade for a bit, Carlos calmly said:
"She wants to stay with me Kathy. She doesn't want to live with you!"

But I told him:

"No Carlos, she told Toni Lisa she was ready to come home and we are coming to get her."

When I looked back at my conversation with Carlos that night, I realized my mistake. Threatening Carlos over the phone put Jennifer in danger. He now knew how much Toni Lisa and Jennifer were talking. If Jennifer were to move back under my roof, his golden goose would be gone. Plus, he was looking at past child support along with current support. Add this to his new wife and child, Carlos was going to be broke! I could hear him in the background talking to Jennifer.

"Talk to your Mother, she is ranting out of her head."

At the time, I didn't recognize the strain in Jennifer's voice. I feel certain now, that they were standing over her, listening to every word she said. Rage and hatred blinded all logical thought. Memories of the way Carlos treated me the entire time we were together, the scars he had left, not just on me, but on Toni Lisa flitted through my mind. I wished he would just disappear from the face of this earth! The next words I heard were from my sweet baby Jennifer.
"Mommy, I am sorry but I want to stay here with Daddy!"

Not believing her, I said:

"Jennifer, I don't like the way they are treating you. You are my baby; I want you home with me. I am coming to get you. Grandma and I will be right there!"

How I despised that man. I intended to do everything in my power to make him suffer. I wanted him to feel the 'Longo' wrath! I slammed the phone into its cradle saying:

"Let's go Mom; I can't stand the thought of Jennifer being with Carlos one more minute."

Mom went to get her purse and keys, but Dad interrupted and said:

"Franny what's going on, what are you two up to now?" "Kathy and I are going after Jennifer!"

He turned to me and said:

"Kathy, I understand you're upset, but can't you do it the right way? You have custody; call your attorney in the morning. Let him handle it legally. He will have them pack her stuff and bring her home."

Dad's plan just didn't work for me! I wasn't even really listening to him.

"Dad that could take forever, I want to get her now!"

When Dad raised his voice over my own, I should have shut up, and listened.

"Kathy, Amber is pregnant. You go over there now, the way you and your Mom are screaming, she could end up losing the baby. This is a law suit waiting to happen. Just call the attorney in the morning." Mom was fed up with the arguing.

"NO, Tony! We are picking her up NOW!"

Dad finally lost his temper completely and threw the remote he had been holding. It hit the metal coffee table and shattered into pieces. We all just froze! This was so out of character. Time just stopped for a couple seconds. All of us jumped when Julie began shrieking. Julie, my brother's wife, was hit by a flying piece of the remote. She stood there, holding her mouth as the blood gushed through her fingers. Dad froze for just a brief second, staring at all the blood. Mom ran into the kitchen and grabbed a towel for Julie. Dad rushed toward Julie saying:

"Julie, I am so sorry."

Julie was trembling, tears poured down her face. I know she was trying to hide her pain, but the agony on her face was clear. We couldn't stop the bleeding so we rushed Julie to the hospital!

During the ride to the hospital, I had plenty of time to berate myself. If only I had listened to Dad. All I had been concerned with was hurting Carlos, as he had hurt me and my babies. I had started trouble again; my poor sister-in-law was just an innocent by-stander. She hadn't deserved this, and poor Dad, I upset him so much he lost his temper. He never did that. I loved my parents, my family; I needed to do as Dad said.

The on-duty emergency nurse escorted Julie and my brother, Frank, back to a room. Dad was so worried; there had been so much blood. We didn't know if her nose was broken or how bad the cut was under her nose. After three hours of waiting, the Doctor came out to speak to Dad. Dad met him half way across the room:

"How is she, is everything okay?"

He was such a good doctor he grabbed Dad's hand and squeezed it gently.

"It will be fine Tony, don't worry everything will be okay. But Julie does need to have a plastic surgeon look at her. Jennifer was no longer center stage. We were all upset with what had happened to Julie, worrying if she would be all right.

My dad told him whatever she needed please, only the best for her.

After being there for over six hours the doctor came out and told us everything would be fine. She would have a tiny scar, but the specialist said after a month or so, it wouldn't be noticeable. During the drive back to my parents' house, I told Dad I would call the attorney in the morning. We were all exhausted, mentally and physically.

Later, I found out Carlos was at his favorite bar the same time we were at the hospital. He was getting drunk, talking loudly, and making threats.

"I'll show them, they think their shit doesn't stink. I taught that bitch daughter of theirs a lesson. Just wait and see what I do; I will teach them a lesson they won't ever forget!"

The bartender said Carlos didn't leave the bar until around two in the morning. When he did leave, he was plastered.

I did not remember much about the drive home. I was dizzy; it was hard to concentrate as I got ready for bed. When I finally laid down my eyes closed. I soaked my pillow with tears. Everything that had happened tonight was swirling around in my mind Jennifer, Toni Lisa, Julie, Dad and the meeting at work in a few hours. Everything was just spinning. Finally, I decided I couldn't sleep and got dressed for work and went in early. It's easier to forget your problems if you're busy.

I called Mom at lunchtime; she had taken Toni Lisa to school. She said everyone was doing fine.

My meeting was at three o'clock, I decided to leave at two thirty I didn't want to be late. My office was located at Florida Ave and Bears, so I had quite a drive. As I drove on the interstate I passed Jennifer's exit, I argued with myself; I wanted so much to pick Jennifer up. I had waited for over a year and a half. I would have to wait a little longer. I promised Dad I would do it the right way.

I was very nervous and excited at the same time. I arrived at the FDIC building ten minutes early! I wore the new outfit and carried the new black brief case I had purchased while shopping with Mom. I was ready for a fight! The receptionist escorted me right into their conference room. Again, my figures were right! FDIC ended up crediting Mr. Burns a little over ten grand for fifteen years of over payment on interest. In fact, FDIC offered me a job that day! After feeling like such a failure for so long, having only finished the ninth grade; all that extra time at the library . . . I was ecstatic!

November 15, 1982 was a special day for me. I had beat the best FDIC I felt I had finally accomplished something. I know it's hard to understand why this was so important, but I had felt like such a failure in everything I had done in my life. I had always labeled myself as the bad girl who didn't finish school. Marrying a terrible man, who had abused me. But in this job I felt needed, smart and respected by business people. I was on cloud nine. Now, I needed to fix the problems with Carlos.

CHAPTER TWENTY–DAY ONE

Jennifer School Picture Taken 11/15/1982

Every Mother's worst nightmare became mine on November 15, 1982. What follows was discovered while police interviewed witnesses, classmates, neighbors, teachers, a crossing guard, and family members.

THERESA: Jennifer got up earlier than normal on November 15, knowing it was a special day for her too. School pictures were going to be taken that day.

She had a special dress she had picked out to wear. It was pink, her favorite color, with little flowers on it. She got all dressed up, fixed her hair and headed out to meet her best friend Theresa. Theresa was one year older than Jennifer, but was in her class.

Theresa listened, as Jennifer still upset from the previous day's argument and told her what had happened. Dad and Mom were fighting. How Amber was right on top of her, telling her what to say, while she was talking to her Mom on the phone. She also told Theresa she really wanted to come back home with her Mom, but she was scared to say anything.

The school bell rang, and they had to go to class. Pictures were scheduled after second period.

PHOTOGRAPHER: The photographer said Jennifer talked quietly to her friends while waiting her turn. She sat on the seat, and faced the photographer. Jennifer gave a big smile, saying cheese. The camera shutter snapped and it was all done.

TEACHER: Jennifer walked back to her classroom. After the class had settled down, Jennifer raised her hand asking to be allowed to read to the class. Her teacher told her that since the chairs were already stacked against the wall, she thought it would be a good idea. All the children gathered on the floor facing Jennifer. The teacher handed Jennifer a book off the shelf and she read until the school bell rang at two fifteen. Jennifer put the book down, got her belongings and skipped out with a happy smile on her face. Jennifer headed to the front of the school to wait for all her friends.

THERESA: Jennifer saw Theresa and walked up to her. The girls giggled as eight-year old Greg and nine-year old David joined them. They usually walked home together, this day being no different. As they reach Linebaugh the boys said their goodbye and left, heading up the street to their home. Jennifer was still troubled at what happened the night before. As soon as the boys had turned off, she started telling Theresa how she was upset with her Dad, and the way he had acted. As they reached 98th and 15th, they had to go their separate ways. Jennifer gazed towards her house. She lifted her face to meet Theresa eyes saying:

"Theresa, will you watch me as I walk the rest of the way home? I'm a little nervous and scared."

Theresa thought it odd. Jennifer had made that walk lots of times. She knew she was upset so told her:

"Sure Jennifer, no problem!"

It was four blocks to Jennifer's house, but Theresa said she watched until she heard her Mom calling.

"Theresa, what are you doing? Get in this house."
"I will be right there Mom."

When she looked back to see how much farther Jennifer had to go, she was gone. Thinking Jennifer had made it home; Theresa went on inside her house.

CHAPTER TWENTY ONE–TERROR

As I remember, I felt elated. Success was a drug itself.

Diana was waiting outside our office, standing at the front door when I pulled into my parking space at work. I could see her waving her hand at me and I thought to myself '*what is going on*'?

"Kathy, we have to go, Carlos just called, and Jennifer did not come home."

"What are you talking about, Jennifer lives with Carlos."

"Kathy let's go, we will take my Dad's car, it has a phone in it."

"I don't understand what's going on. Where is Jennifer? Why did Carlos call you?"

"Kathy let's just wait till we get there."

I became upset with her and asked:

"Get where?"

Then my mind clicked through what she had said. Why hadn't Jennifer come home? OH MY GOD, Jennifer was missing! We climbed into the car and Diana started the engine. As she looked my way she asked:

"Kathy, are you okay?"

My throat had closed and I couldn't speak. Fear consumed me. Everything I had thought so important this morning was nothing! I should have picked her up! A sick panic engulfed me. I was in shock and beginning to shake and cry. I rocked backward and forward while I squeezed the blood out of my arms. Why couldn't I ever make the right decisions? I spoke through gritted teeth and asked Diana:

"Did she run away?"

I didn't wait for Diana to answer. Did Jennifer think I don't love her; did she think I didn't want her to come home? I needed to find her. I needed to let her know how much I loved her. I just didn't know if I was strong enough. Please, Dear Lord, help me. Please, I need you, and she needs you! Please watch over her wherever she is. Our Father . . . . I finished my prayer and refused to believe anything but that Jennifer was okay. My heart would tell me if she wasn't, wouldn't it? Positive thoughts kept me sane until we arrived at Carlos duplex.

When we reached the duplex, Diana hadn't even come to a complete stop when I climbed out of the car. Carlos was standing outside talking to an officer.

The duplex he lived in was such a horrible place; how could I have allowed Jennifer to live with her father. What was wrong with me? Jennifer was my first concern, and I needed to get some answers; I would punish myself later. I needed to find Jennifer and bring her home. Grinding my teeth, I stalked toward Carlos and the officer and demanded:

"What's going on Carlos? Where is Jennifer?"

"I don't know, she didn't come home from school!"

"What do you mean; she didn't come home from school? Didn't Amber pick her up?"

"No, Amber wasn't feeling good, so she told her to walk home."

"She walked all that way from school? How could you do that? Are you crazy? She is just seven years old. What's wrong with you?"

"Don't blame me, it's not my fault. I called the police as soon as I found out."

Carlos' rudeness increased my rage. I wanted to strike out at him! The officer looked at me as if I were the rude one!

I stood and stared at the two of them and thought: 'what is wrong, they should be looking for Jennifer, not standing here writing a book.' It was four o'clock, and going to get dark soon. We had to find her before it got dark. The officer making out his report was my next victim.

"So, what are you going to do officer, just stand there?"

The Officer threw his shoulders back and stood very rigid, looking at me very unkindly! I knew I had made him angry, but I didn't care. In a very sharp, curt voice, he explained:

"I am making out a report for your daughter Ms. Longo; I assume you are Ms. Longo. Then I will call it into the station."

Before I could correct the officer, Carlos butted in and said:

"Kathy, I thought it was best to call the police first, and then we can go out and look for Jennifer."
The officer wasn't happy with interruptions and said:

"Sir, I need to finish asking you some questions for my report."

All I was interested in was finding Jennifer! I didn't care about anyone or anything else. I just knew I had to find her and bring her home. Even if she ran away because I didn't come pick her up; even if she thought I didn't love her! I knew if I could talk to Jennifer I could explain everything. I tossed my hands in the air in frustration and started running up and down the street. As I looked in and around the yards, I hollered:

"JENNIFER! JENNIFER where are you?"

Diana followed me, not knowing what else to do. She was probably scared to say anything. I held off crying, but turned into a mean, ugly, maniac, yelling and shouting at everyone. I hated the world. I was in the middle of a nervous breakdown and being tough and mean was the only way I could handle the situation. My character changed so drastically, I didn't recognize myself. Reckless would have been an appropriate description!

Feeling helpless during my search for Jennifer that day, was my own fault. What she did here, at her father's house, how her room was decorated, who her friends were, was all a mystery to me. If I'm guilty of anything, it was ignoring the life she had made; refusing to believe she could choose her Dad over me. I had hoped she would get her fill of the dumpy life and be done with Carlos. That hadn't happened, and now it was too late!

"Jennifer, Jennifer, please Jennifer where are you? Please princess, Mommy is here . . ."

Finally succumbing to the strain, I broke down sobbing. Diana caught up to me. She held me tight and listened while I berated myself. "I can't believe she is missing, she has to be here. I have to find her. Why did I let her come live with Carlos?"

All the streets looked the same, duplex after duplex. Steel fences surrounded yards with posted warnings: 'BEWARE OF DOG.'

Yards were filled with cars and playing children. I could hear laughter, but none of the voices belonged to Jennifer. I would have known her voice anywhere.

I turned and darted to the other side of the road where two small boys were playing basketball in the street. It was hard for me to talk because my throat was so dry. Running there would have been hard in tennis shoes but I was so anxious I ran in 5" heels and a suit. My breathing was ragged when I asked them:

"Do either of you boys know Jennifer Marteliz?"

David, the taller of the two looked up at me with dark hazel eyes. He wasn't real sure he should talk to me, but finally said:

"Yes, ma'am she goes to our school."

Thank God, I had found someone who knew Jennifer!

"Did you see her today?"

"We walked home with her and Theresa. We turn at the light."

"Do you think she could be with Theresa?"

"I don't know, but Theresa lives right over there in that brown duplex!"

"Did Jennifer say anything about wanting to run away, or if someone was going to pick her up today?"

"No ma'am, didn't she make it home from school yet?"

"No, I am looking for her; if you see her would you let her know. Thank you."

“Yes ma’am, we will, I hope you find her.”

I ran over to the brown duplex he indicated was Theresa’s and knocked on the door. A very pretty little girl answered the door.

“Are you Theresa?”

“Yes ma’am, I am!”

“Would Jennifer be here with you?”

“No, Jennifer is at her house!”

“No, she never made it home today.”

“Yes she did, she wanted me to watch her walk the rest of the way to her house.”

Dismayed, I said:

“You saw her go to her house? You’re sure?”

Theresa’s face brightened as she asked:

“Are you Jennifer’s mother? She has talked a lot about you and Toni Lisa. How you all go to this pizza place and Disney World. I have never been to Disney World. She said she had so much fun.”

“Theresa, I promise when we find Jennifer, I am going to take you both to Disney World. We will all have a good time together.”

“Okay, but I will have to ask my Mom first!”

“Theresa, right now I just need to find Jennifer.”

Theresa remained firm in her answer:

"But I saw her walking home."

"Theresa did you walk with her up to her house? Her Father says she didn't make it home today."

"Jennifer told me she was scared, that you and her dad had a big fight. She asked me to watch her while she walked home. I saw her walk up to her mailbox."

"Theresa, are you sure you saw her go up to the mailbox?"

"Yes, I am positive!"

There was a ray of hope; Theresa didn't have any reason to lie. I couldn't say the same about Carlos. She interrupted my thoughts when she said:

"She is my best friend. We do everything together, and she tells me everything. She told me about you and her father getting into arguments all the time. How she hated her step mom. She told me she was thinking about moving back to your house."

For a short moment my heart soared, and then plummeted just as fast.

"Please Theresa, if Jennifer calls you, or you see her, please let me know."

When we walked away Theresa smiled a shy smile and waved goodbye. I decided to head back to Carlos' house to see if they had heard anything. Diana and I hurried, night was falling, and the fear of not finding Jennifer before nightfall consumed my thoughts. Only the hope Theresa gave me, kept the fear at bay.

On the way back, Diana told me she should call her Dad and let him know what was going on. She wanted to know if I wanted to call anyone. I told her I needed to call my Mother, she would be wondering what had happened to me. I dreaded the thought of telling Mom Jennifer was missing, especially after everything we had gone through last night.

"Mom, I'm at Carlos', Jennifer is missing. She didn't come home from school. The Police are making out a report, but I have been here over an hour and Jennifer isn't anywhere to be found."

I broke down and sobbed like a baby. Mom's voice finally calmed the hysterics.

"Kathy, just calm down, this isn't helping Jennifer. Listen, as soon as I let your Dad know, I will meet you at Carlos'. We will find her, everything will be all right. Kathy, don't you have a picture of Jennifer in your wallet? What about taking it to the TV station?"

"That's a great idea Mom; I'll do that now."

"Kathy, Jennifer could have run away because of what happened last night. We will find her, okay. She needs you to be strong right now, don't let her down. I love you honey, just keep your chin up. We will find her! I will bring Toni Lisa with me."

"Okay Mom and I love you too."

Mom's suggestion motivated me. I knew she was right, but I still felt weak. She had sparked a glimmer of hope. I held onto my sanity by a single fragile thread, never in my life not even married to Carlos had I felt so powerless. Diana interrupted my thoughts when she asked me:
"Kathy, are you okay? What did your Mom say?"

Her question brought me back to the present and as I grabbed my purse I said:

"Mom suggested I take some pictures of Jennifer to the TV Station."

I rummaged around my purse and found my wallet. I was frantic to be doing something positive. I opened my wallet and Jennifer was staring at me with her beautiful warm eyes. I imagined I could hear her calling me, 'where are you Mommy, please come and get me.'

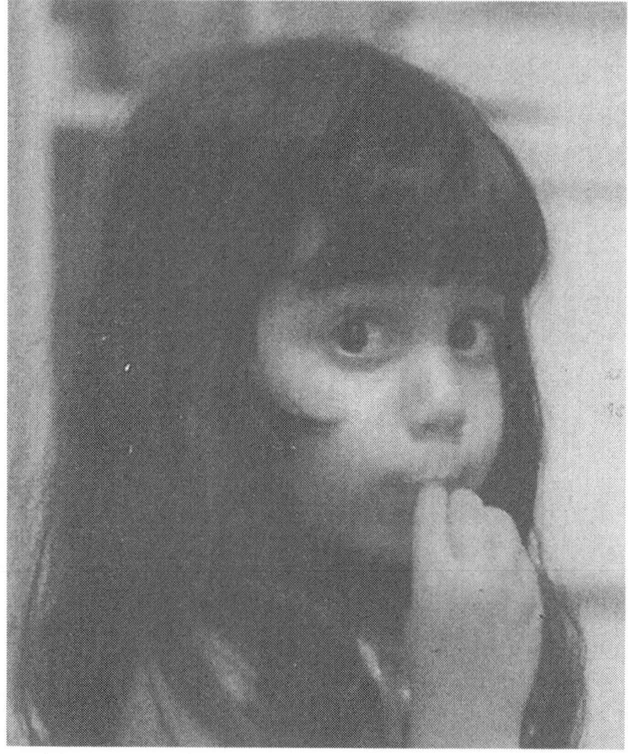

Jennifer

A thousand words couldn't explain how I felt, but one word could—Guilty! I had to have more pictures; Diana drove me to

Mom's house. Once we got there I didn't wait for Diana to stop the car I jumped out. I ran into the den and grabbed our photo album and just threw everything upside down. There—they were more pictures of my precious baby. I grabbed them and ran back to the car.

Jennifer

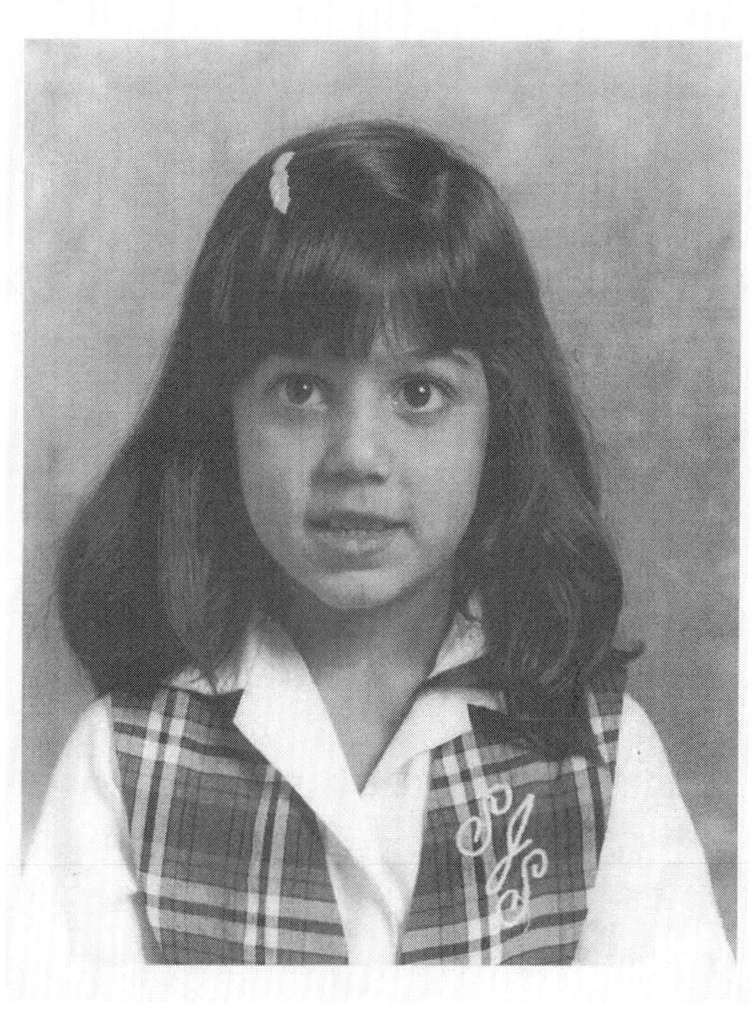

"Diana, would you please take me to the Channel 13 Station?" The clock on the dash blinked five-thirty.

"Sure Kathy."

Diana was truly a good friend. At that moment I don't know what I would have done without her.

I felt dizzy! It was hard to concentrate. All I could see were Jennifer's eyes in the picture. I tried to breathe normal. I needed to concentrate on a way out of this nightmare.

Diana stopped the car at the front door and I jumped out and ran into the building to the front desk. My words just yelled out;

"My daughter is missing. Please I need your help can you broadcast her picture during the six O'clock News, please."

The receptionist backed away from the counter slightly, looking at me in disapproval. She told me they hadn't received a notice from the police that a child was missing. Was I sure?

I felt my face turn beet red and furiously I said:

"Yes, I am sure! It's my daughter that is missing, her name is Jennifer Marteliz."

She turned her back to me to dial the Police Department.

"This is Sarah at Channel 13, I am checking to see if you have any reports on a missing child? Her name is Jennifer Marteliz."

"Okay, I see, I will let her know, thank you."

"I'm sorry but they don't have a report on a missing child. A father called in to report that the Grandmother picked up the child without his knowledge."

Frustrated, I slammed my hands on that counter and assured her in a very loud voice:

"NO, she did not. Jennifer is missing and my mother is out there looking for her."

"I am sorry, but you will have to take that up with the police."

I was totally enraged by her lack of cooperation. I walked, miserably, out of the Station and struggled with emotions that nearly overwhelmed me. I stopped just outside the main doors and attempted to forestall tears. I dug my fingernails into the palms of my hands, and squeezed my eyes tight. As loud as I could, and until I ran out of breath, I screamed! Not words, just pure rage and frustration! I gasped, opened my eyes, and gulped in fresh air. Determination saved me. I was only twenty-eight, but I had been through a lot and had never given up. I wasn't planning to start now. I pulled myself together and decided to do whatever it took to get my daughter back!

I felt like I had just been hit by a car and I am sure I looked like it. As I was getting into the car I explained to Diana what had happened;

"We need to go to the Police Station. Carlos was so stupid; he didn't even report his missing child correctly."

As Diana drove, I stared out the passenger window. The sky had darkened as if affected by my mood. Jennifer was afraid of the dark and I was afraid for her. Diana killed the engine, but her hands stayed clenched around the steering wheel.

"Kathy, I am coming with you this time. You are not going alone."

Her voice was stern. I breathed a silent sigh of relief I did need her. The place was busy. People were everywhere; waiting in line for their turn to talk. Signs on the wall read: 'REWARD DEAD OR ALIVE.' I tried to barge into the front of the line, but the officer asked me to please wait my turn. It was hard, standing there, waiting, and not doing anything.

When we finally made it to the head of the line, I demanded to know why they had lied about my daughter. My accusations and rude manner never even fazed the officer. He simply told me to slow down. He asked me who I was, and what I was talking about. Taking a deep breath, I told him I was Kathy Longo, and my daughter Jennifer Marteliz was missing. I explained that I had taken some photographs of Jennifer to Channel 13, wanting them to air them on the six o'clock news. When the receptionist called the Police Station, she was told Jennifer was with her grandmother. I explained to him that Jennifer was NOT with my mother, she was missing! By the time I finished talking, the tears rolled down my face.

He told me to hold on for just a second he needed to check with the reporting officer. After making a phone call, he just picked up the microphone to his radio, and began broadcasting an all units bulletin. Without looking up, he called Channel 13, and instructed them to include a 'Missing Child Alert' during their news broadcast, giving them the pertinent information.

I felt relieved now that some definitive action was being taken. It helped that this officer actually acted as though he cared.

"Thank you, Officer; you're the first person who has even attempted to help me!"

He apologized for all the confusion and told me he hoped I found Jennifer soon!

I turned around and asked:

"Diana can we go back to Carlos's duplex."

Mom and Dad would be there by now, and I needed to know if there was any news. I decided there was just one thing I had to believe to survive this ordeal with my sanity; Jennifer was still alive, she had to be! That belief would keep me going. I refused to believe anything else.

As we approached the neighborhood the traffic got very congested. I could hear the helicopters overhead, police car sirens. Was this for Jennifer? As we got closer to the duplex, there were hundreds of people walking around. There were reporters and camera men, news trucks and so many police officers. It was amazing. Everyone was here to help us find my baby.

We climbed out of Diana's car, and even before I straightened all the way up, we saw a jumbled mass of television lights, cameras, microphones and people rushing toward us. Voices shouted out questions in unison.

"What can you tell me about your daughter?"
"How old is she?"
"What was she wearing this morning?"
"Are you sure she isn't visiting a friend?"
"Do you think your daughter has run away?"
"Do you believe she has been abducted?"
"Have there been any ransom demands?"
"Do you have a picture of your Daughter?"

How did these people know I was Jennifer's Mother? I didn't care, I was just so happy they were there to help me. My head was buzzing with all the questions. But all I could think about was showing Jennifer's picture so someone would recognize her and bring her home. I had the pictures in my hand and held them up so the cameras could see her, and then I said;

"She is just a little girl, seven years old. She has long black hair, and big dark brown eyes. If anyone knows anything, please call the Police. Please, if everyone could please help me find my little girl."

I wiped tears from my cheeks. Reporters mobbed me from all sides, shoving their microphones in my face, while blinding me with flash bulbs. Before anything more could be said, an officer ushered me away from them, telling me he wanted to speak to me regarding new information. He held his hand out to the reporters, indicating they were to leave us alone.

"Ms. Longo, I've just completed an interview with Tammy Russo. She is a tourist, visiting some friends who live a block away from your ex-husbands' duplex. She claims she saw a rust colored car; the occupant had slammed their door which drew her attention. She believes she saw Jennifer running away from that car between 2:45 and 3:15 this afternoon. She didn't pay much attention to it, thinking it was the child next door. She doesn't recall seeing the tag number, but is willing to be hypnotized to make sure. Do you recall seeing a vehicle with that description?"

I shook my head no and I told him I didn't live here. Jennifer lived here with her Father and Step-mother. When I glanced towards Carlos' duplex, I saw him standing there, with his hands in his pockets, just staring at me with an odd expression. Bells and whistles went off in my head, but before I could think about the look on his face, another Officer approached me.

"Ms. Longo, some of Jennifer's classmates said Jennifer was talking about running away, with one of the other girls in her class. When we find out the girl's name we will let you know."

He wanted to know if Jennifer had been moody or uncommonly quiet recently.

I shook my head and replied:

"Jennifer would never run away, not when all she had to say was, 'Mom I want to move back home'."

The profound numbness that threatened to overtake me began to fade with news from the two officers. Hopeful energy took its place.

Mom found me while I was talking with the officers. She stood there, waiting for them to finish, and held my hand. When the officers walked away, we grabbed each other and hugged hard. Neither one of us wanted to think about what had happened the night before, but we both knew if we had gone to pick up Jennifer, we wouldn't have been in this nightmare! Mom was my rock, my support; I don't know what I would have done without her. Finally, Mom said:

"Everything will be okay Honey. She is fine. We will find her."

Dad finally got loose from the reporters. He hurried over and grabbed me in a bear hug.

"Honey, I'm so sorry, this is my fault. I should have let you and your Mom pick Jennifer up last night!"

I was concerned when I realized my Dad was carrying all the guilt on his shoulders. I couldn't let my Dad blame himself! I was Jennifer's Mother and I should have made right decisions. This abduction was my fault not his! Everyone else in my family had normal lives; happily married with great relationships. Not me, no, I was stuck in a hole I had created by making bad choices.

"No way Dad! Just forget that ever happened last night. I'll tell the police about the argument Carlos and I had, but that's it. Sorry Dad but I am going to be the strong one this time. We are not going to mention last night ever again. Please Dad, for me. Promise me."

Tears welled in his eyes. I was his only child that made him cry. I loved him so much, he was my hero. Why is it, I caused him so much pain?

A commotion behind us caught our attention. It was one of the K9 units going crazy around Carlos duplex! The dog ran from the front door to the mailbox and back. I walked over to the Officer controlling his dog, and asked if I could pet his partner. He was huge, thick black and brown hair, but you could tell he was much more muscular. I knelt down to pet him; his eyes were dark, nearly black. He gazed at me for a fraction of a second, the deep eyes seeming too intelligent for a wild animal. I leaned in close and whispered in his ear; 'Please help me find Jennifer. Please, if anyone can, you can!' Without warning he spun around and pulled the Officer back to the front door of the duplex. Snarling and snapping so loudly that my hands flew up to cover my ears. The officer had to pull the dog back to their cruiser. He walked back over to me and explained there were too many people, his K-9 partner probably lost Jennifer's scent.

Just then an officer ran up to me saying they found they found out the name of the little girl who talked about running away with Jennifer. She lived a few blocks from Carlos' duplex. Mom and I hurried towards her home. I looked over my shoulder and noticed several officers had gotten into their cars and were following us slowly down the street. I felt like they were going to stop us, so we ran. We were out of breath by the time we stood on Laurie Anderson's porch! I felt excited as I banged on her door just thinking that Jennifer could be in the house. Every instinct I had convinced me she was in that house. I decided right then I would hug her until she couldn't stand it anymore. I would give Jennifer a big party with all her friends. Mrs. Anderson opened the door.

"Yes, can I help you?"

"Yes please. I'm looking for my daughter. They say she might be here with your daughter. They were talking about running away together."

"I'm sorry, but your daughter is not here!"

"Can we just look please? She could be hiding and you don't know it."

"No, you cannot; you need to leave right now."

I heard police cruisers as they came closer and panicked. If I didn't act, I might not be able to later. I decided to pay the consequences and pushed the lady aside, ran into her house calling for Mom to check the rooms. I yelled for her to hurry because the police were very close.

The entire family came out of their rooms and screamed at us to get out of their house. 'What did we think we were doing?' They told the officers to hurry up and get us out of their home. I responded by yelling: "Mom are you done? I am!"

"Yes, I've checked these rooms. Jennifer isn't here."

When we left the house, an officer grabbed each of us by an arm. I thought to myself, it looked like we were going to jail! I didn't care; I just wanted to find Jennifer. I decided if I had it to do over again, I would have done the same thing. The officer holding my arm asked:

"Mrs. Anderson, have the Longo's caused any trouble here? If you want, we can have them arrested for entering your home without your permission, disrupting your family!"

"No, I feel for them, I probably would have done the same thing. It's okay, I let them in, let them go, they didn't hurt anything."

"Are you sure, Mrs. Anderson?"

"Yes, I'm sure!"

Looking at Mom and me, she said:

"I will pray for you ladies. You are going to need it."

I grasped her hands with both of mine and said:

"Thank you Mrs. Anderson. We can use all the prayers we can get. I am sorry for barging into your home; I just want to find my daughter."

The officers escorted Mom and I off Mrs. Anderson's property and warned us that we should allow them to do their jobs, they were trained professionals.

I nodded my head and agreed with them, but I didn't mean it. If the situation needed to be repeated, I wouldn't involve Mom. I didn't want anything to happen to her. This was my daughter and I would do whatever it took, even if it meant going to jail!

All the energy I had hoping Jennifer was hiding at Mrs. Anderson's house, disappeared as we headed back to the duplex. I slumped dejectedly and an ache radiated throughout my body. I was exhausted and just walking was difficult. Darkness covered my spirit just like the approaching nightfall blanketed the area of our search. But as we walked, my resolve to find Jennifer bolstered my sagging spirits. By the time we arrived at the duplex, I held my head high and I was re-invigorated and my purpose was clear—FIND JENNIFER.

Searchers began to leave, but assured us they would return in the morning. I understood they had other responsibilities and we thanked them for their help. The number of people who had come out to help search for Jennifer was amazing and their departure was very disturbing.

"Mom, I can't leave here, I am staying until Jennifer comes home!" "Your Dad and I are staying too Kathy. We are not leaving!"

The temperature dropped when the sun went down and it surprised us when Carlos invited us into his home. Carlos had all the lights on but it was still dark. As I walked into the duplex the only furniture in the room were a couch and a TV. As I sat down I could see there were two bedrooms. It looked like Carlos and Amber's room was at the front and Jennifer's room was toward the back of the duplex. Mom, Dad and I sat on the couch and Toni Lisa sat on my lap. Carlos and Amber sat at the kitchen table. It was quiet and it felt very awkward. The Police officers and the FBI decided to stay outside. They were setting up a command post on the street. The two officers that were in charge stayed inside asking us questions about Jennifer.

Everyone had a theory: the police leaned toward 'run-a-way'; the FBI believed we would receive a ransom demand and the media just wanted to know why an affluent family member lived in this area. Carlos and Amber kept their thoughts to themselves. Mom, Dad and I had our own theory.

I sat on the couch and the walls seemed to close in on me. I got up, walked to the window and looked out at the street. The Command Station was lit like a circus, but the area surrounding it was dark. I wandered from window to window and finally found myself in Jennifer's tiny bedroom. There were mementos of her life everywhere. I pulled her dresser drawer open. I thought I might find something to explain this nightmare. I pulled out some of her tiny clothes and held them close to me. My knees buckled under me, and I fell onto my hands, I felt as though I couldn't breathe. I couldn't move but my arms and legs were shaking. My mind couldn't move past the fear, the horror I just didn't understand. Not knowing where or what has happened to my baby. I could hear the cold breeze whip through the windows as though she was trying to call me. There was nothing I could do. Jennifer's words repeated in my head. I love you mommy . . .

I pressed my fist against my mouth to keep from screaming but the tears never stopped.

My mother came into the room. She had heard me crying. We both felt tormented, if only we had picked her up. We never mentioned it, we just knew. Mom knelt next to me and held me in her arms. She said:

"Honey, you mustn't blame yourself." I squeezed my eyes tight together trying to be strong. I then found a new escape to calm myself; I fantasized Jennifer running into the house yelling my name. Mommy everything is okay I am fine. The vision comforted me. I was calmer, but still a mess. I opened my eyes and took a deep breath only to see the pain in my mother's eyes. I felt a lump beginning to build in my throat.

"Are you okay Mom?"

I asked while I could still speak. She didn't respond in any way, she just stood up and held me strong. Mom put her hands around my face very slowly, drawing out the words,

"We can do this."

Mom took me by the hand and pulled us away from that darkness. I was exhausted, heartbroken, and angry. I wished I was dead, but knew I had to keep going. I had to find my baby! I had allowed her to live in a hellhole. It was difficult to accept, every decision I have made had consequences!

I returned to Carlos' living room where Mom discussed getting something to eat with Dad. I saw Carlos walk out the front door and followed him. Standing under the awning in the darkness, I watched Carlos approach a female officer. He was very nervous. I wondered why?

I strained to hear Carlos' words.

"Wow, there have been a lot of people out here tonight. Has anyone heard anything, any leads? Do you have any suspects?"

"Nothing yet, Mr. Marteliz, but we have half the force out looking, following leads."

"But I thought you people didn't get involved with a missing persons' case until they were missing for 24 hours?"

She gave Carlos a strange look and said:

"Typically that is the case, but since your daughter comes from such a high profile family, we got involved early."

Carlos shrugged and walked away muttering to himself. I wondered if Carlos felt guilty for letting Jennifer walk home from school. The one person who loved him unconditionally and he had let this happen to her! I turned around to go back into the house and thought how stupid Carlos appeared. Instead, I should have wondered why he had asked such a question. He should have been happy the police were on Jennifer's case so quickly.

CHAPTER TWENTY TWO—DAY TWO

It was Tuesday, November 16, and there was light coming through the window curtains. It was morning, but I don't remember the time. I didn't care. The only thing I cared about was that my daughter was still missing, and we had not received a ransom demand yet.

Mom and I walked outside, stretching our legs. Breathing that fresh crisp air felt pleasant compared to the closeness of the previous night. Amber was outside and I looked at her knowing she had hit Jennifer! I wanted to do her bodily harm! Carlos had said Amber was sick, that was why Jennifer had to walk home. Amber wasn't sick! Maybe sick in the head but not physically. She looked fine to me! I would have to wait to confront Amber until later; right now, the most important thing I had to do was find Jennifer!

We both stopped dead in our tracks, there were people everywhere. Press vans, reporters, neighbors, police, FBI, friends, People we know and more that we didn't. I thanked God for them! Everyone wanted to help me find Jennifer. The people of Tampa exhibited their true colors for me that day. I love this town.

Mr. Burns made his way through the crowd and greeted me with a big hug. He said: "Kathy, I'm so sorry. Is there anything I can do for you? Did you spend the night here? I should have known. Listen I have a trailer. I will have it brought over here and set up, that way you can have a little privacy. How does that sound?"

He didn't wait for me to answer any of his questions; just like that he was there and made our lives a little more bearable.

"Thank you so much Mr. Burns, I hated staying in that duplex last night. I didn't want to leave in case I was needed. I'll leave when Jennifer comes home."

"Kathy, whatever you need I will get it for you just let me know. We will find Jennifer, don't you worry. Just look at all these people here to help you."

"I know I can't believe it. Everyone has been so great."

Mom drew our attention by yelling:

"Kathy, come watch the news report. The search for Jennifer is being released on all stations."

NEWS BROADCASTER: The scene yesterday was one of panic. As the hours pass the chances of finding Jennifer Marteliz fades. Many people took off work to help look for the little seven-year-old Tampa girl. Jennifer Marteliz, who disappeared walking home from school yesterday.

Why would they say that, 'as the hours pass the chances of finding her fade?' Why? I refused to think that way. I had to keep on track I had to find her! I could not let her sleep in the dark another night. I had to find her!

While everyone discussed the news release, I decided to talk to Carlos. Find out about Jennifer's friends. Find out if he knew any of the neighbors. I looked around and realized I hadn't seen Carlos this morning. Where was he? The thought of talking to him at all made the bile rise in my throat. This loser, my daughter's Father, had caused me such pain while I had been his wife. Now, adding to the wound by losing Jennifer. While I searched the duplex for

Carlos, I wondered where Jennifer's two white cats were. I found him standing in the back yard.

"Carlos what are you doing? Why are you out here? Where are Jennifer's cats?"

When he turned around, he was sobbing.

"Kathy, I loved her too. I don't know where her cats are. Please just leave me alone. I don't want to talk to you, or anyone else, just please leave me alone."

"Alright Carlos, I will leave you alone."

I shook my head and walked back through the house; 'everything is always about him'. We needed to look for Jennifer, but he stood by himself crying! I didn't want to talk to the reporters myself, especially knowing what they must be thinking: 'Why did she let her daughter live here?

When I walked out the front door of the duplex, I saw all the wonderful people who were there to help. It did my heart good to see all of the support. The University Restaurant had set up a station to feed everyone breakfast and lunch. The support was unbelievable!

After speaking to the FBI and police officers at the Command Post, Dad and my brothers purchased maps, and flashlights from everywhere. They marked the maps into search grids, and set up search teams from all the people waiting to help. Each team was given a map, flashlights, and requested to report in periodically.

Frank, my brother five years my junior, impressed me the most. The police officers had told him the missing rust colored vehicle was a major lead. It needed to be found. Not only were the searchers looking for Jennifer, they searched for that vehicle at his direction.

I took one of the maps Frank marked and started to head for my car. Frank rushed over to my car saying:

"Not alone young lady, someone has to go with you."

"Okay, so who is going with me?"

"I have Patty coming with you, just hold on a minute."

Patty was as good as anyone. I understood I needed someone with me, and I didn't argue with him. I wanted something to do. We took my car, a 1982, dark blue, Buick Regal.

Frank had marked a three-mile area we were to search on the map. We found four cars that were a rust color, but I didn't think any of them matched the missing vehicle. I was not very good company for Patty.

I prayed silently that Jennifer would be found and thought about my reaction when she was found. We searched for three hours, going up and down the streets. After we combed every tiny driveway and street on our map, we headed back to the duplex.

As we drove down ninety-eighth Avenue, I remember seeing officers talking to neighbors, going house to house. Jennifer's girlfriend Theresa was with a detective. So I stopped. I pulled to the side of the street and jumped out of the car; but the detective put up a hand and motioned for me to stop.

"Please Ms. Longo; I need to talk to Theresa alone."

"I'm sorry, of course, I understand, I don't want to get in the way."

My mind was going crazy I decided to just leave my car there and walk back. What else could Theresa tell us? Maybe she knew more than she had told me.

The detective allowed Theresa to return to her house and ran over to me.

"I'm sorry Ms. Longo; we brought Theresa to the station and had her hypnotized. While under, she told us she saw Jennifer go up to her mailbox. That mailbox is only ten yards from her front door. Amber says she was at home waiting for Jennifer. We were wondering how that could be. We are arranging to re-question Amber, something just is not right.

I thanked the detective for sharing the information he and Theresa had been discussing and returned to the Command Center with Patty. I noticed the trailer Mr. Burns had promised had arrived. Mom was headed to the duplex with an extension cord.

I didn't find out until much later about the confrontation between Mom and Carlos. Just thinking about it now makes my blood boil. Mom knocked on the duplex door and waited for Carlos to answer. He came out of the door and it looked like he had been sleeping.

"Carlos what outlet can I plug the trailer into?"

"You can't plug it in unless you pay me!"

In disbelief, Mom said:

"Are you serious? Pay you? Pay you for what?"

He shrugged his shoulders and said:

"I need you to pay for my rent, electricity, phone, and water for the whole month if you want to plug that in here!"
Shocked, Mom looked at him in amazement.

"I can't believe you! This is your little girl we are looking for. Maybe if you hadn't let little Jennifer walk home alone, this wouldn't have happened."

As Carlos turned to go back into the duplex, Mom answered:

"Fine Carlos, whatever it takes, just give me the bills. You better hope Kathy never finds out about this though."

I was sitting at the Command Center and watched as two detectives headed toward Carlos' duplex. Carlos saw them coming and didn't look very happy. As inconspicuously as possible, I followed them.

"Hi Mr. Marteliz, we would like to ask you and your wife a few questions."

Carlos rudely turned his back to the detectives and headed into the duplex saying:

"Whatever."

They all walked into the duplex toward the kitchen. I used a bathroom break as an excuse to enter the house myself so I could listen.

"Hello Mrs. Marteliz, we would like to ask you and your husband a few questions, if you don't mind."

I heard her say the same thing Carlos said:

"Whatever."

"Mr. Marteliz, can you share with us the events that led up to you calling the police yesterday.
"Amber hasn't been feeling well, so I called her from work to see if she needed me to pick up anything. That is when she told me

Jennifer wasn't home from school yet. I told her to call the school and check with our neighbors."

"Carlos, was there a reason for Jennifer to be mad at you, and your wife?"

"Well, Jennifer had a problem eating some cereal. She supposedly told her sister that Amber, was trying to poison her."

"What was wrong with the cereal?"

"Jennifer said there were bugs in the cereal. But I looked in the bowl; it just looked like the edges were burnt."

"Tell us what kind of punishment Jennifer would get, if she were bad?"

"Jennifer broke house rules a lot, so she was given a choice; a spanking, or staying in her room. If Jennifer needed a spanking, I spanked her. I used a book because I didn't have a paddle."

"Can you tell us about the relationship between your wife and daughter?"

"In the beginning, Jennifer couldn't stand my wife. But Jennifer realized, and understood that Amber was trying to bring her up the right way, and that the punishment handed out was for her own good."

"How long have you known your wife?"

"I've known Amber for about six months."

The detective must have noticed an abrasion on his face, and scratches on his arm, because he asked:

"Mr. Marteliz how did you get that abrasion on your lip?"

"Shaving"

"What about those scratches on your left arm, and hand?"

"I got those from Jennifer's cats, while I was playing with them!"

"Thank you Mr. Marteliz, we will keep in touch."

I heard chairs scraping the floor and I wondered why the detectives weren't going to question Amber any further. I waited until I heard the front door close before coming out of the bathroom. I saw Carlos. I stood and stared at him in disgust! When he turned around to go back into the kitchen, I walked out the front door. As I headed to the trailer, I saw those same detectives looking around.

"Ms. Longo, could you spare a couple minutes to talk with us?"

I nodded my head and motioned for them to come into the trailer.

"Ms. Longo, we have received numerous leads from phone calls, but we think we need to consider putting up flyers. We know Jennifer had school pictures taken the day of her disappearance. We were wondering if you would give us permission to have that picture flown in from Gainesville. If so, they would arrive tomorrow; then we could have flyers made up using that picture."

"Wow, what a wonderful idea! That would be great, thank you."

After they left, I looked around the trailer. It was perfect. An officer had contacted the phone company and a temporary phone had been installed. There was a tiny bathroom, a small kitchen, and even a little bedroom of sorts. I was very relieved not to have to use Carlos' duplex any longer.

I hated depending on Carlos and Amber's hospitality. I didn't want to be cordial; I really wanted to strike out at them.

"Kathy, hurry your Dad has some news for us."

Mom was standing at the door waiting for me.

"Okay Mom, coming."

I left the trailer and tried to listen to Dad's excited voice.

"Honey, we got a phone call from a psychic named Patricia Sanders. She believes a female, either a prostitute or an exotic dancer, took Jennifer. She claims to have seen Jennifer in a vision, tripping or falling, injuring herself. Supposedly, Jennifer was sitting in the street crying when this woman drove up, stopped, and then took Jennifer into her car. Ms. Sanders believes this woman probably lost a child earlier in her life. Seeing Jennifer unhappy, she wanted to fix it for her."

"Dad it sounds good, but it doesn't help us. Where is this lady? Does she live close to here?"

I knew he was trying to help any way he could and I didn't want to hurt his feelings.

"But honey, at least she is saying Jennifer is alive. That is the most important thing isn't it?"

"Dad, can you ask Ms. Sanders to meet with us." "Kathy, I already did that, she is coming out tomorrow."

"That is great Dad!"
I thought to myself; you never know she might be able to help. I kept an open mind and tried to remain positive. It couldn't hurt! Being negative wasn't going to help anything. It was getting dark

again and I couldn't stop thinking about my baby being out there all alone!

"Kathy, I am sending your Dad and Toni Lisa home. You and I will stay in the trailer tonight."

"Mom, that sounds great, I don't want to leave until we have Jennifer."

Dad put up a fight, but between Mom and I, he finally gave in. He had been through a lot that year; he was a diabetic, He had heart surgery in April, his dad died in June and now this. Our family had been through too much to take the chance of losing Dad too. He and Toni Lisa left around 10:00 pm.

Everyone was gone except the officers in the Command Center. Mom and I decided to go back to the trailer. We talked about what we were going to do tomorrow, to find Jennifer, when the phone rang. We both practically jumped out of our skins. It was so loud, I am sure you could have heard it from across the street! I hurried and answered the phone.

"Are you Jennifer's mother?"

"Yes I am, and can I ask who you are?"

"You don't need to know that. I want to ask you some questions about Jennifer. If she is returned to you will you be a better Mother?"

All I could think about was maybe this woman had Jennifer. Maybe that psychic was right. This woman wouldn't bring Jennifer back unless she knew I was going to take better care of her.

"Oh yes, I promise, I will be the best Mom. She will never ever leave my sight, never again!"

"I want to know how you could let your daughter live with that drunk, and that witch of a woman."

How did this woman know all of this? She had to be close to the family; maybe Jennifer told her. Answering her as truthfully as I could, I said:

"Because I was stupid that's why!"

"Yes you are! Tell me, what will happen to the person who has Jennifer?"

I knew I had to be careful how I answered her questions. I didn't want her mad at me, but I didn't want to lie to her either.

"If that person brought Jennifer back to me today, I would thank that person for returning Jennifer to me, nothing else."

The phone call lasted for over three hours! I was sure she had Jennifer. I believed she was going to bring Jennifer to me so Mom and I turned off all the lights. We didn't want to scare her off. We couldn't even see our hands in front of our faces, it was so dark. It was a long night waiting and whispering. The woman never showed!

CHAPTER TWENTY THREE—DAY THREE

I struggled to get a grip on my disappointment and depression as we drove to Jennifer's school the next morning. I had been sure that last night I would have had Jennifer in my arms and the nightmare would be over! Despair controlled me until I saw Theresa's familiar face. She looked so cute; her hair was in pigtails. She saw us and ran over with a big smile:

"Hi Ms. Marteliz, did you find Jennifer?"

"Hi Sweetie no not yet but we will. Theresa, this is my Mother Frances Longo and my name is Kathy Longo. Mom this is Jennifer's best friend, Theresa. They did everything together."

"Yes Ma'am! I miss Jennifer; I've been having nightmares about her."

"I am so sorry to hear that Theresa, but when we find her, I promise to bring her over to visit you, okay?"

"That would be great Ms. Longo, Thank you!"

As she walked her way back to class, Mom and I headed for the school office. The main entrance had very large wooden doors with the name 'Shaw Elementary School' carved on them in large letters. All eyes stared at us as we walked through those doors. As Mom and I approached the receptionist I said:

"Hi, my name is Kathy Longo, and this is my Mother, Frances Longo. I am Jennifer Marteliz's Mom!"

"I know who you are, we all saw you on TV last night. Have you heard anything?"

"No. Not yet. We would like to see the principal please."

At that moment, the principal came out to greet us.

"Hi, my name is Mrs. Patterson, I'm the principal.

She personally escorted us to Jennifer's classroom and introduced her teacher. Before leaving, she let us know that if she could help in any other way, to let her know. She hugged me and said she would be praying for Jennifer.

I don't know why talking to Jennifer's teacher was so hard. Probably because I felt guilty. I was ashamed that I had never met Jennifer's teacher. I had never been involved in any of her school activities. I hadn't wanted her here, I wanted her with me, I stuck my head in the sand and made believe this part of her life didn't exist.

Jennifer's teacher was so gracious. She had the entire class stand up and greets us, then asked them to read quietly while she talked with us.

"Hello, my name is Ms. Brown, I am so glad to finally meet you. You can be very proud of Jennifer; she was a very well behaved young lady. She always had a smile on her face. She was an 'A' student in all her work. Here let me show you."

I looked at Jennifer's work and tears began welling up, sliding down my cheeks. I took a deep breath and regained control. I wouldn't cry in front of the children. I felt a tug on my shirt and looked down to see this cute little boy. He had big blue eyes and very light blond hair. He looked like he was bursting to tell me something. I told him;

"Hi! Who might you be?"

With his big blue eyes staring at me, he said:

"Hello, do you know where Jennifer is? Are you her mommy?"

"Yes, I am her mommy but, I am sorry; I don't know where she is."

Ms. Brown asked him to return to his seat. Gently explaining:

"I am sorry, but Jimmy and Jennifer liked each other. At lunch time, they would hold hands. We try to discourage that type of behavior, but they were very cute."

There were so many things I didn't know about Jennifer. I had missed out on so much. Ms. Brown told us that Jennifer talked a lot about how she missed her family. She had even explained to Ms. Brown why she lived with Carlos instead of us! I had shortchanged myself by not involving myself in this part of Jennifer's life. What had I done? I felt so empty and I prayed that somehow I would be able to make it up to her.

I thanked Ms. Brown, and told the class goodbye as we walked out. Before we left, Ms. Brown handed me a bunch of Jennifer's paper work and said:

"I think you will enjoy looking at these."

Mom wanted to get back to the Command Center, but I walked around the school, hugging Jennifer's work to my chest. The school bell rang and all the children ran out of their classrooms. I day dreamed a bit and imagined Jennifer running out of her class into my waiting arms.

When we followed the children out those large wooden doors, we saw the crossing guard at her station. She was no more than 4'11", about 100 pounds, with dark hair, Latin descent. She acted very tough with the children, but they all listened to her. She acted as if she owned that piece of road. I introduced myself.

"Hi, I am Jennifer Marteliz's Mom."

She held her hand up to stop me, and with a very commanding voice, she said:

"Just a moment, I need to let the children cross the street. Just stand over there by the telephone pole please."

Five minutes later, she came over to us.

"Ok ladies, what can I do for you?"

"Did you know Jennifer Marteliz?"

"Yes I did. In fact on Monday she bit me on the hand."

"What? She bit you! Why?"

"She said her new mommy was coming to get her and she had to wait right there. I tried to explain to her she had to wait on the other side of the road, but when I tried to escort her over there, she bit me. See, right here are her teeth marks."

"I can't believe Jennifer did that." "Well she did I am not a liar"

"No, that isn't what I meant. It just sounds so out of character for my daughter to bite someone. I am very sorry she did that; she must have been upset about something. Did you see someone pick her up?"
"No, later I saw her leaving with her friend Theresa."

"If it's okay with you, I would like to tell the police what you saw. They will probably want to talk to you also."

"That is fine with me; let me write my number down for you."

After she wrote her name and number on a piece of paper, she hurried back to her station to assist more children cross the street. She was a toughie, but I liked her. You could tell she liked her job, and the children. Her information added a twist to what we already knew. Was it possible that Amber hadn't been home? Was Jennifer afraid to leave because Amber had told her she was picking her up? Maybe that was why Jennifer told Theresa she was scared and wanted her to watch her walk up to the mailbox. I was tired and could hardly think anymore. Last night had been long and tension filled. We hurried back to the Command Center to share what we had learned with the Officer in Charge. Thanking us, he assured me he would personally speak with Mrs. Garcia.

Officer Durand was waiting for us when we got back to the trailer. "Ms. Longo we have those flyers of Jennifer for you."

I handed the flyers over to my Mother without looking at them. I saw her expression and knew Mom was upset. We were all shocked by her reaction. She began waving that stack of flyers around in the air and demanded:

"Who gave you the information on these flyers?" The officer was surprised by Mom's outburst. I don't think she even realized the consequences when she gave up her source.

"Amber, the stepmother she said she knew the child better than anyone else."

Mom's face turned bright red, she was livid.
"Knew her better? She has only been around for six months."

Mom was furious! Her face contorted with the feelings she was attempting to control, but her eyes blazed with anger. I don't recall ever seeing Mom so mad, and we still didn't have a clue why.

Now let me tell you, I've never seen my Mother lose her composure, much less move in anything but an elegant walk. Oh no, she was in a dead run headed for Carlos' duplex. Reaching Carlos' door, she barreled her way through the door after one little fist slammed on the door. We could hear Mom screaming for Amber, but she wasn't calling her Amber. The officer and I looked at each other, turning we ran into the duplex looking for Mom. We rushed through and found Mom in Amber's room! Amber was lying on her bed with my Mother on top of her, slapping her in the face with the flyers!

"You stupid bitch (that is something else I've never heard from Mom)! Why would you tell everyone about the mole on Jennifer's butt?"

Amber pushed Mom off her chest and stood up. She looked Mom straight in the eyes and in a cocky, sarcastic voice, she said:

"Listen here, I knew her better than you. I'll do and say whatever I want."

Crazy is a descriptive word, but I don't think it covers what that officer and I witnessed next. As Amber said her last word, Mom attacked! I could not believe what I was seeing: Here was Amber, standing 5'4", weighing in at around 225 pounds versus Mom, a mere 4'11", weighing around 100 pounds. Mom's attack knocked Amber back down on the bed with Mom on top. Amber was screeching, and trying to push Mom off; all the while Mom is slapping her over and over again. The duplex filled with people trying to stop the fight, or possibly just enjoying it. I finally got a hold on Mom and pulled her off Amber. Her face was still red and the tears streamed over her cheeks. The officer escorted her from Amber's room and she didn't resist anymore, just said:

"I couldn't take it anymore Kathy. That bitch I'm sick of her. This is all her fault. She didn't pick up my grandbaby from school."

I was still in shock, but I held her as tight as I could admiring the spunk Mom displayed. She held me just as tight. I admired her very much at that moment and when we finally looked at each other, I couldn't help but laugh and asked her:

"Mom, do you know what you just did. You beat her up! She is twice your size and then some."

Shaking a little, Mom made her way back to the trailer. Toni Lisa ran to me; I didn't know she had seen what had happened until she hugged me tight and said:

"Mom, I have never seen Grandma like that before. Is she okay? I am worried Mom. Grandma doesn't act like that.

"Toni Lisa your Grandmother was just very upset. It took several of us to get her off Amber. She just did what I have wanted to do for a long time. We have not slept in two days. This has been stressful for us all."

We were angry with Carlos and Amber, but I think we were angrier with ourselves. Carlos refused to allow Amber to press charges against Mom. He did, however, demand that we stay away from the duplex. To this day, I wonder if Dad had offered Carlos money in exchange for that agreement.

Mom's unbelievable actions were the talk of the neighborhood. Amber kept the front door closed as a protective barrier between her and Mom after that.

At 8:30, Dad reminded us about the 9:00 meeting he had scheduled with Patricia Sanders, the psychic. She believed Jennifer was still alive, and that was important to me! Two detectives came with us as official representation. Her office was close to the duplex, so we arrived with time to spare. She was very happy that we all showed up. While everyone was being introduced I was observing Ms. Sanders. I found her to be somewhat odd, but I liked her. She was a small woman with red hair and hazel eyes.

Ms. Sanders's office was small; she had ten chairs set in a circle, all filled with my family. The two detectives remained standing, making the room feel even smaller. There was a large chair sitting in the middle of the circle and Ms. Sanders was sitting in the center chair. She asked me for my hand, saying:

"Kathy is it okay for everyone to hear about your life, or would you like it to be private."

"No, I want my family here with me."

"Okay then, I see you have lived a tough life for being so young. You got married at sixteen; your husband was abusive to you. You have a bright aura around you Kathy, and he was trying to break it. You have two daughters; your oldest daughter lived the pain with you. Your youngest loves him. He still haunts you to this day. He will bring you much sadness. You will never be free from this man. He is very evil." I could not help it, everything she said was true, and I cried.

My mother looked at me and told Ms. Sanders:

"That is not true, he never hit her. He was a bum, and drank, but never hit her."

My Dad spoke in his very calm voice:

"I would have killed him, if I knew he had touched my baby."

Patricia just looked at me, and then asked:

"Kathy, am I saying it right, did he abuse you?"

I looked at my parents and nodded.

"Yes, it's true, he beat me."

After a small quiet second, Dad said:

"I just don't think my heart can take anymore. I can't believe you never told us. We would have helped you."

"Dad, he threatened he would kill you, and that it would be my fault."

Bitterly, Dad laughed, saying:

"That loser kill me? Kathy how could you believe something so stupid?"

One of the detectives asked:

"Tony, how old was she when they married? Sixteen? He was a big influence in her life then. She isn't married to him anymore. We need to move on. We need to worry about finding Jennifer. That is what we are here for."

Nodding his head, Dad said:

"You are right; I need to let this go. She is free of him, and we need to get Jennifer home."

I saw the looks on both my parent's faces and I knew I had hurt them again. It seemed as though that had become a habit of mine. Dad continued speaking:

"Well Patricia, it looks like you have convinced us you do have some power. Can you help us get Jennifer back? Until this meeting, I had not put much stock in people like you. I just figured you did your homework before meeting with clients."

If this was the case with Ms. Sanders, she had done a lot of homework . . . She looked back at Dad and said:

"I hope so."

Turning to Mom, she said:

"Frances, I can do healing also."

I jumped out of my seat and I demanded: "Healing, what are you talking about?"

Mom grabbed my shirt and pulled me back down into my chair.

"I sprained my ankle that is all."

Mom looked at Patricia and said:

"Right?" Patricia nodded her head.

Ms. Sanders drew out her wand and called for Jarrett. He was a spirit from the other world that helped her.

"Jarrett is here to help us find Jennifer. Please hold hands, because we love each other, and we need to put our souls together with the help of God."

Everyone held hands except the detectives. They remained in the background, but I noticed they smirked at each other! I didn't care what they thought. If this worked, and we found Jennifer, well it didn't matter what anyone thought!

"Let us pray that the spirits help us find Jennifer tonight. Jarrett we need your help."

Ms. Sanders held up a picture of Jennifer and said:

"I really believe Jennifer is alive. Kathy, do you have a picture of someone who has passed in your family?"

"Yes, a picture of my grandfather."

She instructed me to get it out of my purse.

"Okay pass your hand over his picture. Do you feel how cold your hand is? Now pass your hand over the picture of Jennifer. Can you feel the warmth? That tells me she is still alive!"

"Mom, look I can feel it. It is warm! Try it."

We passed the pictures around so everyone could feel them. I think after what she said about me, she had made believers out of everyone.

Patricia told me to please get up and sit in her chair. I was instructed not to be scared, she just wanted to hypnotize me.

"I am going to try and put you in Jennifer's body, so you can see where she is, and we can go get her."

When I sat in her chair, she waved her wand over my head and told me to relax, and count down from 100. I still remember that to this day, I was counting:

"100, 99, 98, 97."

After she successfully hypnotized me, Ms. Sanders verbally directed my path.

"You're in a hot air balloon basket gradually ascending into the air. As you float over the landscape admiring the panoramic view below your balloon, it slowly loses altitude. You will become Jennifer when your balloon lands."

Believe it or not, in my mind, that is what happened. I was asleep, she clapped her hands and I awoke. She began asking me questions:

"What is your name?"

"Jennifer." "Do you know where you are?"

"No."

"What do you see around you?"

"A large field with tall, brownish-yellow stalks; there are long leaves of the same color all over the stalks." Ms. Sanders had to retrieve a book of sceneries and she requested that I identify my environment as close as possible. The scene I chose from that book was a cornfield. The questioning then continued.

"How does your hair look? Has your appearance changed recently?"

"My long black hair isn't long anymore; it isn't black, but light brown and very short."

"Can you tell me how old you are?"

"Seven."

"Are you happy?"

Mom said my expression made it seem that I was disconcerted by this question.

"I miss my Grandma, Mom, and Toni Lisa."

"Is there a house where you are?"

"Yes and a large barn. No horses, just chickens, pigs and goats."

"Is there a phone in that house?"

"No."

She told me I would awaken when she clapped her hands and I would remember everything I had seen. She clapped her hands. When I woke up, I felt confused and disoriented. Our session had lasted about an hour but I still remembered the experience clearly. I WAS Jennifer in a cornfield chasing butterflies and I had extremely short, light brown hair. I vividly felt as though I could have touched those butterflies with my hands. I was not afraid, but the feeling was not one of happiness or sadness. I was perhaps a little worried. In a weird way, it felt wonderful to be her!

It was very emotional for me. I felt sick to my stomach; I was back, but no Jennifer. I could not see where she was. When I got up, I was still confused. Mom told me later that I said I couldn't do this anymore! It hurt too badly and I had to leave.

Everyone got up and hugged me. Mom asked me:

"It is okay honey. Where do you want to go?"

I told her I just wanted to go back to the trailer. I felt so close to Jennifer, yet couldn't have her there with me. I felt like I had been caught in a whirlpool and was being sucked to the bottom. It had been just too much to handle! Mom guided me out of the office saying:

"That's fine honey, you did good. Let's go."

We all had not slept for a couple days; it became very important to deal with our exhaustion. I personally collapsed on the bed in the trailer and slept for a couple of hours. It wasn't a dreamless sleep, and I wasn't refreshed when I awoke, but it was sleep.

CHAPTER TWENTY FOUR–DAY FOUR

The police came knocking on the trailer door. They needed me to go down to the station with them. I was escorted to a small, very chilly, dungeon style room to wait. I still wore the suit I had bought for my all-important meeting just three days ago! How twisted life had become in such a short time. I decided after the interview I would go home, shower and change into clothing that was more comfortable. That would make me feel better.

I waited for about thirty minutes before a detective finally came into the room. He looked to be about fifty with a marine type haircut and clear gray eyes.

I sat in the chair he indicated and wondered if he had any children. How would he feel if it was him sitting in the hot seat? It was hard not to feel negative about the meeting, but I didn't expect his first question:

"Ms. Longo, you work for Mr. Clay Burns, correct?"

I answered his question and asked defensively:

"Yes, but what does that have to do with Jennifer?"

"Someone tried to kill Mr. Burns last night!"

I had been wrapped up in the loss of Jennifer and hadn't even called into the office! I was close to Mr. Burns and his daughter and was astounded at the information.

"What? Is he ok? Where is he? Is Diana okay?"

Abruptly, he said:

"Yes, yes, they are fine. Am I to understand you knew nothing about this attack?"

I became angry with him and said:

"Detective, do you really believe I would be sitting here right now if I had any idea my boss's life was at risk? Just what type of person do you people believe I am?"

He had lost control of the interview. I don't think he expected my reaction! In an attempt to regain control, he held up a hand as if to stop me from talking, saying:

"I'm sorry Ms. Longo; I truly thought you already knew about this. Mr. Burns has his hands in many different businesses. One is called 'Floor Planning'; another is a 'Junk Yard' where we believe he is buying stolen goods."

I was in total denial and responded saying:

"That is just plain crazy; Mr. Burns is a good man. He doesn't buy stolen stuff; he wouldn't do anything against the law like that! We work in the same office together, I would know. He couldn't hide something like that from me!"

He changed direction; his questions became more personal. "Kathy, are you having an affair with Mr. Burns?"

"Sir, you are offensive! No! I am not having an affair with my boss! Look, I thought you brought me here to discuss Jennifer, if not then I'm leaving."

"Ms. Longo, this is about Jennifer! The people who are mad at Mr. Burns could be using your family to get back at him."

I shook my head in denial.

"No way! If they were going to take anyone for that reason, they would have taken Toni Lisa, not Jennifer. Toni Lisa has been to my office, but Jennifer hasn't, she lives with Carlos."

His logic didn't make sense to me. How could they possibly think Jennifer's abduction was connected to Mr. Burns? Why would they think I was having an affair with him, he was like a father to me? He had never said anything mean or vulgar to me and I couldn't have asked for a better boss!

The detective interrupted my thoughts to explain:

"Kathy, this case is a mystery to us! We have a group of people, all telling us different stories. There are five people in the station right now claiming they saw Jennifer, but they all saw her somewhere else, all within the same time period. We don't have any solid clues. We are investigating every lead we receive. That is what you want, right?"

How could I argue! He was right.

"Kathy, we are going to continue looking into our lead concerning Mr. Burns. I'll personally let you know if we come up with anything. In the meantime, the department would like you to take a lie detector test. Listen, before you get upset Carlos, Amber and anyone else necessary are going to be asked to do the same. This is one way to eliminate each of you as suspects."

"Fine, I will take your lie detector test. I'll be glad to take it."

Two hours later I was mentally exhausted!

"Are you done with me, I want to go back to the trailer?"

"Yes, we are done here! Wait here just a little bit longer; I'll have someone come in to escort you out of the Station."

I went home to take a shower and change clothes. My heart clenched as I turned into the driveway and shut off the motor. I sat there and stared. This had been our home. The girls and I had picked it out together. All my hopes and dreams for a better life were nothing without my girls!

I walked into the house and memories flashed through my mind. Memories the girls and I had made here. Important memories! The FDIC paperwork was scattered around on the kitchen table. The meeting, which had been so important a few days ago, meant nothing. Sometimes we lose ourselves in self-importance and really, our family is all that matters.

I named each stair as I climbed to the girls' room: regret, grief, anguish, misery, distress, sorrow, heartache, shame, guilt and despair. I entered a very dark place while climbing those stairs!

Their room was exactly how they left it. I remembered being scared to put up the wallpaper they had picked out. It hurt your eyes just to look at it, bright pink, with big white flowers. I had wanted it to be their room, decorated the way they wanted it. They each had matching twin canopy princess beds, with pink bedspreads. Jennifer's stereo sat there waiting for her return. I put one of her favorite records on the turntable and lay on her bed to listen. Memories crushed the breath from my lungs and flooded my mind! I pushed myself off her bed and cried:

"I can't do this!"

After I jerked the plug out of the wall, the stereo played the rest of the record moaning mournfully. I felt it fit my mood perfectly! I ran down the stairs to my room, turned the shower on and stepped into the cascading water. I closed my eyes tight but the tears would not stop. I leaned against the shower stall then fell to the floor. I tried to pretend I wasn't giving into the feeling of despair, but actually, I drowned in it! I don't know how but I got myself dressed and headed back to the trailer. I was struggling to get a grip on myself before I got there. The vision of Jennifer was hard to get out of my head.

My parents were waiting for me by the trailer. I wanted to avoid them because I just wasn't in the mood to act like everything was okay. That I was doing fine. Every time I had to put on that fake smile I felt like a small piece of me died.

I walked up to my parents and gave them both a kiss, that's when I noticed Carlos' car was missing. I asked;

"Mom, Carlos' car is gone; do you know where he went?

"Carlos and Amber left about two hours after you went to the police station Kathy. One of the detectives told your Dad they were going to be interviewed. I'm sure they are still there."

DETECTIVE'S O'SULLIVAN AND TAYLOR interview:

(These are the true statements taken from the police files)

"Mrs. Amber Marteliz, how concerned are you for Jennifer?"

"My concern is for a missing child, as I do not have maternal love for her."

"Have you ever done any drugs before?"

"In my earlier years, I tried amphetamines, marijuana, cocaine, and barbiturates, but I never used any of them in excess. As for liquor, I just drink to socialize."

"Do you think Jennifer ran away?"

"I really don't know. Discipline is a normal procedure at our home. Carlos and I are both involved. I often had to spank Jennifer, and on several occasions I slapped her face."

"Did you have anything to do with Jennifer's disappearance?"

"No, I did not!"

"Ok, thank you Amber."

Back at the trailer Dad had some news for me. He excitedly said:

"Honey, I didn't get to tell you last night, but when I went to leave, Carlos stopped me. He asked me to offer a reward for $500,000.00. The detectives are supposed to get back with me on the best way to handle the offer." "Okay Dad, whatever the police and you think is fine by me."

I watched Dad as he walked towards the Command Center, and noticed his shoulders weren't in a dejected slump anymore. He looked like he was doing something productive. Loving Dad was easy; he will always be my hero! I could hear my dad as he called out to the Detective:

"Have you had a chance to talk with your Captain about my suggestion of offering a $500,000.00 reward?"

"Yes I did Tony! He asks that you do not mention a reward. Captain Garcia said you would have every crazy person in Tampa making claims. Not only that, he says your other family members will be put in danger. He says, it isn't a good idea."

"Okay, that sounds reasonable, you know best."

"Thank you Mr. Longo, you just saved yourself, and us, a lot of grief."

Standing there with Mom, my mind began cataloging information:

1. ***Carlos asked Dad to offer a reward, going so far as suggesting an amount.***
2. ***Carlos and Amber stayed in their duplex, not coming out to assist in the search.***
3. ***Carlos called the police, before looking for Jennifer himself. He was with an Officer at 4:00 pm.***
4. ***Carlos told the Officer not to submit the report until he checked with my Mother.***
5. ***Carlos asked the Officer why they had not waited 24hours prior to becoming involved, like normal.***
6. ***The abrasions, and scratches on Carlos face, arm, and hand.***
7. ***Jennifer biting the crossing guard, insisting she was waiting for her new Mommy, walking home with Theresa.***
8. ***Theresa watched Jennifer walk all the way to Carlos' mailbox. Just ten yards away from their front door.***
9. ***Where are Jennifer's cats?***
10. ***Carlos and Amber had something to do with this. Something was not right!***

I looked up after pouring a cup of coffee and Patricia Sanders was standing in front of me.

"Hi Kathy, I was worried about you after last night. I thought I would just come and check on you. Hello Frances!"

"Ms. Sanders, Hi, thank you! I am doing fine."

"Kathy after you left, Jarret indicated to me that Carlos or his wife Amber could be involved in Jennifer's disappearance!"

One of the detectives, who had participated in the session with Patricia Sanders, was standing in front of Mom. He added fuel to my fire when he said:

"You know we didn't think much of it at the time, but Amber's family owns a carnival. They travel all over the United States and Canada."

Mom shook her head and said: "That can't be, Amber told us her father, Morton Sloan was a very rich man. She even went so far as to tell us she attended private schools."

Now the detective was shaking his head.

"I'm sorry Mrs. Longo, Amber lied to you both. Yes, her father is Morton Sloam, but he is not rich. He runs a family carnival business. Amber spent her childhood being shuttled between his employees. Her mother, Carol Cohen was a nervous woman. You know the somewhat unstable type. She claimed she couldn't handle her daughter. Amber and her family are supposed to come to the station tomorrow. They are scheduled to be interviewed."

While we all thought over this news, another detective approached and asked:

"Ms. Longo, do you remember the woman you talked to for several hours the other night?"
"Yes I do! Did you find her?"

"As a matter of fact we did! Her name is Lisa Andrews. She claims she only called you after she received a message to do so. She claims you kept calling her, and wouldn't stop."

"Detective Taylor, that is a lie! She called me, Mom was there when the phone rang."

He didn't argue the issue any further. He just asked:

"Please, won't the two of you just go home to night, and get a good night's sleep? Even if you can't sleep, just get some rest. If anything happens, I promise to call you. You need a couple hours away from this place, to help you clear your heads, please?"

Mom and I both agreed to do as he asked.

My mom wanted me to go home with her, but I decided I wanted to go to my home. I had all my clothes there. I wanted to just be by myself. Once I got there I went to bed. Lying there, staring at the ceiling and walls, I attempted to sleep. Several hours later, sleep deprived, and exhausted, I heard Jennifer's sweet voice calling me. "Mommy, Mommy," over and over again, clear as a bell. I just don't know if I can do this. As I prayed, I begged God to help me and my family. Our Father . . . I don't remember anything else.

CHAPTER TWENTY FIVE–DAY FIVE

The next morning, while I lay in bed, I watched the second hand move on my clock. I knew the alarm was going to start blasting in seconds but it still startled me. I was depressed and faced another day of hell with my baby missing. My thoughts changed just as quickly as I had thrown off the covers; 'Today could be the day we find Jennifer'. Now I hurried getting dressed. I grabbed a drink of juice and skipped breakfast in a rush to get to the trailer.

Police cars blocked the roads across both lanes. I had to show identification before being allowed to park behind the trailer. Officers were everywhere. All you could see was the sun shining off the badges on their blue shirts. It was a very intimidating scene. I was nervous, and I hadn't done anything wrong! I wondered how Carlos and Amber were feeling.

As I stood by the trailer, I couldn't believe what I saw. Officers and their dogs were all around searching Carlos' car. The doors were all ajar, and the trunk was open. There were officers inside and underneath inspecting everything. Dogs were sniffing around the seats, which had been removed. Carlos, Amber, and Amber's Mom, Carol stood in front of the duplex. They were finally out of their house!

I knew my thoughts were sarcastic, but they had not been out of their house to help look for Jennifer since she disappeared.

Carlos and Amber were scowling and it was plain they were not happy. I watched them, and I loved seeing them squirm, they were actually being treated like suspects. By then I was positive they were involved in some way. They were hiding something. One of the officers said:

"Okay, finished with the Father's car. Let's start on the Mother-In-Laws' car now."

Carol started crying when she saw the officers concentrating on her car. Amber tried to calm her down, but it didn't work. I wondered what the woman was afraid of. Ten seconds later, she began screaming that she couldn't handle the search and she fainted! Amber was frantic, screaming for help. Several officers and Carlos circled them to see if they could help while one officer called for an ambulance. I heard the siren a short time later.

Two paramedics came and worked on Carol for about ten minutes. With two officers helping, they put her on a stretcher and loaded her into the ambulance. My mind raced: What was that all about? She didn't even like Jennifer. Why would she have fainted like that? Did she have something to hide? Could she have been involved in Jennifer's disappearance?

After the ambulance left the officers stopped their search. The officers cleared the blocked streets and the on-lookers figured the show was over. In a very short time the only people around were the officers at the Command Post, Carlos and I. I thought that had worked out very well for Carol; maybe that was what she was after. Why had they stopped their search of her car?

Carlos saw me staring at him. His expression turned to one I remembered only too well from his beatings. I could tell he wanted to be a bully again. He stood rigid, clenched and unclenched his fists, glaring at me and the officers. Abruptly he spun around and stormed off into the duplex!

The plan for the day was to search the park. The thought of looking for Jennifer there was very depressing. It just meant one thing: we were looking for her body. We watched the helicopter skimming the treetops while the wind from the rotors stirred up dust, and blew our hair. The vibration in our ears and the K9 dogs barking felt unreal; then I heard the detective.

"Okay everyone, let's get started."

He set up three lines of 100 people each. The second line was to be fifteen feet behind the first. The third line was to be fifteen feet behind the second. We were to stand an arm's length apart from the person next to us. He then explained:

"If you see any dirt that looks fresh or sand that is piled up, anything that does not look right, don't touch it, just yell for me. Before we start let's have a moment of silence."

There were over 300 people there and it was totally quiet. There wasn't even a bird chirping. Bowing our heads, we prayed. I'm sure my prayer was different from everyone else's. They wanted to find Jennifer! I didn't want to find her in that park!

The park wasn't a place you took your kids to play. Basically, it was an overgrown area where stringy vines and moss twisted through the trees. In some areas, it was mushy and wet. If you had ever driven through the Tampa area, you would have remembered the tall palm trees. Rats live in those trees! Rats, mice and armadillo's all gave me the creeps! I would rather have been in a room of snakes, spiders, and lizards!

We had been searching for about an hour when someone down the line yelled for the detective. They had found something!

"Nooooooo!"

The word echoed through my head. I closed my eyes and drifted away. I concentrated on Jennifer being alive. I wrapped my arms around her tiny little body in a protective circle of my arms. I had refused to accept any other outcome! It would have been the end of me if it had. I couldn't lose my baby! I had so much to make up for, please Dear Lord!

My thoughts were interrupted by whispers. It was a grave. The officer called for shovels and Detective O'Sullivan rushed to my side, wrapping his arms around me. Not just to comfort me but to shield me from all those eyes. He said:

"Kathy, come on, let's get out of here. We will go back to the trailer."

"No! I am not leaving. It's not her! I know she is still alive, I know it in my heart! That is not Jennifer. My baby is still alive!"

"Please Kathy!"

The Detective tried to grab me by the arm.

But I was firm: "No!"

The officers shoveled the dirt at the fresh grave. I took a deep breath shielding my face with my hands. I told myself I could do this that I would make it through this! That was not my baby covered by that filthy dirt! Each shovel sinking into the dirt was bringing us closer to a revelation! Suddenly, Detective O'Sullivan shouted:

"It's a dog!"

There was a collective sigh of relief, and everyone cheered. Me, I thanked the Lord. After that, everyone relaxed a little and chatted along the lines. When I listened to those people, I was so numb, nothing registered. My body did as it was told, but my brain felt limp and I just plugged along. Finally, after four miserable hours, we were done. Returning to the trailer I lost all resemblance of sanity! I sobbed in relief and wept in despair. I just cried!

An individual does not normally realize the personality of their community until there are reasons for everyone to pull together. The people of Tampa did that for my family and me. Some of them actually slept in their vehicles, either too exhausted, or just in case they were needed! They became my extended family. They are what kept me going knowing I have them beside me.

Back at the trailer trying to compose myself I see my dad coming in:

"Hey, Dad."

He was not alone this time

"Hey Honey, I wanted you to meet John Weeks."

I remembered this guy. I had seen him hanging around Dad. He reached out his hand and I shook it. The first touch of his hand had stopped my heart and fear raced up my spine! What was the matter with me? He wasn't a tall man; maybe 5'9", with expressionless, light blue eyes closely set above a once broken nose. The pupils of his eyes were so large; it was hard to determine the color. His stringy, dirty blonde hair, hung limply down the sides of his angular face from a center part. He stood and waited, watching, and listening for my reaction. His hand had been warm, sweaty, and limp like a wet noodle, until I had attempted to draw my hand from his. Then he tightened his grip ever so slightly.

"Hello Mr. Weeks, it's nice to meet you!"

Dad hadn't noticed that the man hadn't released my hand, and started talking:

"Honey, John has been with me since day one, looking for Jennifer. He lives in the duplex next to Carlos."

I placed my left hand over his and pulled out of his grasp. I did not want to embarrass Dad so I acted as if nothing had happened, saying:

"Thank you so much, we need all the help we can get. Did you see Jennifer much?"

He stared at me. His voice was low, and rough.

"I feel so bad. Jennifer used to bring me my mail all the time. She was such a beautiful little girl. I just wanted to tell you that I would do anything for you. I just hope you find her."

A wide grin spread, slowly, across his face. He seemed pleased with himself for some reason.

"Well, I guess I better go. It was sure nice meeting you 'Kathy'! Tony, catch you later man."

I watched him walk away and I didn't understand why my Dad had me meet him. There were so many people helping us search I thought it was odd. I quietly asked Dad:

"Dad, why did you have me meet him?"

"Honey, he has been pushing me every day, to meet you."

In the back of my mind, I was building my own suspect list. Mr. Weeks had just been added to that list, along with Carlos, Amber, and Carol!
As we were eating, Detective O'Sullivan came over.

"Kathy, we believe at least one person should stay at your parents' house in case there is a ransom demand."

I glanced at Mom and she nodded. We both wanted Dad to get some rest. He hadn't completely recovered from surgery just six months earlier. That had been the perfect excuse to get him home.

"Dad, can I get you to go, do you mind?"

"Whatever you need me to do, Honey!"

I turned and looked at Toni Lisa. She had been such a trooper. I knew she was going to be upset with me, but there were just too many people here. Just for peace of mind, I wanted her to go with Dad.

"Princess Girl, I need you to go with Papa, okay?"

"That's not fair Mom. I want to stay here with you and Grandma. I don't want to go with Papa."

"Well, if you don't want to go with Papa, how about I call your best friend Whitney, and see if you can stay at her house?"

"Okay Mom."

I knew she was not very happy leaving, but I just couldn't let anything happen to her! Whatever I had to do, if she got mad at me or not, her safety was first. Toni Lisa's life changed drastically, even though she didn't know it yet! I would put an over-protective barrier around her, one she fought me about, until she had children of her own!

As Dad prepared to leave, Toni Lisa ran around the table, and gave me a big hug saying:

"I love you Mom, don't worry, we will find Jennifer. Even if we don't, she will find us. I know she will, Mom."

"I think so too Princess. I love you and have a good time at your friends okay? Papa will drop you off on his way home."

Dad walked slowly towards his car, Toni Lisa's little hand grasping his. His back hunched with the heavy burden of guilt he felt. We didn't talk about it, but Dad blamed himself for this entire nightmare. We could tell he hadn't been sleeping well, his eyes were red, and there were dark circles underneath them. I was glad the detective had suggested one of us stay by the phone. I didn't want to lose Dad too.

CHAPTER TWENTY SIX–DAY SIX

Dad didn't get a call from Jennifer's abductor but Carlos was on the phone the very next morning. (Or had he?) The call upset Dad enough that he needed to talk to Mom and I.

"Sweet heart, Carlos just called me! He wants me to offer that reward we discussed. I tried to explain to him that Detective O'Sullivan said it could put our other family members in danger. He considered offering a reward a bad idea. But Carlos started arguing with me. He told me the only way we would get Jennifer back, was to offer the $500,000.00 reward."

"Dad, don't let Carlos upset you. He has not bothered looking for Jennifer. He just hides away in that duplex."

"Okay Kathy, if that's what you think, I will let it go."

After I reassured Dad, I decided to confront Carlos. We didn't need Carlos harassing him. Dad had always been a very confident man, more than willing to make the hard decisions. He wasn't himself anymore, what with the guilt and stress from losing Jennifer.

When I walked toward Carlos' duplex I felt nauseous. I thought back to our last confrontation when Carlos ended up storming into his duplex. I suddenly realized I didn't have to worry about him anymore; he no longer controlled me. I pushed out my chin and stood a little straighter when I walked to his front door. Knocking, I waited. I was ready.

Carlos opened the door and stood there staring at me rudely. I heard his teeth grinding and smiled to myself.

"Carlos, stop bothering my Dad, he's sick. You call him again; I'll make you wish you hadn't! What is your problem anyway? Get your ass out of there, and start looking for your daughter. What are you hiding from in there?"

"Kathy this has gotten out of hand. All these people, it's crazy. I just want everyone out of here. I don't want to talk to any more reporters. I was trying to help, when I called your Dad."

He was trying to help, who did he think he was fooling? Not me! The sight of him when he whined about people sickened me. At that very moment, it re-affirmed my suspicions that Carlos and Amber were indeed involved with Jennifer's disappearance! Disgustedly, I turned my back on him and did not bother listening to any further complaints.

Patricia Sanders had phoned earlier, she wanted me to drive her around. She asked me to bring something that belonged to Jennifer. Something very special that Jennifer loved. Her teddy bear, Jennifer never went to bed without him I thought he was perfect.

My Mother Gave Her The Teddy Bear When She Was Born And Jennifer Always Kept Him Close.

I blinked back sudden tears as I drove Patricia up the street toward Jennifer's school. Knowing she had walked all that way home upset me. Patricia got out of the car and walked over to where Jennifer had to cross the street to get home. Nothing! She wasn't getting any insights! When we drove up to the duplex, she stared wide-eyed at Carlos front door. Her voice was filled with excitement when she asked:

"What is this place? Who lives here?"

I wondered why she didn't already know the answer and responded:

"Carlos and Amber"

"Kathy, this is what I have been seeing in my dreams. Jennifer made it here. Listen, I drew a composite of the woman I saw taking Jennifer. I gave the picture to Detective O'Sullivan earlier today. We need to find him so you can see that picture. Maybe you have seen the woman before, because I've seen her here."

Patricia had been so convinced when she saw the duplex; she knew everything she saw fit together. Her excitement was contagious. I couldn't help but get excited as well and said:

"Let's look for him at the Command Center; someone there should know where he went."

When we walked toward the Command Center, I could see that Detective O'Sullivan sat at one of the desks. He stood up as we entered and said:

"Hi Kathy, Ms. Sanders! I see you two are on a mission, are you here to see the picture Ms. Sanders drew for us?"

"Hi Detective O'Sullivan! Yes, Patricia would like me to look at it; she thinks I might recognize the person she drew."

He had handed me the picture and in turn greeted Mom as she walked in the door: "Hi Mrs. Longo, Kathy is looking at a picture, you might want to take a look also. Maybe one of you will recognize the person."

He stood there and waited to see our reactions.

Gasping, I knew immediately who Patricia's picture resembled. I turned a little so Mom would see it too and said:

"Oh my God, that looks like Carol, Carlos' Mother-in-Law."

"Who?"

"The woman who fainted as you and Detective Taylor were searching her car. Remember the ambulance took her away."

Mom took a quick look over my shoulder and said:

"Oh yes, it does look like her."

Excited, I handed the picture back to Detective O'Sullivan and said:

"I don't want to point fingers at anyone, but do you realize through all our searching, all the leads they keep ending up at Carlos' doorstep."

"Wait Kathy, just wait a minute. Captain Garcia needs to be brought up to speed. We may not have the whole picture. He does. You've met him I believe. Haven't you?"

"Yes, I have met your Captain!"

"Kathy, he thinks we need to pack up. There isn't anything else here. We searched the entire area and we need to concentrate on the leads we have. We can do that from the station. He thinks we need to clear out, let these people have their neighborhood back. Wouldn't you agree?"

I looked at Mom and she nodded her head. I wasn't as sure as they were about leaving. It seemed so final, as if I were giving up on finding Jennifer. I decided they were probably right. As I looked back at the previous six days and remembered asking myself if we had missed anything. Was there anything else I could have done? Finally, I said:

"Okay, Detective O'Sullivan, I agree, let's pack up."

I knew I would be back. I had plans of my own.
I would be watching.

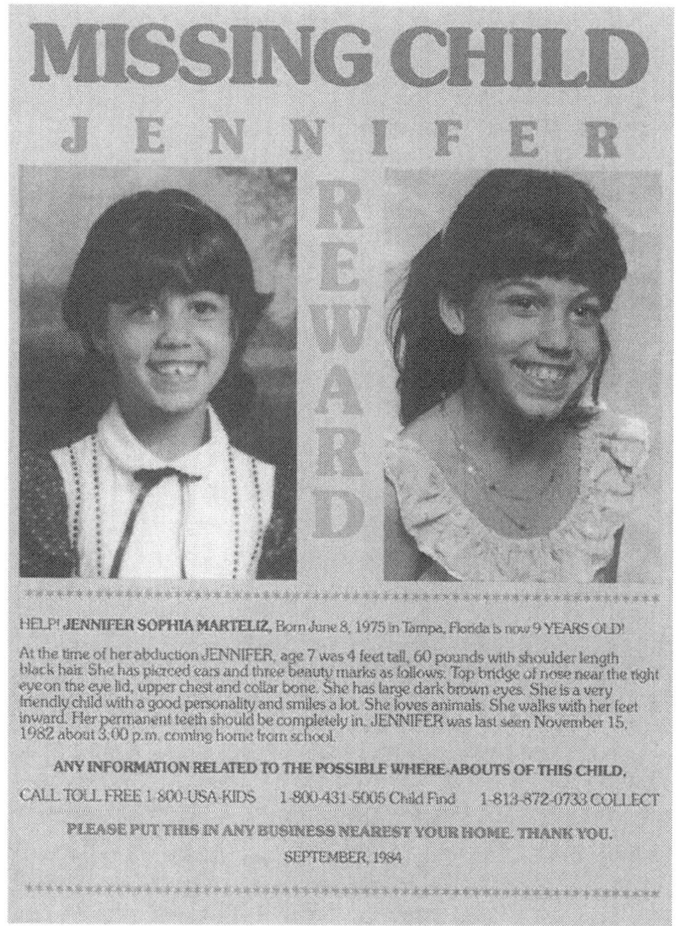

CHAPTER TWENTY SEVEN—

MOVING ON

Mom had made it clear to the entire family that our Sunday traditions were to be kept. It was Sunday and we all went to church together.

When we entered the church, everyone came up to us and expressed their sorrow at our loss. They all were praying for Jennifer and our family. It was extremely difficult to keep from crying. There was a lump in my throat that I had difficulty forcing down. Mom grabbed my hand, holding tight and gave me support that I had badly needed. Mass had started, so everyone went back to their seats. I sat with my rosary and said my prayers as mass continued. The Priest started with prayers for the sick. My mother put her hand on mine and whispered to me very softly:

"Kathy, please put the rosary down, Father is going to mention Jennifer and I want us to say the prayer together for her."

I nodded. I knew how important this was to my Mother. She believed Our Lord would fix this; he would bring Jennifer home to us. We all had gone to school here, including my Dad. Father continued prayers for the sick and needy and everyone responded with 'The Lord hear our prayer'. Then Father said, 'let us all bow our heads, and pray for their safe recovery. Everyone please stand!'

I felt so bad for Mom. I looked at her and she met my gaze. When I heard the Priest ask everyone to have a seat, I had no idea what was to happen next. Suddenly as everyone else took their seats Mom pushed her way out of the pew and walked up to the altar. The music had stopped and everyone was watching Mom. She didn't care. You could have heard a pin drop, it was so quiet!

What was she doing? I'm sure I wasn't the only one who asked that question.

Mom's angry voice filled the silent auditorium as she said:

"You didn't mention my Grandbaby, Jennifer! What's wrong, did I not give you enough money this week?"

She pulled a wad of money from her wallet and threw it at the base of the altar. No one said a word, not even the priest. Time had stopped for us. Her expression, as she turned around, was pained; yet strength of righteousness, and conviction were obvious. As she walked toward us, she motioned for us to leave, saying:

"Let's go! Now!"

We were all in shock, and meekly stood up to exit the church. None of us looked anywhere but at our feet. Mom cried all the way home. None of us could believe what had just happened. Mother was a devoted Catholic; she lived and breathed her religion. She loved the church, and everything it stood for. For her to have acted in such a manner, she had to have been close to a breakdown. She was being consumed by feelings of pain and betrayal; she had just lost herself! Personally, I was inspired by Mom's actions. I was weak and would not have had the audacity to stand up in front of all those people, much less express my anger!

Worried though, I wondered how much more stress Mom and Dad could take. I knew they both felt as responsible as I did; if only . . .

In an attempt to break the tension that imprisoned our entire family, Dad announced he would be doing the cooking this Sunday. That did it. We all, including Mom, had to laugh. Dad, cook? No way! It would have been comical since Mom spoiled Dad. We had never seen him pour his own drink much less cook.

"That's right; I am taking everyone to the Village Pancake House. I am paying for it, so it's like me cooking!"

Dad accomplished his goal, the tension was gone. I couldn't remember any other time Mom hadn't cooked Sunday dinner for her entire family.

The Nuns From St Joseph School

When we got home, there were three cars in our driveway. We hurried to the front of the house to see who it was. I was relieved to find our visitors were the six nuns and four priests from St. Joseph Church. Mom broke down and cried, when she realized who was visiting. They had brought her a St. Anthony statue, and a beautiful rosary.

She invited them in and the Priest performed Mass at the house for our whole family and for Jennifer. The pain was still evident for Mom, but we could tell she felt much better.

Later that evening Patricia Sanders called and invited us back to her office for another session. She believed that Jennifer had the color orange around her. She tried to hypnotize me again, but it never worked.

Every morning, I called Mr. Burns and told him we would find Jennifer today. I would see him at work the following day! How naive I was; after four weeks, I had to go back to work. Bills came in, and I had been using my savings account. Money started coming up short, and I refused to borrow from my parents. I wasn't with Carlos anymore!

When I returned to the office, Mr. Burns had a vase full of roses sitting on my desk. Everyone greeted me as I walked in the door; they all made me feel so good. I thanked everyone and smiled at their nice gesture, but still, all I could think about was Jennifer. I had a picture of her in my mind, her eyes stared at me. The vase of roses couldn't rid me of a dead feeling. The only time I felt alive was while I searched for my daughter. I know, I always said 'Today, this is it!' But that is how I felt, that is what I wished and prayed for.

I had been gone from work four weeks and there was so much work sitting on my desk! Before Jennifer's abduction and the resulting search I had only taken one vacation. I liked my job and it had been hard to get me away from work. Now there was nothing on my mind but finding Jennifer. It was all I thought about all day while I watched and waited for the clock hands to move!

CHAPTER TWENTY EIGHT—
MICHAEL MILLS

Captain Garcia, himself, called me a few mornings later, at work. He said he would like me to take another lie detector test! This test was to be conducted by a private investigator the department used regularly. The investigator's name was Michael Mills and his office was located on Sligh Avenue, not ten minutes from my office.

I arrived at Mr. Mills's office and introduced myself. He had a nice firm handshake; nothing inappropriate. He stood 6'4" and towered over me; he was slim, with dark wavy hair, friendly deep blue eyes. He treated me courteously and I knew I liked him immediately.

"Kathy, I know you have been through a lot. I can't even imagine the pain of losing a child. I hurt for you! I want to make this quick and painless for you."

He had me sit in the chair in front of his desk. He pulled another chair up next to me, and leaned down to briefly explain what he was going to do. I told him an officer had already tested me. He said his method was a little more complicated. He started sticking small round buttons on me, holding them in place with tape. His tone was soft and gentle and I felt like I could trust him. Closing his kit, he walked around his desk and sat down behind a screen where I couldn't see him. He started the questioning process.

Suddenly, I had to ask him:

"Why are they having me retake this test, I have an alibi. I was in a meeting with the FDIC between 2:45 and 3:15. They already checked me out."

After eight hours of repetitive questions (so much for quick and painless) he finally turned his machine off. His interrogation had been unbelievable! He walked back around his desk and sat in the chair next to me. He said:

"Kathy, I know, you know something you're not telling us. Nothing will happen to you, if you tell us what happened to Jennifer."
I was angry at what he implied and I turned in my chair to face him directly.

"Mr. Mills, I don't know what you're talking about. I don't know what has happened to Jennifer. Do you really think I would be sitting here if I knew where Jennifer was? I can assure you, I wouldn't be."

"Don't get defensive Kathy; I'm just trying to help you. I promise you nothing will happen to you. You are Jennifer's Mother. Did you have someone pick Jennifer up and now with all the publicity, they are afraid to bring her back?"

"Your joking right, I don't think this is funny. No! You're wrong, I had nothing to do with this, I just want Jennifer to come home."

"Kathy, we have a problem! When I ask you the question, 'Do you know who picked Jennifer up?' You continually failed with your answer. The last break we took, I called Captain Garcia, he and your Father are on their way here now. Are you sure you don't have an explanation for failing my question?"

"The only thing I can say is that I believe my ex-husband and his wife have something to do with this! Even if I fail your questions, how can anyone think I could or would kidnap my own daughter? I've never even spanked my daughters. Do you understand that I have custody of Jennifer? You must be doing something wrong!"

Captain Garcia arrived first. Mr. Mills excused himself to talk to Captain Garcia. I could hear my dad's voice. I felt relieved knowing he was there.

"Tony, this is Michael Mills, He is giving Kathy the lie detector test and we have a problem. She says she doesn't know where Jennifer is, and it is showing she is not being truthful."

Dad was my hero as usual. He backed them down when he said:

"Mr. Mills, I know my daughter didn't have anything to do with this. Do you people have some type of truth serum you could try?"

My poor father came to my rescue once again. I felt like a disabled child. My parents seemed to always watch over me! I could hear Dad's voice in the other room, but I couldn't make out what they were saying. Not because I didn't try!

Mr. Mills walked back into the room and seriously asked:

"Your Father and Captain Garcia are here Kathy. Are you sure there is nothing you need to tell me?"

"I am sure! I want to see my Dad!"

"Kathy, your Father wants me to ask you the question a different way. If this does not work, he said you would agree to take a truth serum. Is he right, would you agree to that?"

"Of course, yes, I would!"

"Your Father and Captain Garcia are watching us on a closed circuit TV Kathy. Are you ready?"

I nodded my head and he plugged the wires back in and stepped back around the screen. I felt as if I sat in an electric chair, waiting for the zap of death to course through me. The questioning began again.

"Kathy, do you know and can legally prove who picked Jennifer up on November 15, 1982?"

"No!"

"Kathy you show you are being truthful when I ask if you know legally who took Jennifer. Who do you believe picked up Jennifer."

"I believe in my heart that Carlos and Amber had something to do with Jennifer's disappearance."

"Well Kathy you passed with flying colors. I am so sorry, this has never happened before. You believe so strongly Carlos took Jennifer, you kept failing when I asked if you knew who picked her up. You have a very strong and determined mind."

Explained like that, I could understand how I kept failing. There wasn't a doubt in my mind that Carlos and Amber had been involved with Jennifer's disappearance.

"Kathy, I am going to help you for free. You have to promise me one thing though; I want you to open your mind to other possibilities. We will start all over, investigating each and every lead."

After Mr. Mills disconnected me from his machine I felt like a pardoned prisoner. I felt excited and I'm sure I never smiled bigger than when I heard his offer.

"Michael, that would be great! I would love that! That means I can come with you to check the leads out, right?"

He laughed and said:

"Of course you can Kathy; I will teach you how to follow up on leads. Before you know it, you'll be a private investigator."

"This is great; everything that happens in our lives is for a reason. God sent you to me, to help me find Jennifer!"

Things began to look more positive to me. Michael Mills had joined in the search for Jennifer. He not only worked for the police department, he was also a Professor of Criminology at the local College. Captain Garcia and I didn't see eye to eye; he thought I should have stayed home and let his Department do their jobs. He didn't know me at all. I had to be involved in looking for Jennifer! I would have felt as though I had failed Jennifer if I had done nothing! It was the only thing that got me up in the mornings, hoping and praying that today would be the day we found Jennifer!

As much as I had enjoyed my job prior to Jennifer's abduction, it wasn't where I wanted to be now. It was hard to stay focused. Just getting dressed for work was hard for me. Everyone tried to console me, saying I just needed to be strong and put everything into God's hands. It had become a little easier when Michael Mills joined my team. There would finally be something positive to look forward to after getting off from a long day at work!

It was five o'clock, and I ran to my car to go meet Mr. Mills two blocks from Carlos' duplex. He was dressed in a blue suit and looked very professional. As vain as it sounds, I was proud to work with him. He told me the first step in our investigation was to visit every house Jennifer passed on her way home from school. At our first stop, he introduced us:

"Hello, my name is Michael Mills, and this is Kathy Longo. We are looking for her daughter, Jennifer Martilez. She was abducted on November 15th. Did you see or hear anything out of the ordinary that day?"

Everyone was very nice to us and remembered having heard about Jennifer. It was always the same answer, 'sorry but we don't know where she is! It took us two weeks to check every house. I worried at first, visiting people after five, but it turned out to be a great time. Everyone was home from work. We ended up with two good leads from canvassing the neighbors. Michael got three leads from the FBI, and police department. The authorities had been willing to share information with him, but not with me!

CHAPTER TWENTY NINE—

LARRY SMITH

One of the police suspects was Larry Smith, a taxi driver, who lived across the street from Jennifer. Neighbors had told the police that Jennifer loved to go to his house to play with his birds. His birds resembled chickens, although smaller, with wings dappled with black dots. Detective O'Sullivan had requested him to take a lie detector test, but he had refused. Michael and I decided to pay him a visit. When we started walking up to his chain link fence, I had noticed his birds. It was no wonder Jennifer liked to play with them as they were very cute. We opened his gate, and he ran out of his home looking like a crazy man. He yelled:

"Get off my property, leave me alone."

He stopped abruptly and with a softer voice said:

'I am sorry, aren't you Jennifer's Mother?"

"Yes, I am!"

Looking at Michael, he said:

"Sorry, the cops have been at my home almost every day this week. I'm tired of them accusing me of hurting Jennifer. I haven't done anything wrong. I just could not handle the harassment anymore."

I told him it was okay. At one point, I had felt like they accused me, so I understood. Michael had grabbed my hand and pulled me back toward the sidewalk. I thought we were done and told Mr. Smith goodbye. When we walked toward the car, Michael told me:

"I need you to go back to Mr. Smith's by yourself Kathy. Talk to him, he seems to be able to relate to you. Maybe you can get him to take a lie detector test."

I felt excited; Michael trusted me to talk to Mr. Smith. But I felt uneasiness talking to Mr. Smith alone and said:

"You think I can do it Michael?"

"Yes I do Kathy, but I want you to be careful. We don't know this guy. He very well might be the person who kidnapped Jennifer."

I wasn't scared; my own death had never scared me. The only thing that scared me was NOT being able to find Jennifer. My job was to convince Mr. Smith to take that lie detector test requested by the police. It would eliminate him as a suspect and provoke the police into concentrating on Carlos. I walked back toward Mr. Smith's house; I was elated that Mr. Mills trusted me to do this. I knocked on Mr. Smith's door and he opened it right away.

"Hi, again! It's me, Jennifer's Mom; could I talk to you for just a few minutes, please?"

I didn't know if he liked me, or just felt sorry for me. I was willing to play on his emotions if it meant he would talk to me.

"Okay, come on in. My place is small but I call it home. I am a writer; I became a taxi driver to help pay the bills."

Mr. Smith was right, his duplex was smaller than Carlos', but in contrast, it was very clean. The walls were paneled and the floors were wood. None of the furniture matched, and his bed was on the floor. He offered me a glass of water and said he didn't have anything else in the house to drink. I accepted his offer because I didn't want him to think I was afraid of him.

We ended up talking for about three hours. We discussed Jennifer, my work, his work, him being a writer, just anything I could think of to put him at ease. I wanted to make sure I had connected with him before making my request. Finally, I brought the reason I was there out into the open. I held my breath as I asked:

"Larry do you think you could go to the police department and take a lie detector test?"

Before I let him answer, I told him I didn't think he had anything to do with Jennifer's disappearance. Jennifer told Theresa that she was afraid of something and she would not have stopped to look at the birds if she had been afraid of Mr. Smith. I wanted his name cleared officially.

He started yelling at me:

"Is this why you are here? I will not go, they can't force me, and I want you out of here now!"

He was extremely angry; I felt he had to have been mad at more than just my request. It seemed as though he was mad at the world. I was afraid he was going to kick me out of his home and I started pleading with him:

"Larry, just listen to me a minute, we have just been talking for about three hours now, and I don't believe you have anything to do with this. I swear to you."

I told him why it was so important to me that he clear himself! If the police exonerated him, they would finally concentrate on Carlos.

"Please Larry; you will be helping me a lot if you'll take the test. You said you would do anything to help me."

When I finished, he looked at me and very calmly said:

"You got me there, I just . . . . I will go to the station in the morning and do it. But I am doing this for you, not them!"

"Thank you Larry."

I was so relieved he consented to be tested it was a bit of a shock when he asked:

"Kathy, why do you suspect your husband? Wasn't Jennifer living there?"

"Yes she was, but Amber wasn't treating her very good and Carlos was never home. I had threatened that Jennifer was coming to live with me. Carlos had a lot of unpaid child support he was going to have to catch up on, plus a new baby on the way. Personally, I think he did it for some ransom money. But it got too big too fast for him to follow through with the scam. By then, the people he had holding Jennifer couldn't let her come back home."

"I am so sorry to hear that. Will I see you again; I really enjoyed talking to you?"

"Larry, do you remember the gentleman I was here with earlier? He can't help me on the weekends; he needs to be with his family.

Maybe you would let me hire your taxi. There are some places I need to go, that my car would be recognized."

He would be helping me and at the same time I could help him.

"That would be great. Do you want to go this weekend?"

"Sure do. I already know where I want to go. Thank you, Larry!"

I finally walked back outside and saw Michael pacing back and forth on the sidewalk. He was extremely upset and acted as if he just had a heart attack! I had been gone so long he had been afraid for me.

"Kathy, do you have any idea how long you have been in there? Three hours! What the hell were you doing in there? Really Kathy, I thought I was going to have to rescue you."

At first, I laughed, but sometimes I laugh when I get nervous. I didn't want him mad at me: I needed his help and I wanted him to trust me. I explained:

"Michael, I am sorry, but I had to get his trust! I believe he is innocent. He has agreed to take the lie detector test. He said he would go to the police department tomorrow morning."

"He said that?"

"Yes he did."

Getting Larry to agree to the lie detector test was definitely a feather in my hat. Michael wasn't angry at me anymore, but he suggested:

"Let's call it a night. I'll take you to your car; you did a good job in there."

We went back to the car and I waved when I pulled away. I drove fast as I dared to get home. Mentally, and physically, I was exhausted and barely managed to get myself through the front door to my room. I lay on my bed fully clothed contemplating the evening. Soon after my head hit my pillow, I was sound asleep, but it didn't last; I kept drifting in and out as memories of Jennifer's face kept flashing through my mind. I finally got up.

My Grandmother used to tell me when I had a nightmare, to put a glass of water under my bed. It helped then, perhaps it would help now!

When I went to the kitchen, the house was quiet and it made me realize I missed hearing Toni Lisa's TV on at all hours of the night. Her room was above mine, so I generally had to force myself out of bed, go upstairs, and turn the TV off. I reflected on the fact that I used to get so mad when she left the set on but now I wished I could have heard her TV. Toni Lisa had moved in with Mom, but I had decided against moving back, since my evening escapades would worry my parents. I didn't consider that house my home any longer, just a place to clean up and sleep. I had even changed the kitchen into an office. I headed back to my room with the glass of water, determined to give Grandma's remedy a try.

Today was Friday! I had made it through another night. I woke up early and felt optimistic about the weekend. Jennifer seemed close enough, I could feel her!

I had been back to work for two weeks and was trying to catch up. Thinking about Jennifer made it hard to concentrate on my job, so work seemed a prison to me, a necessary prison!

Michael called and said he wasn't going to be able to meet with me tonight. When it hit 5:00 pm, I still rushed away from the office. I called Larry to make sure we were still on for Saturday, and if 8:00 pm would work for him.

"Hi Larry, this is Kathy!"

On the phone, Larry told me about his day and acted as if he was excited to talk to me too.

"Kathy, I did it! The officer was shocked when I walked in, saying I was ready to take their lie detector test. He wanted to know what changed my mind. I told them you talked to me, he just shook his head. They told me I passed the test with flying colors. Kathy, I'm cleared!"

"Larry, I can't thank you enough. Now they have to focus on other suspects, not you. How do you feel about 8:00 tomorrow night?"

"Okay Kathy, I will see you then!"

CHAPTER THIRTY—TONI LISA

Generally, my spare time had been spent searching for my daughter, Jennifer. Toni Lisa, her sister, was being shortchanged on attention. I decided to make it up to her tonight. Maybe she would feel like spending time with me. I called her at Mom's.

"Hi Princess, how would you like to have dinner and a movie with me?"

"Hi Mom, I would love it, but Wendy is over, can she come too?"

I missed Toni Lisa. I just wanted to see her alone and was disappointed at this turn of events. I understood she was getting older and she wanted to be with friends her own age.

"Sure honey, I don't mind."

Toni Lisa and Wendy looked beautiful. They were dressed in sparkles from head to toe. Toni Lisa brought joy back into my heart! I had been so negative and sad and they had just given me such a lift! It felt so good and my stomachache was even gone.

"Let's go girls; I have a new restaurant I want us to try. It's called the 'Melting Pot'. The Melting Pot was packed and it was almost three hours before we were seated. We never made it to the movies, but Toni Lisa loved the restaurant. I promised the girls a rain check for the movie and we headed back to Mom's house. Both girls hugged, kissed, and said they had a good time. To tell the truth, I had the better time; they were like a spring tonic. Up until our evening out, my world had faded; Toni Lisa refreshed the color for me.

The time I spent with Mom that night helped. Without knowing it, Mom had supported me like no one else could have. I explained my plan for the rest of that evening to her. She was reluctant to have her daughter out that late with someone she didn't know. Eventually, she understood how this might benefit in our search for Jennifer and she asked that I not tell Dad; she didn't want him to worry. It was a relief Mom would know where I was going, and who I would be with. Guess you could have said I knew I was doing something stupid, but because Mom knew it was a little less stupid. When I left that night, I felt renewed.

CHAPTER THIRTY ONE–MISSION

Before I met Larry, I decided I should probably change my appearance a bit. I went from having long black hair, to having short, red hair. It definitely changed my appearance.

We had decided it would be best if I left my car in a well-lit parking lot while we rode around in his taxi. While I drove to our meeting, I couldn't help but chuckle at my reflection in the rear view mirror. I parked a little distance from his cab and walked over to his door. I tapped on the window and said:

"Hi Larry, I'm ready. Are you?"

Larry wasn't sure it was me!

"Kathy? Is that you?"

I put my hand up behind my head and struck a pose like those models you see in the magazines and said:

"Yes, it's me! I'm in disguise."

He said, as he laughed and shook his head:

"Well it worked Kathy; I didn't know it was you. That short red hair sure looks different."

I knew he had tinted windows in his cab but I just wanted to make sure I wasn't recognized. Especially since I had planned to sit across from Carlos' house first thing tonight!

"Kathy, I understand now. But you don't have to worry, they are used to seeing my taxi parked there. We can go wherever you want, most people don't even look twice at my cab."

He told me he understood I was on a mission, and he intended to help me any way he could. I couldn't believe I had been so fortunate; first Michael Mills, and then Larry. The Lord was surely helping me. There wasn't any other explanation for the coincidences!

We sat across from Carlos' duplex and got an eye full! Men who looked like bikers came and went from his house. They looked rough, tough, and scary; muscles, tattoos and long hair! I couldn't help wondering if Carlos had been running drugs from his home. Had he done it with Jennifer there in the house? I saw a very different world from mine, and sensed that, yes he had. The realization made my blood boil! Guilty feelings resurfaced when I remembered that I had worn blinders and had never really seen Carlos' world!

My dark thoughts were interrupted when headlights glared inside the taxi. A car was parked in front of Carlos' duplex but the guy that got out of the car wasn't a biker! He was more upscale, a better dresser. Carlos came out of his house, but didn't invite the guy inside. Instead they stood on the porch and talked. I wished I could have heard what they were saying because it had looked like the man was upset. Carlos did all the talking; it appeared like he was trying to calm the guy down. Eventually I saw them shake hands.

Curiosity drove me crazy. What could they possibly have been talking about? Carlos walked back into the house but Mr. 'well dressed' stood there seemingly confused. He looked around, and then headed to the porch next door. I hadn't seen Carlos' neighbor sitting in the dark on the porch.

"Larry can you read that guy's tag number? Are we close enough for you to see it? He is headed over to the neighbors; please Larry, go over there, just make believe you are taking a walk, and you're stopping to talk. Please?"

Larry was almost as curious as I had been. He finally gave in after I pushed him from the taxi. Turning back toward the cab, he asked:

"Kathy, you sure about this, are you going to be okay by yourself?"

"Yes! Yes! Go Larry! Go see what they are talking about."

I watched as Larry approached the two men. A couple other men were walking towards them from down the street. Mr. 'well dressed' waved his hands in the air, talking fast. What had he said that drew everyone's attention?

I had noticed activity at Carlos' front door again. The biker guys had left; they hadn't stayed very long. Maybe, Mr. 'well dressed' had scared them off. Better yet maybe he scared Carlos, and he told the bikers to leave!

Carlos came out of his house again. He carried out the garbage, left it out by the street and went back into the duplex. He closed the door and turned off the porch light; making it very clear company was no longer welcome.

I smiled to myself. Bringing that garbage to the curb had given me another idea. The thought of it grossed me out, but I couldn't pass up an opportunity. Garbage sitting by the street is no longer on private property. I had decided I was taking Carlos garbage! I was thinking about the garbage and Larry startled me when he opened the taxi door. In an unhappy tone, he said: "Kathy, that guy is talking about you! He said he was Carlos' drinking partner. Carlos had not been to the bar since Jennifer disappeared, so he decided to come and check on him. He claims Carlos told him, the night before Jennifer disappeared, how he had met you. Said he got you pregnant when you were 16. Carlos announced to the entire bar that the Longo's acted like big shots, assuring everyone that really, they were nothing. Carlos told him you were a wild cat when he met you, that it took him beating you, to tame your attitude. Then Carlos bragged that tomorrow was payback time. He would be getting even with all the Longo's. The Marteliz family was going to teach them a lesson. Kathy, he told us he had come here to confront Carlos about what he had said that night. Now Carlos is denying everything. He just told him that he was talking about taking you to court, winning custody of Jennifer. Then Carlos told him you got upset, kidnapped Jennifer, but that he knew where you had her. Kathy this is very important you need to call your detective friend."

"You're right Larry. Can I use your phone?"

I knew it was late but I justified a call to Michael Mills by telling myself what I had found was an important lead. I apologized for calling late and told Michael I needed him to come to Larry's house as soon as possible.

Michael Mills was standing in front of me within 10 minutes, and he was angry. Very angry! My appearance had disturbed him for a second, but he didn't say anything about my red hair.

"Kathy, I need to talk with you outside. Alone!"

Michael pulled me outside by my arm and stood staring at me for a full 10 seconds. His eyes were the clue to how angry he was and he barked:

"What are you doing here so late Kathy? Are you looking to get yourself killed?"

I laughed and it wasn't the response he had expected, or wanted from me.

"Michael, it's okay, Larry has been with me, we were in his cab, and no one could tell it was me in there. It has worked out great so far. In fact, I need you to get a report from a man talking with Carlos' neighbor. He and Carlos were arguing about Jennifer tonight."

Still angry, but a little curious about the new information, Michael said:

"Fine Kathy, I'll get the report, but you need to re-evaluate what you are doing. This isn't smart. You need to go home; you don't belong out here on the streets at this time of night!"

Looking back, I really don't know how I kept up that schedule; had to be adrenaline. I don't think I ever slept. I worked all day, spied until 3 and 4 o'clock in the morning, then got up the next day to go back into work at 9:00 am.

Michael took the report, making it an official document. He told me he would give it to Captain Garcia tomorrow. They could check the information out. His body language told me he was still angry I had put myself in jeopardy.

I thanked him for coming out so late. I didn't want him mad at me, he was helping find Jennifer and I didn't want to lose that. I couldn't help being depressed. Captain Garcia would shelve the report if he knew I had been involved. Captain Garcia accused me of interfering in his investigation. I accused him of not doing his job. Neither of us liked the other. He had been a thorn in my side since Jennifer had been kidnapped. As time passed, the thorn had grown. God introduced me to people who willingly helped me search for Jennifer. But Satan had his own team working.

Michael informed Larry he would be taking me to my car, I'm sure Larry thought he would never see me again. Surprise! The next Sunday night I met with Larry again. I really liked using his cab, no one suspected anything. We watched Carlos bring out the garbage but this time he didn't go back into the duplex; he got in his car and drove off. Larry opened the back of his car while I ran and grabbed the bags and threw them in the trunk. Larry suggested we go through them at his house. We sat on Larry's clean floor and spread out the trash. It was bad! In fact, it was gross. When we finished a couple hours later, all we had to show for the enormous mess was a phone bill, gas charge card, and a credit card slip that showed Carlos' social security number.

It was late, but I guessed Carlos had gone to the bar. I asked Larry if he would take me to the bar in his taxi; I wanted to collect license numbers. Larry said he wasn't tired and sure, we could go to the bar. He said he would clean up the garbage mess later. That offer meant a lot to me. I felt yucky after we had searched that trash.

I had planned ahead and had a camera with me. I took pictures of the people as they left, plus wrote down a description of their vehicle, and their tag number.

Carlos didn't leave until the bar closed. I felt the night had gone well. Larry dropped me off at my car at 2:45 am and as I headed home I thanked God for helping me make it through another night. I prayed for Toni Lisa and Jennifer, promising Jennifer I would be seeing her soon. We shouldn't make promises we cannot keep!

CHAPTER THIRTY TWO–RANSOM

The weekend had gone by so fast and I hated that I had to go back to work, knowing I still had not found Jennifer. I refused to give up! I would never give up, not until the day I died!

I had barely walked through the office door when Diana handed the phone to me and said:

"Kathy, it's your Mother! She sounds upset!"

"Thanks Diana!"

I took the phone and noticed there was complete silence in the office. They all listened. I answered, and heard Mom say:

"Kathy, you need to come home NOW! We need to talk! It's important Honey!"

"Okay Mom, I will be right there!"

My boss, Mr. Burns heard me talking, and said:

"Go, Kathy! Everything will be okay here! Just go!"

I ran out of the office. I don't even remember driving to Mom's, praying the entire way that Jennifer was still alive. Okay, maybe they had found Jennifer and she didn't want to tell me on the phone.

Could she be at the house waiting for me? No! Maybe Carlos told the police where Jennifer was, and they were going to get her? No! Maybe . . . I was preoccupied with these questions the whole drive. I parked the car and ran into the house where Mom was pacing back and forth in the kitchen. Breathlessly I asked:

"Mom, what is it? Did they find Jennifer?"

Mom stopped pacing; she looked worried, yet excited at the same time.

"No honey! We just got a ransom demand. The caller told me to bring $100,000.00 to Lowry Park in one hour."

I grabbed the counter to steady myself as my heart took flight, and then crashed to the ground.

"Mom, how are we going to get our hands on $100,000.00 in one hour? Did you call Dad?"

She shook her head and firmly said:

"We can't tell your Dad Honey! He would call the police, and we will never get Jennifer back. We have to do this alone!"

I accepted that Mom was in control. She had thought this out.

"Okay Mom! I'm ready but, what about the ransom money?"

She had put some rags in a duffel bag and it was sitting on the chair.

"We are going to just show up, and see what happens!"
Putting her arms around me, she said:

"Maybe, just maybe this will be the end to this nightmare!"

Shaking my head, I dejectedly said:

"Mom even if that is true if we get Jennifer back my life will never be the same. I don't know if I could ever let her leave my sight. I just don't think I can go through this again. Listen to me, we don't even have her yet, and I am talking about losing her. I think I'm going crazy Mom!"

Mom turned around, grabbed the bag from the chair and took my hand in hers, we headed for the door.

"One step at a time Honey, let's go get Jennifer!"

"Yes, lets!"

We walked out the door hand in hand. We did this together, just as we had been going to do the night of the big fight. We were finally going to bring Jennifer home!

We had decided to take Mom's blue Mercedes convertible; we wanted the kidnappers to see us. We drove in silence. All I could think about was getting my baby back. Mom turned onto a small path not meant for cars that led to an open field where she parked. Mom broke the silence as she said:

"Today is the day Honey, our Lord is bringing Jennifer home."

I remember crying. My prayers were to be answered. Jennifer was coming home! As we sat there, the sound of sirens kept getting closer. We heard a helicopter, then all hell broke loose; the helicopter was flying above our car! Police sirens blared and tires squealed as squad cars stopped around us! What the hell was going on? I jumped out of the car and started screaming, 'I just want my daughter back I . . . . just . . . . want . . . . Her . . . . back . . . ! I could not stop screaming! Tears blurred my vision as I collapsed on the ground. I thought at the time that death would have been preferable to my pain!

My poor Mother tried to be the strong one. She grabbed my shoulders and told me:

"Kathy, please honey, please get up! It will be okay honey. They will call again. Please Kathy, we have to be strong, we can't let them see you like this. They are winning Kathy stand up and hold your head high. Come on honey, we will get through this stand up."

It took every bit of energy I had just to get up from the ground. There were officers all around us, standing not saying a word just watching us. Mom put her arms around me and helped me back into the car. Getting behind the wheel, she turned the car around dodged their cars and slowly drove us home. Neither of us spoke. I just wanted to curl up somewhere and die.

When we got home, I was still numb and didn't want to talk. I told Mom I had to go back to work but what I really did was get in my car, turn the radio on to mind numbing loud music and drove. The longer I drove, the madder I got. The music didn't keep me from thinking. I wanted to blame someone and I chose Captain Garcia. Who better? He had blocked all my attempts at finding Jennifer. This was just another one of his tricks.

I parked the car and noticed I had subconsciously stopped at the police station. Maybe not, since anger was my motivation, I couldn't see straight. I had intended on showing Captain Garcia the extent of that anger. I did not care what happened to me, my life could be over as far as I was concerned. I barged past his secretary right into his office and demanded:

"WHY WERE YOUR MEN AT THE PARK?"

"Kathy, do you want to get killed? You and your Mother just pulled a very dangerous stunt. Especially considering you went without telling anyone. You both need to stay at home, let us handle this investigation; we are trained in these matters. You are not! Stop interfering!"

How dare him! Jennifer was MY daughter and I refused to wait for her to be found while that bastard sat in his office. I was at the limit of my control when I glared into Captain Garcia's cold dark eyes and said:

"This is my daughter we're discussing Captain Garcia, and I intend to remain on her case. I am not afraid to die, if that is what it takes to get my daughter home. With or without your worthless assistance, I intend to find Jennifer."

I turned my back to him and stormed out of his office!

CHAPTER THIRTY THREE–KICKER

I felt a little better and drove straight to Michael Mills's office. As I walked up to his door, he opened it for me and said:

"Hi Kathy, I am glad to see you. I was just about to call you. Captain Garcia called, he isn't very happy with you or your Mom!"

He held his hand up to me, indicating he didn't want me to say anything and continued:

"You don't have to explain to me, Kathy! I think I understand what is going on between the two of you. But I do agree with him, it was a very dangerous thing to do, going to that park without letting anyone know. That being said, we need to discuss options.

Without any formal chitchat, Michael go straight to the point.

"Kathy, in my way of thinking, you're absolutely right. Carlos and his wife are involved in Jennifer's abduction. Amber stated in her deposition that Jennifer did not come home from school at 3:20 pm like normal. However, in a taped interview with Amber, she told me she went outside her residence looking for Jennifer at 3:00 pm, because that was Jennifer's normal arrival time from school. Therefore, at 3:20, Jennifer was not missing, just late.

Carlos stated he did not have time to leave work; pickup Jennifer from school, return to work, and make that 3:20 call to report Jennifer missing.

Look at this Kathy; I have his time sheet, which shows Carlos did not report for work that day. Now Theresa, the little girl Jennifer was walking home with, said they got to her house at 3:05 pm. That would mean she would have seen Amber at the mailbox, waiting for Jennifer. Theresa never mentions Amber being at the mailbox."

I was elated! I wanted to hug him.

"Finally, someone believes me. I'm so happy you're helping me investigate THEM now! Finally, we're on the right track! This is what I've been saying all along. Thank you Michael."

"I'm not rushing into anything Kathy; this has to be done right. I want to give Carlos a Lie Detector Test, but Captain Garcia refuses. He says the City has spent too much money, and manpower on this case as it is."

I was barely keeping my anger contained as he added:

"Here is the kicker Kathy, I told him I would do it for free. I plan to schedule the test so Captain Garcia can attend, thereby making it official. He will view the entire procedure via closed circuit TV."

"When Michael?"

With a small grimace, he said:

"Not until January 6th. You have to be patient. We're taking baby steps I grant you that, but at least they are forward." Everything takes so long. I have to wait a month, 30 days, I feel so useless. I just have to hold my breath for ten seconds and let it go. "Michael how can I be patient I want her home for

Christmas? How can we celebrate Christmas without her?"

Christmas had nothing to do with it, I just wanted her home. I was trying to think of anything I could use to speed up that lie detector test!

"Kathy, I understand, but don't give up hope. We might still get her back for you! It would be interesting to know who it was that called your Mother for the ransom!"

"Michael you have been so good to me. I can't thank you enough."

Michael Mills had become a dear friend. Putting up with me wasn't easy. Considering all the hours he had invested in Jennifer's case, it meant a lot that he had never charged me a dime. He called Jennifer his special project.

CHAPTER THIRTY FOUR—

MISSING CHILDREN'S CENTER

On December 13, 1982, a woman contacted me from the Missing Children's Center. She wanted to let me know they were sponsoring a Christmas party that weekend and asked if I would please bring my Mother and Toni Lisa.

"Kathy, this is not for fun, this party is for all the parents' of missing children. This is a trying time for all of you. We have a stocking for each missing child. We are going to hang them as an acknowledgement that yes, they aren't with us, but we still miss them."

"We will be there!"

Mom had been working closely with the Missing Children's Center. She volunteered twice a week.

Attending the Missing Children's Christmas party was emotional for all of us. It was a reality check to see Jennifer's name on a stocking, along with over a hundred other children!

Light The Way Home For Missing Children

Missing Children Float For The Gasparilla Parade

CHAPTER THIRTY FIVE—

ORLANDO LEAD

The party went really well. We all held hands and prayed to God for strength to continue our lives. Everyone cried as each stocking was hung on that tree. Afterwards Grace a volunteer for the Center, came up to me and excitedly asked:

"Kathy, whatever happened with the lead from Orlando?"

Grace answered the Center's hot line in her spare time. I heard her words but couldn't comprehends what she was saying so I asked:

"What lead, Grace?"

She was upset at my question. She had been anxious to hear what had happened and said:

"What Lead? What do you mean, what lead? Carlos didn't tell you? Oh my, Kathy, I knew I should have contacted you myself. Carlos assured me he would relay the information to you. On December 5, at five in the morning I get a phone call on the missing children center hot line. I was half asleep and I heard the Operator telling me it was a collect call, asking if I would accept the charges. Kathy we are not allowed to accept collect calls! When I told the Operator that, the caller started talking very fast. She claimed she saw that missing girl, Jennifer Marteliz getting on a bus from Tampa, headed to Orlando. She got off the bus in Orlando with a man; it was definitely her. When I tried to instruct her to call my home number, the Operator disconnected her. I asked the Operator if I could have the woman's phone number, that I represented an Emergency Hot Line for Missing Children. She said the call was made from a phone booth at a greyhound bus station in Orlando. Kathy, I looked in the phone book but could not get a number for you, so I called your ex-husband, Carlos. He told me not to worry about calling you; he would do it himself. I am so sorry; I should have looked a little harder for your number."

Upset was not an expressive enough term for how I felt! Questions flooded my mind. Why in God's name hadn't Carlos called me, or given my number to Grace? Did he know the man with Jennifer? He definitely did not want me knowing about any leads. What was he covering up?

"Grace, that's okay. Please don't worry, you're doing a great job and you didn't know. Thank you for everything you do for all of us."

As I hurried to the Center's office to call Michael Mills, my mind raced. Jennifer was alive! Someone had seen her! Thank you God!

"Michael, I'm at the Missing Children Christmas function. One of their hot line operators had received a call regarding Jennifer. We didn't hear about the tip until now because Carlos was supposed to forward the information to me. I just know he is hiding something. The operator said the call came from the Greyhound Bus Station. Michael I need to go to the Bus Station and talk to the bus drivers. Can you come?"

"Kathy I can't tomorrow! But knowing you, you're going to go anyway. If you actually find the guy you're looking for, ask him to come to my office and we will record the interview."

Michael was correct. I would not have waited; I was at the Greyhound Bus Station at seven am. It had been extremely congested with people, but it was easy to tell who the drivers were by their uniforms. Talking to everyone was a slow process. I had to find the drivers, show them Jennifer's picture and request information. I had been ready to give up and start again the next morning when I saw the last driver for the day pull in. I waited for all the people to get off the bus, and then I asked him about Jennifer. My excitement mounted as he said:

"Yes I had her on my bus. I remember her because when she got on she was alone. Then this man came on the bus, sitting right behind her. It was very weird, as if he didn't want anyone to know that he was with her, but he was. It definitely caught my eye. Why would this guy be on a bus with a little girl, yet not want anyone to think he was with her? She looked drugged, her face was expressionless."

I finally managed to talk to someone who had actually seen Jennifer. I remember I had goose bumps on my arms. I grabbed his arm, ensuring he would not get away from me and told him:

"She has been missing since November fifteenth. I always felt in my heart that my daughter was still alive. But now you have seen her, it's for real. This is so exciting for me. I have a private detective working on the case, his name is Michael Mills. Please, could you come to his office? He will have a sketch artist there. It will help us to create a picture of that man you saw with Jennifer."

"Sure, no problem! Anything I can do to help the little girl. Would tomorrow be okay, I'm off work?"

"That would be wonderful! Thank you!"

I gave him Michael Mills's address and he told me he could be there around 1:00 o'clock.

He was right on time. Michael asked me to please wait outside the office. It was easier for the sketch artist to concentrate if there weren't too many people in the room. I am sure Michael was suspicious that I would talk too much. I did talk too much when I got excited, or nervous. It didn't take long; the sketch was finished within thirty minutes. The driver described the man as being slim, probably weighing about one hundred and eighty pounds, dark hair and dark eyes, with very large eyebrows. He wore his hair slicked back, and had a mustache that went to the bottom of his mouth. The artist handed the composite to Michael. He looked at it for a minute then handed it over to me. The blood drained from my face.

"Oh my God Michael, he looks just like Darlene James' boyfriend!"

Michael thanked the driver for his help, and informed him if we found Jennifer with the assistance of this picture he would be eligible for the reward.

"I don't want the reward. Just wanted to help in any way I could. My heart goes out to you."

I felt elated; I jumped up and kissed him on the cheek! "Thank you ever so much, you have been a tremendous help!"

He was a very nice man! He had come here on his day off to help, and he did not want anything. That was a sample of the heart of Tampa residents! Their generosity did not really surprise me anymore. When Michael escorted him to the front door, I rooted through my suit case and pulled out a book I had been working on. It contained information and pictures of the people I suspected might have been involved in Jennifer's case. When Michael came back into the office, I proudly lay the book on his desk to a page of pictures I had taken. These were some of the people who came and went from the bar where Carlos liked to drink.

"Look here Michael; this is the bar Carlos goes to when he drinks. He met his wife Amber there. A woman named Darlene James owns it. See here, this is her boyfriend. He looks just like the man your artist drew."

"You're right Kathy. It looks as if the sketch artist was looking at his picture when she drew this. I will contact Captain Garcia in the morning. We need to get Darlene James and her boyfriend in here for questioning."

CHAPTER THIRTY SIX—CHRISTMAS

Our entire family, and close friends, gathered at my parent's home for Christmas Eve. My precious daughter Jennifer would not be there. I did not want to go. How was I going to make it? Putting on, that fake smile as if everything is ok. But I couldn't let Toni Lisa down. I just could not do that to her. I had to go.

I was not feeling very well when I headed over to my parents. Being sick to my stomach was normal these days, but tonight felt different. I had to drive by Jennifer's street. I stopped in front of the duplex to satisfy a compelling need to confront my guilty feelings.

My poor Jennifer, where are you? Why can't I find you? Baby, I am so sorry I wasn't strong enough. That I wasn't able to tell you No! Giving in to your demands, I let you live in this dump. How could I have listened to everyone, allowing a seven year old to decide what was best for her? Seeing it all clearly now, it was too late. Fear of losing your love, my only excuse. Now I have lost your love and you too!

I remember seeing a light turn on in the duplex as I thought about all that had happened.

They knew where she was! They could stop this pain. These monsters have ruined my children's life, they have ruined my life. How I despised them.

I got out of the car and in total despair; I pounded on the front windows screaming:

"GIVE ME BACK MY DAUGHTER, NOW! I WANT MY DAUGHTER BACK!"

I went from window to window; I scratched and banged on the glass, whatever I could think of to disrupt their peaceful little lives. They peeked out at me, the cowards never saying anything! I know they heard me! The entire block heard me! Carlos quickly covered the windows with aluminum foil so I couldn't see inside. I felt helpless, out of control. I was hoarse from crying and screaming when I finally went back to my car. Everything I had done to get Jennifer back had failed. Carlos never showed any pain or guilt for Jennifer. Amber was pregnant; he was getting a replacement for Jennifer. It wasn't fair; Amber shouldn't have been able to have a child, when she had lost mine!

I felt a little better as I drove to my parents' house! Stopping at the duplex had helped me focus.

Christmas presents for the girls filled the back seat and trunk of my car. I was determined Toni Lisa was going to have a good Christmas! I felt my mind wandering back to our last Christmas with Jennifer. How Jennifer's Christmas had been ruined because of me.

When the girls and I finally got our own home, I wanted to celebrate Christmas Day in our home, just the girls and I. I had ten presents for each of my girls, a continuation of Mom's tradition. I asked the girls how many presents they wanted to take to Grandma's for their Christmas Eve celebration, and how many were they going to leave at home for Christmas Day. Toni Lisa said half, but Jennifer wanted them all to go to Grandma's. Once again, I let my children decide instead of making the grownup decision. I left five for Toni Lisa and two for Jennifer at home.

On that fateful Christmas Day, it broke my heart when Jennifer cried because Toni Lisa had more presents than she did. I tried to explain that Toni Lisa did not have as many presents at grandmas, but she was only six, she did not understand. So I told myself for next Christmas I would do it the right way, both the same. But that Christmas never came. You never know what tomorrow will bring.

I may not have had Jennifer physically with me, but she was in my heart.

Toni Lisa ran up to hug and kiss me when I stepped out of my car. Her beautiful little face was bright, and cheerful. Smiling in the face of such childish glee wasn't difficult.

There were about eighty people there to celebrate the holiday and Toni Lisa had a great night. She got lots of gifts. For once, talking her into going to bed wasn't a problem she was exhausted. We knelt by her bed; prayed for Jennifer and wished her a Merry Christmas. When I drove home that night, my car was packed again; I wasn't the only one who bought gifts for Jennifer!

CHAPTER THIRTY SEVEN—

DARLENE JAMES

Michael Mills and Detective O'Sullivan made a point to stop in at 'Las Crackers' bar. They wanted to talk with Darlene James and her boyfriend, Anthony Vegas. It was 9:00 o'clock and the pair had just finished cleaning up the bar. They were on their way out when Detective O'Sullivan showed them his badge, introducing himself and Michael:

"Good morning, I am Detective O'Sullivan with the Tampa Police Department and this is a private detective, Michael Mills!"

Darlene James was an intelligent woman. It was apparent she has been around the block a time or two with officers of the law. She could hold her own in a casual interrogation.

"Yes, what can I help you with?"

"Ms. James, are you aware of the missing girl, Jennifer Marteliz?"
"Of course!"

"I will get straight to the point; we would like you and Anthony Vegas to come down to the police station. Evidently, the young girl's father is in here quite a bit. We would like to get statements from the both of you. It would be greatly appreciated."

Her expression changed from suspicion to blatant boredom.

"I'm off tomorrow; I should be able to make it around 9:00!"

Detective O'Sullivan wrote in his note pad and said:

"Thank you Ms. James, and if Anthony Vegas could come with you that would be great."

Darlene James and Anthony Vegas arrived at 9:00 o'clock sharp. They were not happy! When they walked into the small interrogation room, Detective O'Sullivan thanked them for coming down to the station.

"We will take you one at a time for the lie detector tests. Ms. James I thought we would start with you first, if that is okay?"

Darlene James was on her feet before he got out his last word.

"What? Lie detector test, I didn't agree to that. I thought you wanted to talk about Amber and Carlos. I will not take a lie detector test I want to call my attorney! In fact, just forget the whole thing!"

She grabbed Anthony Vegas' arm and pulled him to his feet; they stormed out of the station.

The following day she had her attorney call to explain that 'Ms. James would not be submitting to a test, or questioning, unless, of course, she was being charged with a crime'!

Michael Mills couldn't believe what he was hearing when Captain Garcia told him they couldn't do anything. He argued with him saying:

"We have a witness who claims Darlene was on 98th Avenue the day Jennifer disappeared. Our witness says she was smoking heavily and looked very nervous. We also have a sketch that looks just like Anthony Vegas."

Shaking his head, Captain Garcia firmly said:

"More evidence is needed if Darlene is going to be pulled in for questioning."

Poor Michael, he called to let me know what had happened during his meeting with Captain Garcia. We made plans to meet at 5:00 o'clock.

Very frustrated Michael left Captain Garcia's office but maybe now he would believe what I had been telling him. I believe the police department had no more use for Michael, since he was helping me. Something wasn't right with Captain Garcia or the way he treated Jennifer's case. I knew as long as he headed the investigation I would never find Jennifer!

We returned to Jennifer's neighborhood to check out the rest of our leads. We went to Carlos' house first, but when we got there, the house was empty! Where could he have gone? Was he with Jennifer? I tried to open the door, but it was locked. Michael got impatient and said:

"Kathy, please get away from there, let's go!"

"No Michael, I want to check inside!"

I checked the windows and found one open! The window was very high. I tried to get Michael to open it but he refused to help. He was by the book and considered what I wanted to do as breaking and entering! I looked around and found a crate that I could put under the window. When I pushed up on my tiptoes I could pull myself thru the window. I opened the front door for Michael, but he refused to enter Carlos house. I told him to please give me five minutes and I'd be out. To my amazement, Jennifer's things, clothes, stuffed animals, bedroom set, everything was gone! The entire duplex had been emptied. I closed the front door and met Michael in the front yard. I told him:

"There is nothing of Jennifer's left in her room. They have taken everything out Michael, everything."

"That is very odd Kathy. But I don't see how you can report it without incriminating yourself. We came here to check on our leads, let's just get to work."

There were a lot of kids playing in the street. Two little girls, who looked to be around the same age as Jennifer, were playing jacks. I asked them if either of them knew Jennifer. One said she had classes with her. Michael asked where she lived and she pointed at a man sweeping his driveway.

"That is my Daddy!"

We walked over to him and Michael introduced us:

"Hello, my name is Michael Mills. I am a private investigator working with the Longo family. This is Jennifer Marteliz's Mom, Kathy Longo. We were wondering if you knew Jennifer?"

"Yes, I knew Jennifer. I have two daughters who went to school with her."

Michael looked at the car in the garage.

"I noticed your car, it seems freshly painted."

"Yes it is! I really feel bad about this, but my car is the car everyone was looking for. I was scared to say anything, but I had taken my car in to be repainted. After work, when I went to pick it up, it had only been sanded. I had to drive it home like that. The following day I took it in and had it painted. I heard all over the news, how they were searching for a rust colored car. I didn't want any trouble, my wife is from Cuba and I couldn't have the police asking a bunch of questions. I am so sorry."

Michael nodded and asked him:

"Did Jennifer run past your car and do you remember what time it was?"

"Yes, she ran right past me. I had to stop to let her get across the road. My daughters were home when I got there, so it had to be around 3:00 o'clock. I am really sorry, but I just couldn't get involved with the police. Please forgive me!"

I had been upset by his confession. We had wasted so much time looking for the rust colored car, and it had been parked only a block away!

After Michael shook hands with the man, he led me away by the arm and said:

"Kathy, I can see you're upset, but look at it this way we can cross that lead off our list. We found the car."

"You're right Michael, it's just hard."

"I understand Kathy, but remember; tomorrow is 'lie detector test' day, okay?"

The following is a typed record of Carlos Marteliz's lie detector test as it was given by Michael Mills.

January 6, 1983

Tester: Michael Mills
Tested: Carlos Marteliz
Witness: Captain Garcia

Michael: Mr. Marteliz, please answer all questions with a yes or no only, do you understand?
Carlos: Yes!
Graph: Indicates Carlos is telling the truth.

Michael: Is your first name 'Carlos?'
Carlos: Yes!
Graph: Indicates Carlos is telling the truth.

Michael: Did you lie when you said you did not know how Jennifer disappeared on that day?
Carlos: No!
Graph: Indicates Carlos has lied.

Michael: Did you lie about Jennifer's where a bouts on November 15, 1982?
Carlos: No!
Graph: Indicates Carlos has lied.

Michael: To your knowledge did Jennifer come home that day from school?
Carlos: No!
Graph: Indicates Carlos has lied.

Michael: Did you yourself pick Jennifer up that day?
Carlos: No!
Graph: Indicates Carlos has lied.

Michael: Regarding the disappearance of your daughter. Was she picked up by some one in Oklahoma?

Carlos: No!
Graph: Indicates Carlos is telling the truth.

Michael: Was she picked up by a friend?
Carlos: No!
Graph: Indicates Carlos has lied.

Michael: Was she picked up by a relative of yours?
Carlos: No!
Graph: Indicates Carlos is telling the truth.

Michael: Was she picked up by a relative of
Amber's?
Carlos: No!
Graph: Indicates Carlos has lied.

Michael stopped the test!

Carlos cried as he said:

"I blame myself for letting Jennifer walk home. I wish I could say one of my friends got her and tell you where to go get her."

Michael asked Carlos:

"Why have you failed when you're asked if you know who took Jennifer?"

Carlos looked down he could not meet Michael's eyes as he said:

"I believe my wife's family could be involved."

Michael asked Carlos:

"Would you wear a wire?"

Carlos responded:

"If I was given immunity I would."

Michael nodded his head and told Carlos:

"I will be back in a moment."

Michael went to an adjoining room where Captain Garcia had been watching the test on a closed circuit TV. Michael asked him:

"Did you see what happened? Carlos is willing to wear a bug. Let's wire him up!"

Captain Garcia shook head, and said:

"We can't do that, I can't offer him immunity!"

In a frustrated tone Michael asked:

"You were watching right? This could end it all right now, let's do this!"

Shaking his head again, Captain Garcia responded:

"Sorry, I can't."

Michael had passed beyond frustrated. He was angry and it showed when he said:

"Are you really sorry you can't, or is it that you don't want to wire Carlos?"

Captain Garcia's very calmly said:

"I can't Michael! I am not the boss you know! I have to ask my superiors, before this goes any further. How about we approach Carlos again?"

Captain Garcia got out of his chair and walked into the room where Carlos sat crying. Before anything could be said, Carlos asked:

"What if it isn't my wife? I would feel horrible that I did something like that to her."

Captain Garcia looked down at Carlos and said:

"It is up to you Carlos, talk to a lawyer first. You're free to go!"

Michael threw his hands in the air, spun around and left the room in disgust! He couldn't believe what had just happened. Michael was hooked. Not only did he now believe me that Carlos was involved with Jennifer's abduction, but Captain Garcia's actions could be questioned too! He called me after Captain Garcia and Carlos left his office. I could tell he was depressed about the results of the test, but he tried to be positive for me. He told me that we would just have to work harder. Michael had decided the next step to catching Carlos was to check out his work schedule.

Carlos worked for Tampa's Maintenance Department and he had to punch a time clock. Michael was given permission by the City Manager to question all employees attached to the Maintenance Department. There were some interesting results from Michael's questions. Carlos had not worked on November 15, 1982. Yes, his time card had been punched, but that was because of an arrangement the foreman and Carlos had worked out. The shop foreman would punch Carlos time card, while Carlos was out working on side jobs. They would use the city's materials for the jobs then split the money. Plus Carlos would still receive a check from the city. Again, Captain Garcia said he wouldn't be able to use this against Carlos, because of the method used in obtaining the information.

CHAPTER THIRTY EIGHT—
ANNA MARTELIZ

During the seven years I was married to Carlos I had made friends with his female family members. I received a call from his sister-in-law, Anna. She claimed she was at Marias' home visiting. Maria was Carlos' sister. She told Anna that Carlos claimed Jennifer was safe, not to worry about her. I had been so excited about her statement I didn't think about any legality when I asked:

"Anna, could you try to record Maria saying that, please?"

Anna was married to Carlos' brother and she had received more than her fair share of abuse. She hadn't gotten away from it the way I had. She was still living with an abusive man. She said:

"Kathy I could get into big trouble if I were caught! The only reason I wanted to tell you what I had heard was because we were such good friends! You know what; I'll do it for Jennifer. I'll meet up with you at McDonald's at 5:00 o'clock if I can get Maria on tape, okay!"

"Thank you so much Anna. You don't know what this means to me!"

I waited in the parking lot at McDonalds. Anna drove up at 5:25, pulled in next to me and handed me a tape. We were furtive and acted like secret agents, sun glasses and all. She put her car in reverse and said:

"Kathy, I'm praying for you. Please remember, no one can find out that I helped you. Please!"

Mom had been waiting for me and when I got to her house the recorder sat on the table ready to go. I put the tape in and we sat hunched over the recorder listening.

'Hey Maria, I just came over to visit. Listen I was thinking about what you told me the other day, you know, about Carlos?' 'I know Anna, I can't believe it either.'

'Maria, I couldn't sleep thinking about what you said, are you sure you heard him right?'

The TV was on very loud but you could still hear Maria say:

'Yes I am sure Anna, I will never forget what he said for the rest of my life. The other day, Carlos walked in while I was crying. I told him I was upset about Jennifer! You know, wondering where she was. I asked him, how are you holding up. Jennifer and her dad were always together. He put his arms around me and said Jennifer was safe, that I shouldn't worry about her. I asked him what he meant by that? How could he know Jennifer was safe? He told me Amber's family had Jennifer. They were going to keep her safe until everything cooled down; then they were going to demand a ransom for her return. Anna, I couldn't believe my ears. I asked Carlos what he thought he was doing? He was going to end up in jail. He told me to forget about it. He would handle the Longo family. I probably shouldn't have told anyone what Carlos said, but you're family Anna. Please, just don't tell anyone what I've told you. Please! My brother would kill me.'

'Maria, I would never say anything.'

I stopped the tape, looked at Mom, and said:

"Mom, can you believe what she said? Jennifer is alive. It's like I have been saying all along. They took her for the ransom money! Remember that first night we were in the duplex, the FBI told us they were tapping all our phones. That must be how they found out about the ransom call. Carlos must have been checking to see if the phones were still tapped. What should we do Mom?"

"Kathy, we have to give this tape to Captain Garcia. He is in charge of Jennifer's case. He will know what to do. This tape proves Carlos knows where Jennifer is being held."

I disliked and mistrusted Captain Garcia, but realized Mom was right. During the drive to the police station, I prayed Captain Garcia would change and do the right thing. Maybe now he would help us, instead of fight us!

"Okay Mom!"

The police department was packed, but I knew where to go. The Captain's office door was closed, and his secretary suggested we have a seat and wait. While we waited, Mom told me she would do the talking. I laughed because everyone knew my mouth got me into trouble. It wasn't long before Captain Garcia came out of his office and acknowledged us.

"Hello ladies, what can I do for you today?"

"Captain Garcia we need your help. We have a tape of Carlos sister stating: 'Carlos told her, Amber's family took Jennifer for the ransom money'."

"Can I have that tape Mrs. Longo? I would like time to review it, and then I will give you a call?"

Captain Garcia took his time making that call. It was around 3:00 o'clock when I answered the phone on the first ring.

"Hello Kathy, this is Captain Garcia. I wanted to let you know we picked Carlos up and brought him down to the station. I had him listen to the tape you gave me. He didn't seem real surprised; he just laughed and said his sister Maria was crazy! Kathy, I'm sorry we had to release Carlos until we could check the tape. I just wanted to let you and your Mother know. I will call you sometime next week."

I did not really understand what Captain Garcia had in mind, and it surprised me he had been so nice.

"Okay Captain Garcia, thank you!"

Later that night, I got a call from Anna.

"Kathy, this is Anna. How could you betray me like that? I made it clear that no one could find out about that tape. After the cops released Carlos, he was furious. Carlos' brother, Sam, called a family meeting. Kathy, they decided to have Maria committed into the crazy ward at the hospital. Kathy, I'm dead if they find out it was me who gave you that tape!"

"Anna, I can't believe they did that. They had her committed just to get Carlos out of trouble?"

"Well they told Maria it would just be for two weeks, and that if she didn't agree Carlos could go to jail for life. They tried to get her to tell them who she talked to, but she said she couldn't remember. Kathy, she looked right at me when she agreed to enter the crazy ward."

"Anna, I am so sorry! I didn't know Captain Garcia was going to do that. I should have known he would do something like this. How does Carlos do it Anna? How does he get away with this? You would think his brothers would make him bring Jennifer back home."

"I know Kathy; they stick together no matter what. I'm sorry. I tried to help."

"I appreciate what you have done Anna. You will never know how relieved I was to find out about Jennifer. It has been killing me to think I would never get her back. Thank you for everything."

After hanging up with Anna, I called Captain Garcia to tell him what Carlos and his family had done to Maria! I didn't expect his response:

"Kathy, I don't believe Carlos had anything to do with Jennifer's abduction. He just isn't smart enough to trick the police department and the FBI. You need to focus on something else, stop looking at Carlos."

"Captain Garcia, every lead I've gotten has involved Carlos and Amber. I can't believe you think he is innocent, but I guess I should have expected that from you."

"Kathy, I have a famous psychic coming to town tomorrow. Let's see what she comes up. I will call you okay?"

Captain Garcia hung up the phone before I answered.
He does not know this but I have the original tapes.

CHAPTER THIRTY NINE—JOHN WEEKS

Captain Garcia had picked Anne Schmidt, a famous psychic, up from the airport. He handed her a pair of Jennifer's earrings, some clothing, and a doll she slept with at night.

"These items belonged to Jennifer, can you feel, or see anything?"

Ms. Schmidt held the earrings tightly in her closed fist and hugged the doll.

"These earrings are holding a lot of Jennifer's energy, like a recording. I believe she accepted a ride or got into a vehicle with someone she knew. Do you have a street named Skipit or Skip or something like that here?"

Skeptically, he answered:

"Yeah, there is a street called Skipper Road."

Eagerly, she said:

"Let's go there!"

Captain Garcia drove them to Skipper Road. As they passed a grouping of trees, Ms. Schmidt grabbed his arm and said:

"Stop, go back to the house in those trees!"

Captain Garcia turned the car around and drove into the driveway she indicated. Ms. Schmidt said:

"The man in that house is responsible for Jennifer's abduction!"

Captain Garcia got out of the car, walked up to the door, and knocked. He introduced himself when the door opened:

"Hello, I'm Captain Garcia with the Tampa Police Department; I have a few questions if you have a moment?"

The man simply said:

"I wondered how long it would take before you found me!"

His simple statement surprised Captain Garcia. After regaining his composure he continued:

"I am here regarding the disappearance of Jennifer Marteliz!"

"Yes, I know! I used to live in the same duplex as Jennifer; she brought me my mail. My name is John Weeks!"

Captain Garcia stood there in shock, the psychic from out of town, brought him here! This man had lived next door to Jennifer prior to her abduction!

"Mr. Weeks, would you mind coming to the Tampa Police Station at 9:00 o'clock in the morning. I have a few questions I need you to answer for me?"

Captain Garcia handed him his card, then returned to the car. Still amazed, he said:

"That was impressive!"

Ms. Schmidt told him:

"I don't have anything else for you right now. You need to see what comes of this man."

Captain Garcia dropped Ms. Schmidt off at her hotel. He said:

"I will have an officer pick you up in the morning and drive you to the airport. I want to thank you for coming all the way down here. You may have broken this case wide open for us today. I'll be in touch!"

John Weeks showed up at the police station right at 9:00 sharp. Captain Garcia decided that Detective Lync would help him with the interview.(This is the true statement from the police files)

Detective Lync: 'Mr. Weeks, can you tell me what you did on November 15, around 2:30 in the afternoon?'

John Weeks: 'I took my girlfriend to work at University Community Hospital. Then I went to Suncoast Teachers' Credit Union to cash a four hundred dollar check. Then I went across the street to use the pay phone; called my drug dealer to get some drugs. He told me to go to the Holiday Inn on North Dale Mabry. I waited there for about ten minutes; he didn't show, so I went to the lobby desk, got change for the phone booth and called him again. He told me to go to the Mama Mia Restaurant; I met him there and bought eighty dollars' worth, then went home.'

Detective Lync: 'Okay Mr. Weeks, thank you very much for coming in.' Captain Garcia told Detective Lync to check out Weeks's story. In his report Detective Lync stated Weeks had indeed cashed a check at the Sun Coast Teachers Credit Union at 2:41pm. They remembered him at the Holiday Inn but couldn't verify it was November 15th.

Detective Lync then visited with Weeks's girlfriend to determine Weeks' behavior that day. Annette stated that she and Weeks had started out as lovers but the relationship rapidly turned platonic. Mid December they had separated entirely. Detective Lync asked if she had any objections to the temporary impoundment of her car as evidence. He told her that Weeks would have had to use her car to abduct Jennifer. Annette agreed to the impoundment. Nothing was found in her car.

Captain Garcia reviewed the information Lync had gathered and told him:

"Okay, go pick Weeks up and bring him back in for questioning."

After being taken to an interrogation room, John didn't wait for the questioning to begin. He claimed he was a psychic and that he knew what had happened to Jennifer.

Captain Garcia and Detective Lync were skeptical. Captain Garcia said:

"Okay Mr. Weeks, why don't you tell us what happened!"

"Well I see a person get Jennifer in a vehicle; someone she kind of knew. He took her to an abandoned house, telling her that her grandmother was inside the house. Jennifer entered the house and was strangled by a second male by accident, after she struggled with him. Her body was wrapped in a bed sheet or bedspread of some sort and she was buried in some location."

Captain Garcia asked Mr. Weeks if he could show him where he was talking about. He said:

"Sure drive me around and I will show you."

John Weeks had them drive to an area on Livingston Road, approximately two miles north of Skipper Road.

John Weeks claimed:

"I am feeling vibrations stop here!"

They get out of the car and he walked to a large pile of leaves, where he began scraping his feet, spreading the undergrowth around. He said he believed Jennifer was buried there!

John Weeks claimed again:

"I am feeling vibrations!"

He walked to the back portion of the property and located a vacant house. He entered the house, went straight to the attic entrance, and climbed up into the attic. Leaving the attic, he went to the crawl space where he crawled under the house. Weeks crawled back out, walked to the northeast corner of the house, counted out a number of steps and began scrapping the dirt with his foot. After they had searched for two hours, Weeks asked to be taken to an area around 9th Street and Fowler Avenue.

Without getting out of the squad car, he asked for a piece of paper and a pen. He jotted notes down about the persons responsible for Jennifer disappearance. As he wrote, he said:

"There were two men one was about twenty four years old 5'7" with blond hair and wears a blue uniform. The other was an older man, about 5'11" with short hair and a big nose. The blonde guy doesn't have anything to do with the killing, but knows he can never say anything! These men are close; lovers, brothers, father and son, father and step-son, business partners, or something like that. The older guy is a friend of the Marteliz family, and Jennifer has seen the blonde guy several times."

John Weeks went on to say the motive for the abduction of Jennifer was money. Originally she was not supposed to have been killed, but something had gone wrong. He told them that was all he had at that time.

Captain Garcia and Detective Lync decided that was enough, for now, and took him home. As they drove back to the station they decided John Weeks was either crazy or definitely knew something about Jennifer's abduction. Captain Garcia decided to turn a copy of their interview over to the FBI.

The FBI had already completed a profile of Jennifer's abductor. They felt the person who had taken Jennifer was likely a drug user with a minor record of assault, trespassing, and other nuisance type offenses. This abductor had more than likely, not spent any time in prison. If he had been confined in jail he would have had great difficulty adjusting to institutional regimentation due to an independent nature. This person would have known Jennifer prior to the abduction. He would have gained her trust through his pleasant nature, and by his ability to manipulate others. More than likely the abductor was an adult, white male between the ages of thirty to thirty five. The FBI felt he had been acting in concert with one or more other individuals. The perpetrator was probably employed in some type of semi-skilled occupation where he would have been selectively competent by choice.

I felt the FBI profile fit Carlos perfectly. For Captain Garcia, John Weeks fit the bill. It had seemed to me that from the time of his interview with Weeks he refused to look at anyone else. As for the FBI, I was never told what they thought about the Weeks interviews.

CHAPTER FORTY—TONY LONGO

My father, with his kind eyes, compassionate, caring wisdom. The voice of reason, he wanted only to help me. So unselfish, he lived to take care of his family. Now he had a plan to bring Jennifer back home.

The doorbell rang. When Dad opened the door, he was surprised to find Michael Mills on his doorstep. He told Dad he wanted to speak to him privately. He needed to show Dad the results of his investigations. They went into the study.

A. Darlene James was struggling to keep her bar, 'Las Crackers', open.

B. Amber had worked at 'Las Crackers' for a short time. Amber and Darlene had become good friends.

C. Amber and Carlos had met at 'Las Crackers.'

D. A witness identified Darlene James waiting, smoking cigarette after cigarette, on 98th Avenue. This was the same street Jennifer, walked to get home.

E. The bus driver who had seen Jennifer on his bus had helped an artist draw a composite of the man with Jennifer. It was the spitting image of Ms. James' boyfriend, Anthony Vegas.

F. Carlos and Amber were going to have to pay child support when Kathy removed Jennifer from their home.

G. Amber was going to have her own baby soon and wanted Jennifer out of the picture.

H. Then there was the interview with Carlos.

Michael felt Darlene James, her boyfriend, and Amber had decided to work together. They would share the ransom which they believed, would have solved all their collective problems.

My dad stepped in before Michael could say another word.

"Michael, I have a plan. I am going to make an offer to Darlene that she cannot refuse."

Michael looked worried but he knew something had to be done.

"Tony, I am sorry but I don't want to hear your plan its best I don't know. But I wish you luck!

After Michael left, Dad called his best friend, Andrew. Now I want you to understand about Andrew, he was a big man. He had to weight about three hundred pounds with very dark hair and dark scary eyes and stood 6'5". He fit the image Dad was after and Andrew would have done anything for Dad. After they met and discussed their plan, Dad purchased a black briefcase which he filled with $100,000.00 in twenty's, fifty's even hundred dollar bills.

Dad and Andrew decided it would be best to show up at night. They drove into the 'Las Crackers' parking lot at 9:00pm sharp. The bar already had several customers. Their presence demanded attention as soon as they walked through the door, obviously out of their element but still a notch above the rest. They both dressed in black suits and black shirts. They looked like mafia men, which I'm sure is what dad had intended. Andrew walked up to the bar, turned and faced the room, watching the people. Dad asked the bartender to call Darlene. Darlene recognized him as Jennifer's Grandfather as soon as she walked out of the back room. She never let on, but asked how she could help him. Dad set the case in front of her on the bar and opened it, so she could see the contents. Her eyes were huge when she looked inside the briefcase then back at him! Dad told her not to say anything, that he knew she was having financial trouble. All he wanted was the safe return of his granddaughter and the briefcase would be hers—all contents included. Dad closed the briefcase, handed her a business card with a hand written phone number on the back. After she took the card, Dad and Andrew left. Dad had been very sure Darlene would call him, but she never did!

CHAPTER FORTY ONE—SUICIDE

After Michael had told me Carlos failed his lie detector test, I decided to look at Amber's family as a source of leads.

Amber's mother, Carol, lived in an apartment building not far from Carlos' duplex. The first thing I checked was her phone records.

I called the phone company and pretended I was Carol. I informed the phone company I had lost my bill, and requested that they read it to me over the phone. I was able to get a record of calls that dated back to November when Jennifer was abducted!

Carol had made eight long distance calls each month. Once a week she called her son Jack who lived in Texas. She followed the Texas call with a call to her mother who lived in New York. These two calls were like clockwork.

I called Carol's mother's number, which was answered by a nursing home receptionist. Then I began checking into her son. I found he worked for Morton Sloan, his Dad. My information on him had been sketchy. I visited the court house and found Carol had divorced Morton Sloan and had been left destitute! Her husband had been very successful hiding all his assets!

Additionally, I found that Carol had a trust fund. She didn't live like she had any hidden money! She drove an older Toyota four door, but did live in a nice apartment complex. Neither her car nor her home indicated that she had extra money available. I questioned the trust even more. I canvassed her neighbors, like Michael had taught me. One neighbor remembered Carol bragging, while doing her laundry, that she would be 'Coming into some money soon'. She was going to move into a beautiful townhouse in Carroll Wood. I wondered what money could she possibly have had coming to her?

Carol had fainted when the detectives searched her car. Had she picked up Jennifer? Was the fainting spell a ruse to keep from being questioned? Did she think she wasn't going to get caught? I never got answers to my questions about Carol. Six months after Jennifer disappeared, Carol committed suicide. She was found in her bathtub, her wrists slit. She left a letter that said she couldn't take 'it' anymore and that she wanted to be cremated!

CHAPTER FORTY TWO—GEORGIA TO CHICAGO

I had begun investigating Amber's father, Morton Sloan. He had given a phone card to Amber to use when she needed to call him. I found out she had used the card on the day Jennifer had been kidnapped! She said at three o'clock she was standing outside her duplex waiting for Jennifer, but in fact she had used that card to call her brother-in-law, James, at 3:05 from a phone booth three miles away!

Morton Sloan lived in Georgia. I decided after work on a Friday to rent a car and drive all night. The drive was very peaceful and it gave me time to think. It was early morning before I finally arrived. Sloan's home was located at the bottom of a long hill and I could see his black Rolls Royce in the driveway. I stayed for four hours taking pictures of nothing! I didn't see anything, or anyone. I got bored at his home and decided to check out his business. I only drove five blocks before I found the address. It was a large warehouse and the huge painted sign on the building read 'Carnival Supplies'. I remember thinking to myself: 'What a perfect place to hide Jennifer, in a traveling carnival'.

Time came for me to return home. I know it sounds crazy that I drove all that way and came up with nothing but the excursions made me feel active in the search for my baby!

There is a town called Gibsonton about 20 miles from Tampa. It was home to a large community of people who worked in the carnival industry. When I drove into town, it was lined with food stands on both sides of the road, but they were all closed. I asked a station attendant where everyone was and he told me everyone hung out at the coffee shop down the road. I walked into the coffee shop. It was packed, and I felt out of place. I was the stranger, and they all stopped talking, and stared! I didn't know what to do so I just asked in a loud voice if anyone there knew a man named Morton Sloan. The mood in the coffee shop changed immediately. Now we were all friends. They all either knew him or knew of him and Morton Sloan suddenly became the topic of conversation. I found out he didn't go anywhere without his two Dobermans. They were his body guards! One man said that his main business was dealing drugs and he covered the enterprise up with the carnival business. They said Morton Sloan didn't handle pot, only heroin and cocaine. I left my name and phone number at the coffee shop, hoping anyone with information would call.

It worked! Several days later I received a call from a woman named Penny. She lived in Gibsonton. She claimed to have psychic abilities and wanted us to meet. We decided Denny's at 10:00 pm.

Mom and I got there fifteen minutes early. We asked the hostess if we could sit in the back.

"Sure sweetie, just follow me."

She sat us in a booth at the back of the restaurant and handed us a menu. My mother told her no we didn't want anything to eat. But I stopped her and said;

"I would love a piece of Banana Cream pie."

My mother laughed and said she would have one too. As we were eating our pie, Penny walked in. She saw us, waved off the hostess and walked over to the booth. She sat next to me, covered my hand with hers and said:

"When I see Jennifer in my vision she is just as beautiful as you! Kathy, I make a lot of money as a psychic, but I won't be charging you. I just want to help you find Jennifer!"

I can say I just met my first gypsy or what I would imagine a gypsy to look like. Black wild hair, beautiful royal blue eyes and big red lips. She was very pretty and a great personality. A little weird but I liked her. She made sure I kept my attention just on her:

"Kathy look into my eyes, in my vision, there is a very dangerous man in Chicago holding Jennifer. His address is 9720 Stage Road! Kathy, you must go there quickly, he doesn't intend on staying there long! You need to be very careful; this man has a long reach."

I thanked her for wanting to help, but she interrupted me and said:

"Kathy, you must listen to me this is not a joke, you must go there right away."

"Penny am I hearing you right, you mean right now,"

"Yes, please go, I will finish your pie for you now go."

"Ok, can I have your phone number? I might need to contact you."

Penny stops me right in the middle of my sentence.

"No, I will call you."

My mother and I both got up, paid the bill and left. She said she would pray for us, that we would need it. As we got into the car I said,

"Mom that was weird! None of the other psychics we have met with gave us a specific address. They just say near water or in a beige house. Do you think she is really a psychic or just has information she wants to share?"

"Kathy, what I think is we need to head for Chicago, and we need to go now! I'll arrange for our plane tickets when we get home."

Our flight arrived in Chicago at 10:30 am. Mom had made arrangements for a three day stay, booking our hotel and rental car in advance. We dropped everything off at the hotel and drove straight to the address given to us by Penny. We pulled up to a trailer park where we decided to watch for a while. It wasn't long before a black Rolls Royce with two Dobermans pulled up to the trailer!

"Mom that is Morton Sloan's car. Amber's dad, what's he doing here?

We had been so intent on watching the car driving up to the trailer we didn't notice two men that walked up on either side of our car. When they climbed into the back seat, it freaked us both out! The taller man of the two pulled out his badge, and asked me:

"What are you ladies doing here?"

"We are searching for my daughter; she was abducted on November 15th."

"Miss, we have a stake out in process, we would appreciate it if you would drive out of the trailer park. An officer will meet you at the entrance to escort you to the police station."

We hadn't been in Chicago for a day, and we had already gotten in trouble with the law! When we arrived at the police station, an officer escorted us to a conference room, and offered us drinks while we waited. It wasn't long before two officers arrived and arranged themselves across from us at a big table. He said:

"Okay ladies, why don't you tell us why you were parked in the trailer park."

For an hour, Mom and I shared our tale. The detective finally informed us that we would be interfering in an investigation of child pornography. He asked that we stop watching the trailer and even went so far as to threaten us with arrest if we didn't care to listen. After seeing how determined we were, he relented a little and explained:

"Ladies, I have had officers watching that trailer for 6 months now. Morton Sloan is suspected of running a child pornography ring. He brings children, with the consent of their parents who are being paid, to that trailer in order to photograph them in the nude!"

My reaction to the detective's statement was the same as when Carlos had socked me in the stomach! I gasped air into my lungs, hunched over to hug my stomach. This couldn't be happening! Not Jennifer, not pornography! I had pretended that Jennifer was being held by a decent person; that was how I had handled the nightmare, but now reality shattered my illusion!

"I can't leave! If it is possible that monster has my daughter, you will have to arrest me."

"Young lady that can be arranged, but before we take that step, I would like you to listen to me. There is nothing you can do for your daughter. You would be hurting her more by interfering with this investigation. We are very close to shutting Mr. Sloan down. If your daughter is here, you will be the first person we call. I promise you!"

We were escorted to the airport and assisted with the necessary flight arrangements. I endured the flight home but bitter tears burned my face as I imagined what that monster could have been capable of doing to Jennifer. I felt hopeless and realized all I could do was pray. Pray that Carlos would never let them do something like that to his daughter. The only daughter who actually loved him.

After I dropped Mom back at her house, I drove over to check out Carlos's duplex. Mr. Sloan's Rolls Royce was sitting in Carlos' driveway! I had no idea how many hours it took to drive from Chicago to Tampa, but Morton Sloan and his dogs were there!

CHAPTER FORTY THREE—DIRTY COP

Waiting for news from Chicago had been difficult. I filled up my spare time working with Larry; watching Carlos' house, watching the bar, taking pictures, getting tag numbers and collecting garbage. I had no intention of admitting defeat or stopping my search!

A car with Texas plates showed up at 'Las Crackers' bar and we decided it was probably Amber's brother since he lived in Texas. If it was her brother, that would provide a connection between Darlene James and Amber's family. I took tag numbers and vehicle descriptions to the police department for identification. When I walked into the station it looked like a war room. Phones rang off the hook, and everyone seemed to be diligently working assigned jobs. Eventually, I was able to grab an officer, and I asked if he would please check tag numbers for me. He said sure, wrote my phone number down, and told me he would call back when he could. After waiting a week, I called the station and they didn't know what I was talking about! I hadn't written the officer's name down, nor had I kept a copy of the tag numbers. It was a mistake I wouldn't make again!

Garbage night at Carlos' duplex was always a challenge, and I dressed appropriately: grubby clothing! One night there were a lot of dirty diapers, baby food jars, and generally gross trash! I could have told anyone interested what Carlos, Amber, and their new baby ate on a daily basis! Every piece of paper I found always had some kind of food on it or worse. Larry was great, but even more so when he helped me go through the garbage. Generally we didn't find anything of importance, however, this one night would be different!

I sat on Larry's' floor and wiped the goop off some small slips of paper. I recognized the tag numbers I had taken to the police station a week ago! These were not copies, they were originals. I had a very difficult time wrapping my mind around the latest discovery!

I waved the papers in Larry's face and explained the importance of the numbers.

"Larry how could this happen? What's going on?

I was yelling and crying in frustration at the same time. I had wanted to leave for the station right then, but it was late at night and I am sure Captain Garcia was sleeping in his nice warm bed. I attempted to calm myself the best I could so we could finish searching the garbage. After three more hours we were finished, and found nothing else of importance.

I showered when I got home and tried to sleep before making the trip to the police station. I arrived at the station before Captain Garcia. When I saw him walk toward his office I had the strongest urge to run up and hit him. What I did do was just as unacceptable. I engaged Captain Garcia in a shouting match right in front of everyone! I remember taking the papers from my purse, throwing them at him and demanding:

"Those are the papers I brought to this station a week ago for identification. Maybe you can tell me why I found them in Carlos' garbage. Are you getting paid off? Are you a crooked cop?"

"How dare you say that to me. You and Carlos are as different as day and night. He comes in showing the department respect, thanks us for our hard work and lets us do our jobs. You on the other hand;

you come in here accusing the department of being paid off. Get out of here, stay out of police business."

I began to run out of steam and said:

"I just want my daughter back. If you get her back for me, I would kiss your ten toes! I am not like Carlos; I can't sit at home doing nothing, I have to find her. I can't sleep at night! I only see her face, crying for me to come get her."

He was so mad he could not process anything I said! He would not talk, he just pointed at the door. As usual he was ignoring information I had collected!

After my confrontation with Captain Garcia I had intended to head to Mom's house and lay down for a bit. I still haven't figured out how Captain Garcia beat me there, but his car was in the driveway when I pulled up. He and Dad were in the den with the door closed. I could hear them talking, but I couldn't make out what was being said. I was sure they were discussing my actions that morning but I didn't care! I still wanted to know why those papers had been in Carlos' garbage! Mom started laughing when she saw me standing there with my ear to the door. She motioned for me to join her in the kitchen, but I had no sooner sat down when we heard the front door slam. Well, Captain Garcia must be mad at me! Dad walked into the kitchen and I knew by the look on his face that their meeting had not been good!

"Kathy, Captain Garcia is very upset with you; he says you're hurting Jennifer's case. Not helping! You have everyone on your side rooting for you! The reporters are making the police look like the bad guys. Then you went to the police department this morning, screaming insults at him in front of the entire station." "Dad you know I love the police department, I just hate Captain Garcia! When Detective O'Sullivan was in charge of Jennifer's case, we got along great. This all started when Captain Garcia would not do his job."

"Kathy, he said you came into the station this morning accusing him of accepting bribes. That is a serious accusation. He is the Captain. Kathy you need to respect his position, even if you don't respect him."

"But dad I found slips of paper with tag numbers I had written. Those are the same papers I gave to the police last week for identification. You want to know where I found them, in Carlos' garbage. How did Carlos get them?"

Dad put his hand on my shoulder and said:

"Princess, I am begging you. If you don't quit now we will all be sorry. Captain Garcia has implied this case is bigger than you can handle!"

"Dad I am not afraid of him! I'm not even scared of dying. She is my daughter. I would give my life for her. You would give your life for me!"

"Kathy, please! I've already lost a granddaughter; I don't want to lose my daughter too. Honey, your Mom and I wouldn't know what to do without you. You are making charges against the police and they don't like it!"

"Okay Dad, I will be good."

With a sigh of relief, Dad says;

"Thank you, honey!"

I wanted to make Dad feel better. I was stubborn and driven; there was no way in hell I would quit. After Jennifer had been found, everything will be okay again. At least that was how I felt. Besides, what could Captain Garcia do to me? I had not committed a crime!

I was a mother on a mission to find her daughter. That's all I wanted! If they helped me find her, I would have been forever grateful and out of their hair for good! The relationship between Captain Garcia and I didn't improve. It got worse!

CHAPTER FORTY FOUR—MR. PARDO

I routinely listened to the TV in the morning while I got ready for work. A week after the fight with Captain Garcia my routine was shattered when the news commentator announced:

"THE MOTHER OF JENNIFER MARTELIZ IS BEING ARRESTED TODAY! FURTHER NEWS AT 11:00 AM."

I wondered if the broadcaster meant Amber or me. I called Dad, and he suggested that I come home immediately! He had seen the same report and was going to call our attorney, Mr. Pardo, who happened to also be a family friend. My entire family respected, and believed in him. I felt very lucky he was on our side.

Mr. Pardo's car was already in front of the house when I drove up. After we settled down, he said:

"Kathy, I just got off the phone with the police department, and it is you they are going to arrest. You work for a Gary Burns. He does what is called 'floor planning.' I was told he charges a very high interest rate to his customers . . ."

"Mr. Pardo, he doesn't ever charge interest. He charges a flat fee for each car. I don't know what they are talking about?" "Kathy, just listen to me. They are arresting everyone in your office. I know you have been through a lot, but I am here to get you out of this okay? You are only an employee. You did as your boss asked. He has had this business for thirty years: way before you even began working there."

"I think they are doing this to get back at me! They told Dad that I had better stay out of Jennifer's case or else."

"Kathy, let them do their work."

"I am not going to do that. They are not doing their jobs. I've found out more than they have. I don't care what they do to me! I won't stop until Jennifer is found!"

"Kathy, I understand that, but if you are in jail you can't look for Jennifer, right?"

With my head down and a soft voice I said:

"Right."

"Kathy, I see you have fire under your feet. We need to cool them down. You are going to have to stop yelling at everyone. Try to work things out with people in a civil manner. We know Jennifer is your daughter, but the world does not stop turning for you. You have to slow down."

Dad had been quiet until then.

"Mr. Pardo, I have been trying to tell her but she is on a roll, running down anyone who gets in her way."

I felt sorry for myself. Why was everyone so awful to me? Didn't they understand that I was just looking for Jennifer? Mr. Pardo put his hand on my shoulder and said: "Kathy, tell me what you do at your office."

"I am in charge of the office. I take care of the accounting for his many businesses."

"Kathy, how many years of college do you have to back up your ability as his accountant? I also want you to tell me about each of his businesses."

"I didn't even finish high school much less attend college. I taught myself accounting at the library. I really don't want anyone to know that please."

"You what? Kathy if it comes down to it, I will have to bring it up. It will be as a last resort. Now tell me about Mr. Burns' different business adventures!"

"Well, he has a car lot on Hillsborough Avenue. He buys cars from the auction house then sells them on the lot. He has a real estate business, where he purchases homes and sells them or rents them out. Not expensive homes, the lower priced homes. He's also a mortgage broker; he gets loans for people."

"Kathy do you know what interest rate he is charging them on those homes?"

"Yes, the going rate is 12%."

"Well, that can't be what the police are looking at. Okay keep going."

"He has a business he calls floor planning. I like this business the most. It's fun!"

"Kathy, that's why you are being arrested, tell me about that business." "Mr. Burns doesn't charge them interest, just a set fee he calls a customer service fee for each car. Dealers from different car lots bring him their car titles. Mr. Burns gives them the money they paid for the car after deducting the service fee."

"Okay Kathy, if I understand you right, it doesn't matter if the car cost $1,000.00 or $100.00, you charge the same fee."

"Yes, Mr. Pardo! If they sell the car and pay him, then he gives them their title back."

"Okay Kathy, I understand, I am going to call the police station and let them know you are turning yourself in."

Starting to feel nervous and scared I said:

"Will I have to spend time in jail?"

"No Kathy! I will post your bail. After that, we will start working on your defense. Everything will be fine."

"Thank you Mr. Pardo!"

I saw my father's face and his dark eyes glistened with tears. A lump formed in my throat. Once again, I had hurt Dad! He asked Mr. Pardo:

"Can I come with you?"

"No Tony! It's best that you stay here. We shouldn't be gone long!"

The station parking lot was mobbed with reporters. They were on all sides of the streets waiting for us to show up. I don't understand this I am just looking for my little girl.

"I guess Captain Garcia is showing me just what he can do." "It's okay Kathy; we can handle this. We will just wait until noon to turn you in. Everything will be okay."

We went to Mr. Pardo's office and he turned on the TV. We were surprised because the news now claimed: 'Kathy Longo, mother of Jennifer Marteliz has not turned herself in. She is now wanted by the law'.

Mr. Pardo called the jail to request we be allowed to enter via the rear door of the station. But they didn't know Mr. Pardo; he is always one step ahead of them. When we arrived he drove to the front door of the Police Station and there wasn't a reporter in sight. Mr. Pardo had just proved how he had earned his reputation; all the reporters were at the back door! The sheriff's department handled bookings for the jail. The booking officer told us the police department had called and requested I be treated like a common criminal. He couldn't understand why they were acting like jerks. I was finger printed and had my picture taken while Mr. Pardo posted my bail. When I was finally released the officer helped us avoid the reporters. I hoped he realized how much we appreciated that gesture of kindness.

It took six months of hell before Mr. Pardo cleared us all of the charges. The police finally admitted to a lack of evidence and dropped all the charges. My family all agreed that the police were trying to make me look bad in the eyes of the public. There were far too many people helping me, and the police department had received some bad publicity! Thank you, Mr. Pardo, for always being there for me and my family.

CHAPTER FORTY FIVE—

ALFRED CHAPMAN

My life was divided between pre and post abduction! I had close friends from 'before' but now my life has changed. My new friends were from a world I knew very little about! Now I routinely rubbed shoulders with private investigators, cab drivers, newspaper and TV reporters.

Mom and I were sitting at the kitchen table when the phone rang. The man on the other end was Fred Dallas, a reporter for WQYK in Virginia. Mom motioned for me to pick up the extension so I could hear their conversation. He told Mom that a man named Alfred Chapman was to be featured on their show the following evening. He was suspected of killing over thirty women in the southern states. Neither one of us was sure why he had called, until he said Alfred Chapman had claimed he had abducted and killed Jennifer!

That was all I had to hear. I could not pretend any longer I had to say something.

"What? He said he killed her?"

"Yes, but we believe he is just saying this to get off death row. He is scheduled for execution in thirty days!"

I don't know if he thought he was still talking to Mom, but I was the one who said:

"You can't do that; I want to talk to him!"

"We were hoping you would feel like that Mrs. Longo. Chapman says if you agree to appear on TV with Detective George and him, he will tell you where to find Jennifer's body."

"Who is this Detective George?"

"He is Chapman's arresting officer. He works out of the St. Pete Police Department there in Florida. We will schedule flight arrangements for you and Detective George, Mrs. Longo. I look forward to meeting you tomorrow night around 7:30 pm."

I thanked him and we both hung up. Mom had dragged out the phone book for St. Pete when the phone rang again. Detective George was calling and he wanted us to meet with him at the precinct to discuss Alfred Chapman. Before he hung up he said:

"Mrs. Longo, Alfred Chapman is a liar; he would say and do anything to get off death row. Please do not fall for any of his lies. I'm checking our files to see if he was even in Florida during the month of November last year. If you could come on down, to St. Pete, I can fill you in a little better with my files in front of me."

Mom told him we were on our way. It took us twenty minutes to get there and I told Mom;

"I hoped the St. Pete Police Department wasn't like the Tampa Police Department."

She told me,

"Honey you're not being fair! The Tampa Police Department had been great except for one sour apple."

We walked into the St. Pete Station and it felt as though everyone was watching us. Several officers got up to greet us and made us feel welcome. I whispered to Mom that I wished they were handling Jennifer's case but she just shushed me. Before we sat in the chairs offered, Detective George came through the door and introduced himself:

"Hello ladies, I am Detective George; if you will please come to my office. It will be a little more private there."

He told us he had been interested in Jennifer's case and he would like us to share everything we knew with him. He had called the Tampa Department, and they had told him I was very active in the search. They told him I carried a suitcase around that contained more information about Jennifer's abduction than they had been able to collect. That made us all laugh: but it was true. He was curious about my arrest, but said I didn't have to tell him anything if I didn't feel comfortable. Mom asked him how much time he had, which again caused us all to laugh; but we proceeded to answer his questions.

After we had discussed Jennifer's case for a couple hours, Detective George explained Alfred Chapman. He shared that Chapman was known to have raped and killed at least three children and thirty women. The police didn't know how many more victims were unaccounted for. Chapman was intelligent, sought attention and publicity. The TV program was a result of Chapman seeking both. Detective George advised that it would be a mistake to under-estimate Chapman's motives. He must have heard about Jennifer's high profile case and now he was using it to get publicity. Detective George assured us Chapman didn't care what anguish he caused, so he suggested we play hardball with him while on TV.

It was his understanding that Mrs. Longo, not Ms. Longo was to accompany him to Virginia for the show. He joked that Mom was probably the better choice because of my temper. Again, we laughed!

Before we left his office, Detective George told Mom and I that after he was finished with Alfred Chapman, he would be interested in looking at Jennifer's case. I couldn't help but feel a little excited. Fresh eyes might find something new!

Letting Mom go to that prison was hard for me. I felt I should have been the one to confront that monster! Plans had already been made and Mom was on her way. She appeared on national TV with Detective George the following day. I remember feeling bad knowing Mom had to listen to Chapman's filth. He claimed to a national audience that he had killed her Granddaughter. While watching the program, I decided he was a liar on his way to hell, and that I didn't have to listen. There was an 'off' switch on the TV and I used it. I didn't waste any more time on him; I went into the kitchen, opened up my suitcase and went back to work on Jennifer's case.

Detective George had been right about Alfred being a liar. He had not been in the state of Florida during the month of November. I was relieved to know he hadn't killed Jennifer. That little speck of doubt had been chipping away at me.

Good to his word, Detective George began working on Jennifer's case. At his request, I had shown him the contents of my suitcase. After he had reviewed everything, he also concluded Carlos was involved with Jennifer's abduction. I made copies for him and he told me he would get back with me later.

CHAPTER FORTY SIX—OLD CABIN

I have realized the world is littered with evil people. But for every evil person I have encountered, I have met two good people to help me fight them.

A gentleman, who introduced himself as Charles called me from the St. Pete Foundation of Missing Children and informed me he knew where Jennifer was being held. He had received a call on the Center's hot line and had been given instructions that I had to follow if I wanted to find Jennifer. I had to travel by taxi; I had to come alone and I couldn't tell anyone where I was going. He asked if I understood the instructions:

"I promise, anything you say, I will do it; Please, I just want my daughter back."

He set the meeting for 7:00 o'clock at the McDonalds Restaurant on Gulf to Bay in Clearwater. He had not said anything regarding a ransom.

I thought to myself, 'how would he know if I told Mom or not?' My rebellious streak probably saved my life. I had decided to drive to my parent's house rather than use the phone. I didn't know if the phones at my house were still being tapped. I knew the phones at work weren't. Mr. Burns had purchased a machine to check his phones.

After she listened to Charles' plan, Mom had insisted I at least tell Detective George. I thought to myself, 'Here we go; now another person is going to know'. After I told him, Detective George checked into the St. Pete Foundation of Missing Children. There wasn't an organization by that name; Charles had lied to me. Detective George still wanted me to meet with Charles as planned. But he would be there with reinforcements. I called Larry and like always he was there to help me. We arrived in his cab just in time for my appointment. I went into McDonalds to call Detective George, but he didn't answer, so I left a message on his machine. I went back outside, and Charles was there waiting for me.

"Hi, you must be Kathy Longo; I am Charles with the Foundation of Missing Children. It's nice to meet you!

He was an older man, in his fifty's, with short white hair, eyes like a weasel, and he hadn't shaved in weeks.

"Hi, I am excited to see my daughter can we go now".

"Yes, I am ready to take you to your daughter. Did you come in that cab?"

"Yes, just as you told me, and I didn't tell anyone about our meeting tonight!"

"Great, why don't you get into my car, and I will take you to Jennifer."

As he talked, he was guiding me toward his car. A young lady that worked the counter in McDonald's ran out and told me I needed to come back inside for my change.

"Hold on a second Charles, I will be right back. I need to go get my change."

"Okay, but hurry so we can go get Jennifer!"

I ran back into McDonalds. I was glad Charles was on the opposite side of the counter, he couldn't see me! The young girl told me I had a phone call. I picked up the phone and it was Detective George. He explained he was in position to follow us when we left.

As I got into Charles's car and closed the door, he said:

"Are you excited? It won't be long now!"

I glanced over at Charles before answering. He had a big smile on his face, as if he had won $100,000.00.

Charles pulled out of the McDonalds parking lot; officers appeared from hiding places I didn't know existed, and squad cars pulled across the McDonald exits.

Detective George jerked Charles out of the car and threw him to the ground. He handcuffed him, jerked him back onto his feet with one hand, and then read him his rights. After Charles said he understood his rights, Detective George began questioning him right there in the parking lot!

"Where is Jennifer Marteliz?"

"I don't know, I swear!"

"Why did you have Ms. Longo meet you? Listen real good, I'm not playing games with you, tell me now."

"Okay, I will take you to Jennifer."

Except for five officers, Detective George instructed the other officers to return to their normal duties. He shoved Charles into the back seat of the car, opened the front door for me, and then climbed in next to Charles. Two squad cars followed our car as Charles gave the driver directions. I started to get excited thinking, maybe he did know where Jennifer was being kept. He had to be taking us to Jennifer! We drove to a very old cabin. The cabin was old enough I didn't believe anyone lived there.

The four officers in the following cars got out to investigate. One returned to report there was no one in the cabin, nor had there been in a long while.

Detective George lost his temper, dragged Charles out of the car, and slammed him against the door, saying:

"Last chance; tell me where Jennifer is or you're going to spend a long time in jail. Your jail mates don't like child abusers; they take great pride in serving their own type of justice."

Charles caved when he heard the threat and said:

"Someone told me she was here, that's all I know!"

"Wrong answer! You're going to jail and you're going now! I don't want to hear another word from you!"

"Please! Wait! Please! I lied! I don't know where Jennifer is. I was going to kidnap Kathy so I could demand a ransom for her. This is where I was going to bring her. Please, I figured if her Dad was willing to pay for his Granddaughter, he would pay more for his Daughter!"

"You make me sick! Attempted kidnapping is still going to put you in the slammer!"

Detective George shoved Charles back into the car and told two officers to lock him up. After they left, he walked over to me, put his hand on my shoulder and said:

"Kathy, I am sorry you had to go through that. Are you okay?"

"Yes, I have to admit I was getting a little excited. I thought he might actually know where Jennifer was. Thank you!"

Larry had followed us to the cabin but he had waited until everything had calmed down before he drove up behind the squad car. I got into the cab and I could tell Larry's adrenaline still pumped, because he said:

"If the cops hadn't shown up, I planned on following you myself."

Larry had been such a sweetheart over the past few months. What a night, for a moment I had thought just maybe . . .

"Thank you Larry, you have been such a good friend. I hope one day, I'll be able to show you I can be a good friend too!"

He just smiled and said:

"Life is funny Kathy, under different circumstances, we might never have met. Here we are friends, from two sides of the tracks."

CHAPTER FORTY SEVEN—LETTER

"Larry it's garbage day, would you mind if we drove by Carlos'?"

"I don't mind! Are you okay after everything that happened tonight?"

"Yes, but I need something to keep my mind busy. Maybe we will find something good tonight!"

There had been four bags set to the curb for pickup. We sat on the living room floor at Larry's and sorted through Carlos' garbage. I remember it was later than I thought, and I had realized I was getting tired when I heard Larry. He was excited when he said:

"Kathy I found something here; it's a letter from Jennifer, Kathy! Look!"

"What? Let me see it! Larry, it is! I can't believe this"

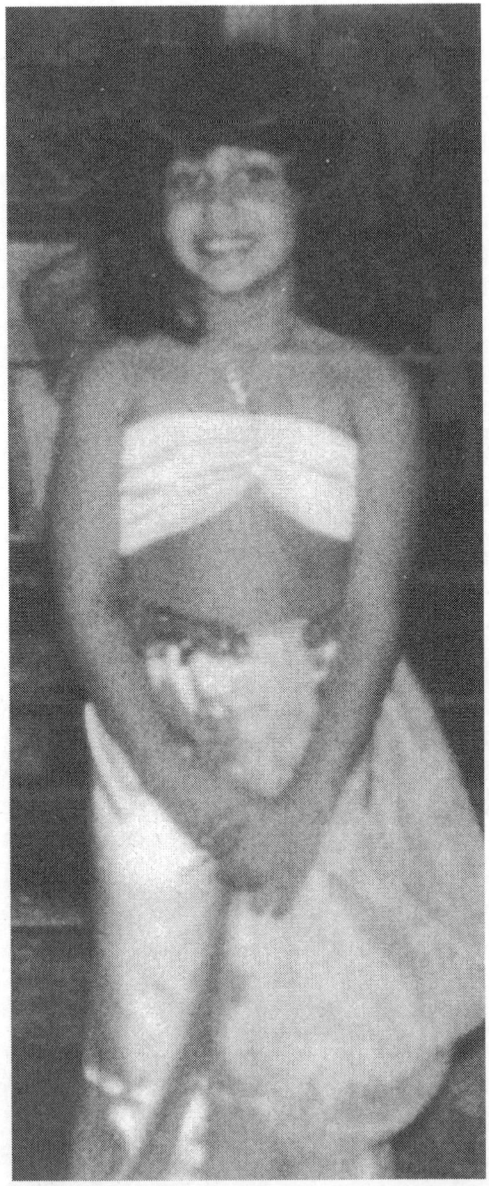

The Outfit That Jennifer Is Talking About In Her Letter

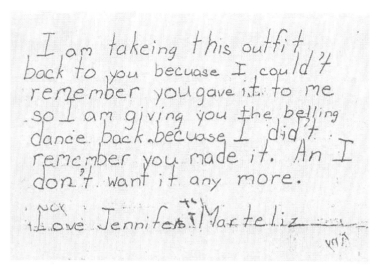

I am takeing this outfit
back to you becuase I could't
remember you gave it to me
so I am giving you the belling
dance back becuase I did't
remember you made it. An I
don't want it any more.
Love Jennifer Marteliz

THE LETTER I FOUND WRITTEN BY JENNIFER

"Larry this is unbelievable, my sister made her that belly-dancing outfit. Jennifer asked me if she could take it to her father's. She wanted to wear it for Halloween. Larry, that was two weeks before she was abducted. This proves she is alive. I have to call my mother; I don't care how late it is."

I hurried to call Mom. We had been so disappointed about what had happened at that cabin. This small piece of paper had recharged my spirit and it would do the same for Mom.

"Mom, I am sorry to wake you but Larry found a letter written by Jennifer in Carlos' garbage!"

She asked me to read Jennifer's letter to her; as I was reading, I could hear her crying.

"Mom please don't cry you are going to get me started."

"Kathy, would you bring her letter here, I have to see it for myself?"

"Sure mom, I will be right there."

It was 3:45 in the morning. I asked Larry if I could leave the garbage on his floor and check the rest of it the next day. He knew how important the letter was and he agreed Mom should see it. Thanking him, I left for Mom's.

"Kathy, we have to give this to the police, you know that right?"

"I know Mom!"

"They need to make sure it is Jennifer's hand writing. I know you don't get along with Captain Garcia; but we need the police department, they have resources we don't have!"

"Mom, if I've learned nothing else from this experience; I now know adults don't always get to do what they want to, this is one of those times. I'm really tired Mom, would you mind if I slept here for a while, then went to the police department?"

With a smile on Mom face she asked:

"Would you mind if I went with you to the police department?"

"Of course not Mom, I would love your company."

I decided to go to my old room, which was now Toni Lisa's room. I tried not to wake her, but she had heard my car when I pulled into the driveway. I heard her sweet voice when I quietly entered the room:

"Hi Mom, is everything okay?"

"Yes honey, just go back to sleep."

"I can't Mom! What is going on? Please tell me, please. They didn't find Jennifer dead did they?"

I was shocked to hear her question!

"NO! NO! Toni Lisa, why would you say that honey?"

"All the kids at school are telling me that is what their parents are saying. That if she has been gone this long, she has to be dead!"

Sitting on the side of the bed, I hugged her.

"That is not true honey! Sometimes people just don't think about what they are saying. I found a letter from Jennifer in your father's garbage.

I turned on her light and pulled the letter out of my purse I handed it to her and asked her to read it. Toni Lisa couldn't believe what she read. Excitedly she claimed:

"Jennifer wrote this Mom, and I remember she took that outfit to Dad's. She was going to wear it for Halloween."

"I know Princess. That is why I am here so late, Larry found it while we were searching through your Dad's garbage. I brought it here so Grandma could see it."

I went to sleep that morning, comforted by the closeness of Toni Lisa's little body. The next thing I remembered was hearing Mom call me.

"Kathy, let's go, your Dad will take Toni Lisa to school."

Half asleep, I hurried to change my clothes and freshen my makeup. When I got outside, Mom was already in the car. Slowly climbing in, I heard Mom's excited voice:

"Kathy, I can't believe you fell asleep. I was so excited, I couldn't sleep."

"I don't know Mom; Toni Lisa was awake when I went in, we talked for a while, cuddled for a while, and fell asleep together."

"Toni Lisa needed that honey; she loves you so much. I know she misses you, and you spend so much time looking for Jennifer. You have always been very close with Toni Lisa. You have always kind of leaned on her, and now you are doing everything without her, on your own."

I got very defensive with Mom and said:

"Mom I am doing the best I can; I don't want anyone taking Toni Lisa; that is why she lives here, and not at home with me. I have to find Jennifer! I can't just sit at home; I think I would go crazy just thinking about everything. I have no life much less sleep; between looking for Jennifer, doing my work, and spending time with Toni Lisa, I feel numb most of the time. I feel as though I am just going through the motions. I thank God all the time, that I have you and Dad. Mom, the Missing Children's Center has asked me to talk to other parents' of missing children. I can't do it! It makes me sick to think about not finding Jennifer. Their souls are crying so hard and I know this because mine is. I just can't face that."

Mom had tears in her eyes as she listened to my little speech. She patted my hand and said:

"I know honey; we just need to take one day at a time. That is the only thing we can do. I love you Kathy."

"I love you too Mom!"

I dreaded the thought of talking with Captain Garcia. Mom and I went to his office; he got right up to greet us, but the tension was apparent.

"Hello Captain Garcia! I found a letter in Carlos' garbage, written by Jennifer."

He held out his hand when he asked:

"May I see the letter?"

"Of course, that is why we are here!"

I handed Jennifer's letter to him. He read the letter, then looked up at Mom and me, and asked:

"Can you explain this letter to me?"

"Yes! This letter was written after Jennifer was abducted. Two weeks before Halloween, Jennifer asked if she could wear the belly-dancing outfit at her school Halloween party. I told her that she could. In her letter, she says it does not fit her anymore. Jennifer was abducted two weeks after Halloween. That costume should have still fit her. She also says in her letter that she doesn't remember who made the costume for her. None of this would make any sense unless she was still alive, and wrote this letter recently."

"Kathy, I don't want to bust your bubble here, but I need to give this to the FBI! We need to find out when, and if Jennifer wrote this letter."

I looked at him very sad and said;

"I have to give them the original, right?"

He smiled and said:

"Yes Kathy, they have to have the original, but I can make a copy for you."

"Captain Garcia, can I have twenty copies?"

My request had been so sincere and earnest that it broke the ice and all three of us laughed. He said:

"Kathy, I will make you as many copies as you like."

We shook hands and I left his office with twenty copies of Jennifer's letter. I surprisingly left Captain Garcia's office and I wasn't upset or angry. That was a first! We walked out of the Police station and I told Mom:

"I guess that wasn't so bad."

"No it wasn't, and your Dad will be very proud of you."

I hated giving up that letter. Jennifer had written that letter, and it proved to me that she was still alive.

I returned to Larry's house to finish going through Carlos' trash. Larry normally slept during the day because he ran his cab at night. His lights were still on so I figured he was awake. I knocked on his door and he opened it with a big smile on his face.

"Kathy, I've been trying to call you. Your mother said you had already left her house, but she didn't know where you were going."

"I thought I would come back here and finish getting that mess out of your living room. Would that be okay with you?"

"Yeah, sure! But Kathy, the reason I was trying to call you is because I know why they had so much garbage at the curb. They have moved to Georgia. I have their new address; directions, their new phone number, everything was in the trash!"

"Larry, you can't be serious. They have moved out? I have to go to Georgia! I need to know where they are living Larry. How long would it take for me to get there?"

After he looked at an atlas for several minutes, he said:

"I would think about eight hours. I will drive you if you will pay for the gas.

"Larry, that would be great, you sure you don't mind? I'll take you up on that Larry, let's go, we can take turns driving."

"No thanks Kathy, I've seen you drive. I don't want to die yet!"

I was still laughing when I called Mom to let her know what I was doing. I also called my boss. We stopped at my house where I changed clothes and grabbed a bunch of snacks so we wouldn't have to stop to eat. Our plan was to drive to Georgia, see where Carlos and Amber lived, and then head right back home. I brought my pillow so I could sleep, but we talked about Jennifer and then Larry told me his story.

Larry's parents had been upset with the choices he had made in his life. He had married, made great money, and had a beautiful home. His wife had a job but she also had a boyfriend (his best friend)! He walked away from it all, becoming very bitter. He hated the world! He had not talked with his father for over ten years, and only talked with his mother a few times each year, usually to ask for money. His parents were rich, but he hadn't seen either one of them since his divorce. He said he didn't trust people in general and that his birds were his only friends!

"Larry you are my friend! I am sorry you have had such a tough life. I am sure things will get better, you might sell one of your books and become a millionaire."

"No Kathy, I am happy with my life. Sure, I would like to be able to pay my bills on my own; but I like living here, and being by myself. Yes, you are my friend, my only friend! I'm sure when you find Jennifer I will never see you again. We are complete opposites Kathy, you like people, I don't; we are only together because of Jennifer."

"Larry, I know you will always be my friend and one day I will be able to show you. I will never forget all you have done to help me find Jennifer. I thought I had a lot of friends, but when Jennifer disappeared my life changed. My life is on hold until I find out what happened to Jennifer."

It took a while, but we found Carlos's new home in a nice looking apartment complex. I was glad I had brought my camera. I took pictures and wondered how they had been able to afford living there since they had a new baby and no income. We canvassed the neighbors just like Michael Mills had taught me. We asked if Carlos and Amber had a child with them. The neighbors all said 'yes' a newborn. I felt good about the trip, and I was happy Larry had been my company. He never truly realized how good of a friend he had become. I suffered a serious personal loss when he died of cancer in June 1985.

CHAPTER FORTY EIGHT—
AMBER MARTELIZ

Michael Mills had not quit, even after Carlos' failure on the lie detector test. He worked hard, pushing the police to investigate Amber.

Detective O'Sullivan had made an appointment with Amber for the interview. He conducted her interview and assured Michael he would ask her all the questions on Michael's list.

"I promise Michael. As soon as I've finished testing Amber, I will call you."

Amber had walked into the police station with her typical arrogant attitude. She acted like a snob!

O'Sullivan:
'Mrs. Marteliz, can you tell me what actions you took the day Jennifer was abducted?'

Amber:
'At about three o'clock, I walked to the mailbox and stood there for about ten to fifteen minutes, waiting for Jennifer. She was late.'

O'Sullivan:
'Mrs. Marteliz, have you ever waited for her before?'

Amber:
'Yes. Normally I'd see Jennifer walking down the street, then go back into the house until she got there.'

O'Sullivan:
'Mrs. Marteliz, did you see her that day?'

Amber:
'No. I waited until three-fifteen. My husband called shortly after and I told him that Jennifer hadn't gotten home yet. He was worried, so I told him that I would check with one of her friends to see if she knew Jennifer's whereabouts.'

O'Sullivan:
'Mrs. Marteliz, who was the friend you went to see?'

Amber:
'I don't remember. Some little girl I saw in the street. She said she saw her in school but not afterwards. So I went back to my house and the phone was ringing. It was Carlos and I told him Jennifer still hadn't arrived.'

O'Sullivan:
'Mrs. Marteliz, do you remember what time this was?'

Amber:
'Yes. It was three-twenty-seven pm. Carlos gets off of work at three-thirty and I told him, he only had three minutes left to work and not to come home before the end of the work day.
'

O'Sullivan:
'Mrs. Marteliz, have you made any phone calls to your father?'
Amber:

'Only twice. When I was seventeen and when I was eighteen years old.'

O'Sullivan:
'Mrs. Marteliz, have you used any telephone credit cards belonging to your father?'

Amber:
'My husband hasn't even met my father and I don't know his telephone credit card number!'

O'Sullivan:
'Mrs. Marteliz, have you made any phone calls from a pay phone during the period that Jennifer was missing?'

Amber:
'No! Matter of fact, Carlos did not even know my father's name until a few days ago when my father called at my house.'

O'Sullivan:
'Mrs. Marteliz, thank you for coming in and helping clear a few things up. Are you here to stay, or are you going back to Georgia?'

Amber:
'We are staying. We just got back three days ago.'

Accusations Michael had made against Amber, regarding her use of the payphone while she had supposedly been at home waiting on Jennifer, didn't stand up with Captain Garcia. He claimed it could have been anyone using Morton Sloan's phone card. The only thing that bothers me about that is the phone call was made to Carlos' brother and he said Amber called him. When her times hadn't matched up, Captain Garcia assumed she had made a mistake on her original statement!

CHAPTER FORTY NINE—SUSAN MARTELIZ

Out of the blue, one evening, I received a call from Susan Marteliz. She introduced herself:

"Hi Kathy, this is Susan! I doubt you remember me, but I helped in the search for your daughter."

"Hi Susan, what can I do for you?"

"When I was helping with the search for Jennifer, I met Carlos' brother, Jim, and we got married. I have some information you need to hear, but I can't talk now! Would you meet me at Lowry Park tomorrow morning at 9:00 am?"

"Sure Susan, I will see you tomorrow morning."

I hung up with Susan and immediately called Mom to tell her of the latest surprise. I told her I would pick her up at 7:30 and I was treating her to breakfast. That night I went home early I wanted to be ready for tomorrow. I had no idea what she had to talk to me about. So I decided to go prepared, getting my recorder out, I replaced the old batteries with new ones. Then I inserted a brand new tape. I never knew what tomorrow was going to bring.

Sometimes I felt so helpless; I knew I wouldn't make it another day. It had been over a year now and all I had to show for my efforts were pieces to this jigsaw puzzle I called Jennifer's case! Oh, my precious daughter where are you.

Mom and I loved to eat at Village House and we had both looked forward to spending time together. We looked for Jennifer in different ways: My search involved finding leads, then following them. I knew Mom would have loved to go with me, but she did something more important, she took care of Toni Lisa. Mom also worked with the Missing Children's Center. She and her friends organized mass mailings to all the different schools, police departments, doctors and dentists. They had just finished mailing 10,000 flyers to the Dental Association Members! Mom wrote so many letters, she actually sprained her hand. Mom was also an avid fund raiser and event organizer; golf tournaments, fashion shows, dinner theaters, all benefiting the Missing Children's Center. We talked at numerous schools, on talk shows, even at the State Fair, promoting child safety. Mom and I were pleased to meet with John Walsh, which was a blessing. My heart broke when they found his son. He worked very hard to get children listed on the FBI computers. In fact, Jennifer was the first missing child listed with the FBI, because of John Walsh.

I didn't remember the last time we ate at the Village House together. It was nice to spend time with my Mother! It was nice not having to rush!

"Mom, what is it with Lowry park?"

We both laughed!

"This time I am going to be ready. I brought a tape recorder. I will keep it in my purse so they don't know I have it."

After we enjoyed ourselves awhile, Mom said:

"Kathy, we need to talk about Toni Lisa. I hate to bring it up honey, but she is doing badly in school. She has gone from being an 'A' to an 'F' student. Kathy, Jennifer isn't the only daughter you have lost, Toni Lisa needs you!"

I wasn't enjoying myself anymore. I knew Mom was right but I just couldn't spread myself any thinner than I already had. I kept saying tomorrow I'll find Jennifer; tomorrow we would get our lives back! My wishes never seemed to come true.

"I promise Mom! I will make weekends for Toni Lisa. She can have her friends over and we will do whatever she wants."

I can't stop looking for Jennifer. That would have been the end of me! After finishing breakfast on a sour note, we headed to Lowry Park. It was only fifteen minutes away and this time we parked in the parking lot! We sat on a concrete picnic bench by the swings to wait for Susan. We couldn't help getting excited as we speculated about what she had to say.

Two young women with three children approached our meeting place. One woman was obviously pregnant; she said:

"Hi, Kathy, I am so happy you came. I don't know if you remember me, my name is Susan and this is my sister Sara. I helped search for Jennifer that first night Jennifer went missing."

I didn't really remember either woman, but how could I say that?

"Sure I do. Thank you so much!"

"Kathy, I met Carlos' brother that night and we got married. I'm six months pregnant with his child."

"That's nice, I'm so happy for you!"

She couldn't contain her story anymore, it spilled out.

"Kathy, the other night, at 2:00 in the morning, we got a call from Carlos. He and Amber had just moved back from Georgia. Carlos wanted to talk to Jim right then; so we dressed and went to their house. They were unloading their car when we got there. Carlos ran to Jim and pulled him out to the street to talk. I went to help Amber take boxes into the house. As I picked up a rather large box, I dropped it! Kathy, it was full of pictures! I felt so bad, I tried to hurry and pick them up; that is when I saw the picture of Jennifer! I took a good look at that picture. Jennifer was older than those flyers you had, but it was Jennifer. She was carrying Amber's newborn. Kathy I know he was born six months after Jennifer was abducted, so I held it up to the light and looked at it real close. Amber saw the mess I had made, and then noticed the picture I was holding. She started hollering at Carlos to help her and she grabbed that picture out of my hand!

Later, after everything had calmed down, and their car was unloaded, I started asking questions about the picture. They gave me a dirty look and Jim told me to shut up. I did as I was told. I am very afraid of Jim, but I could not help myself. When we got into the car to leave, I started to tell Jim about the picture again. Kathy, he didn't look surprised, he just told me to keep my damn mouth shut and don't tell anyone! He said I wasn't to mention the picture again!

Kathy, I know what I saw, it was Jennifer! I swear to you. I have always felt bad for you. I know how hard you have looked for Jennifer, and I couldn't sleep thinking about it. If Jim finds out I told you, he will kill me. He is very abusive! Kathy, I have nowhere else to go and I'm getting ready to have his baby. Please promise you won't say anything."

I would not have thought of betraying Susan's confidence. I could relate to her abusive relationship. I had been married to her husband's brother! I could imagine her dilemma, just the courage it took to come here and tell me this story was amazing! I felt bad for her. I knew what she was going through; that feeling of being trapped. She was standing there telling me Carlos and Amber had a picture of Jennifer, six months after she was abducted, holding their new child. I heard myself making her that promise:

"Susan, I can't thank you enough for coming out and telling us. I know it would have been a lot safer for you to just ignore what you saw. It means a lot to me, and I'll make you that promise. But after living with Carlos, let me tell you, the abuse never gets any better—it gets worse!"

Sara, her sister, was crying when she said:

"I worry for my sister. I hate that she is married to him. She is so much younger than Jim, and he has put her through hell!"

"Susan, we have a private investigator helping us. His name is Michael Mills. Would it be okay if I told him about the picture?"

"Yes, you can tell him."

"Is there a way I can get in touch with you?"

"I will give you my sister's phone number. She can get a hold of me."

"Okay, I want to thank you again Susan. I know this had to be hard on you!"

We left Susan and Sara at the park. While we drove home, I asked Mom:

"Mom could Carlos and Amber be that stupid; to keep a picture of Jennifer holding their child? Are they that sure of themselves. They must think they can't be caught!

Mom didn't have any answers for my questions.

I called Michael Mills and told him everything Susan had shared. He wanted to give Susan a lie detector test! He didn't trust anyone! I explained to Michael that Susan's husband was abusive, and had warned her she better not tell anyone about the picture. Even if she had passed the lie detector test, we wouldn't have been able to go to the police with our information. Michael said:

"Kathy, let me give her the lie detector test first, then we can worry about the police later."

I called Sara and asked if she could have Susan call me. Less than five minutes later Susan called me back. I explained to her that Michael Mills would like her to come in to his office and take a lie detector test. She agreed, but said it had to be done while her husband was at work. We arranged for her to come to Michael's office at 10:00 am the following day!

Susan showed up at 10:00 sharp and at 1:00 o'clock Michael called to tell me she had passed the test. She had told the truth about the picture. I already felt she was telling the truth, but the test confirmed it for Michael. Excitedly, I asked:

"What is next Michael?"

"Well Kathy, I've talked to her; she is sitting here with me now. I told her we need to go to the police department with this information. She is worried about her husband finding out, but she is willing to go to the police."

"Michael are you sure? I know if Detective O'Sullivan was working on Jennifer's case he would honor your promise, but Captain Garcia won't!"

"Kathy, it will be fine. Susan is okay with it. She wants to help you find Jennifer!"

Michael called me at 5:00 o'clock, and said everything went great. Susan's statement had been documented and the police would notify him after they confronted Carlos. I told Michael I was worried how Susan would explain where she had been all day to Jim. I didn't want anything to happen to her; He didn't know the Marteliz family the way I did! He assured me she would be fine and told me I made a bigger issue of her statement than Susan had. I asked him:

"If they can commit their own sister to the crazy ward to keep from getting caught, what do you think they will do to Susan?"

"Let's wait and see what comes of this Kathy. This is a big break for us; we need this."

I was told that after Susan left the station Captain Garcia was very upset. No one understood why he was upset. He broke his promise to Michael and had Jim picked up from work. I could imagine how angry that had made Jim. He was taken to an interrogation room where Captain Garcia explained why he had been picked up. Captain Garcia told Jim that his wife, Susan, had gone to the Longo's with a story about a picture of Jennifer in Amber's possession.

"Are you aware of this picture?"

Of course Carlos' brother wasn't going to snitch on his brother.

"No!" Captain Garcia then asked:

"Why would your wife say something like that?"

Jim Marteliz claimed:

"Susan is upset with our family for personal reasons! I'm upset that she has taken it this far. I'll have a talk with her when I get home. I promise!"

Captain Garcia's next statement made Susan's situation even more dangerous:

"Your wife said she is afraid of you. On several occasions you have beaten her up is that true?"

Jim was good with his lies, he said:

"I would never hit a woman, especially my pregnant wife."

Captain Garcia believed him and let him go home to Susan! They shook hands and acted like nothing was wrong. When Jim pulled up into his driveway, Susan heard tires screeching and knew Jim had found out! Stomping up the steps, he slammed the front door open so hard the top hinge broke.

"Where are you, you f . . . ing bitch?"

Susan was so frightened she ran out the back door! She knew she couldn't let her husband get a hold of her. The last time he had come home in such a rage she had ended up in the hospital with a broken arm and more! She ran down to the gas station, holding her stomach the entire time! After finding some change in her pocket, she called:

"Kathy please, you have to help me! Jim knows. If he catches me, he'll kill me! I have to leave. I can't stay here any longer!"

"Susan, come here. You can stay at my Mom's! We can take care of you!"

"Kathy, he will find me! I can't stay there. Can you give me some money? I can stay in a motel until I can figure something out!"

"Sure Susan. Come to my Mom's house and I will give you some money!"

I hung up the phone and told Mom what had happened. I should have known Captain Garcia would betray a confidence! Not even a full minute after I had hung up with Susan, the phone rang. It was Captain Garcia:

"Kathy, you cannot tamper with a witness. It is against the law!"

"What are you talking about?"

"Don't act stupid with me Kathy, your phone is tapped!"

"But he will kill her! She is just trying to help me, and she is pregnant!"

"That is why we have a witness protection program where she can go until she testifies."

"Captain Garcia, she just wants a little money to hold her over until she can figure out what she is going to do. I have to help her!"

"If this goes to court, she will be of no use. They will claim you paid her!"

"This is your fault. Why did you have to call her husband? Michael explained to you her situation at home, and you told him anyway. This is why I didn't want to tell you about Susan. But no, Michael said it was the right thing to do!"

"Kathy, we had to hear his side of her story. Did you ever think she might be lying? Maybe she was just trying to get money from you!"

"Captain Garcia, who's playing stupid now? You know better than that. Michael told you he gave her a lie detector test and she passed with flying colors. Are you stupid enough to believe Jim, he hasn't taken a lie detector test?"

"Kathy, I understand you are grasping at anything.
But you need to let us handle this now."

"Captain Garcia, listen very carefully! No way, not in this life time! I've seen the way you handle things. Maybe I should investigate your family history to see if you're related to the Marteliz brothers. What do you think of that?"

He hung up! I didn't care. I believe at that moment I hated Captain Garcia as much as I hated Carlos! I wondered to myself, if he were being paid by someone. They could have been working together keeping Jennifer from me, but I didn't know why. If I were to do as he said, what would happen to Jennifer? Would everyone just give up? Who would look for Jennifer? Sorry, I couldn't take that chance! He would just have to realize I wasn't going to stop looking for her!

I tried not to cry as I dialed Michael Mills's number. I was shaking so badly I don't know if it was because I was so mad at Captain Garcia or I was sick over everything Susan was going through.

"Hi Michael, everything just fell through. I just can't believe this!"

"Kathy, I know what happened. Captain Garcia called me and he didn't believe Susan. He thinks she is just trying to get money from your family."

"I promised her, Michael!"

"I am sorry Kathy, but they can arrest you and Susan. You need to think before you act."

"Maybe you should have listened to me Michael. You have experienced the road blocks Captain Garcia can put up. You knew she wasn't lying because you gave her the test. Michael, whatever happens to Susan, it will be our fault! I'll talk to you later."

I sat in the kitchen waiting for Susan to show up. I didn't know what to tell her. I called her sister Sara and explained what had happened. I told her how sorry I was that Captain Garcia threatened to arrest us both. I told her if I gave Susan money they would accuse me of tampering with a witness. We would both end up in jail. I had made a promise I wasn't able to keep, and I was very sorry. I hoped Susan would forgive me one day. I would never forget what she had tried to do for Jennifer. Sara must have gotten hold of Susan because she never did show up at Mom's house that night. I slept there, hoping she would show, but at the same time hoping she didn't. I never heard from Susan again. As I lay in bed, Mom came in the room kissed me on the forehead and said:

"You okay Kathy? I know it has been a long heart breaking day for us."

I remember trying not to cry.

"Mom, I am so tired of fighting the world. We get a lead; I get excited, hoping that this is it; Jennifer is coming home! Then I fall and I fall so hard Mom. Sometimes it is difficult to get up." "I know honey, I know!"

Captain Garcia called Mom the next morning. He wanted Mom to tell me Susan had come into the station claiming she had lied. She told him she had cooked up the entire story to get money from us. My heart ached for Susan! I knew that one day God would punish Captain Garcia. I hoped I was around when he did!

CHAPTER FIFTY—TOM SMITH

I hated being on TV, but Dad always said: Kathy, reporters are your best chance for finding Jennifer. The circulation of Jennifer's picture, with continual updates, will remind people to watch for her. I knew he was right, but it was hard.

Tom Smith hosted his own talk show on Channel 28. He called me to discuss the possibility of a follow-up story on Jennifer's abduction. We set up a meeting for 6:00 o'clock at my parents' home.

It must have started raining because I didn't hear his car pull up. When I looked out the window he was standing there soaked. I hurried and opened the door.

"I am sorry I didn't hear you knocking."

"That's okay, I thought maybe you changed your mind."

He was very handsome, with curly blond hair and deep blue eyes. There was something sincere about him. I invited him into the kitchen and made him a cup of coffee.

"Kathy, thanks for seeing me! I've heard a lot about your search for Jennifer. As I told you on the phone, I'm interested in airing a follow-up program. Would you be willing to answer some questions?"

"Yes, I would be glad too."

"Okay, what is it you do to search for Jennifer?"

"Well, actually I have a suitcase of leads I've been following."

"May I see it?"

"Sure, I'll go get it."

I opened the suitcase I carried everywhere with me. I pulled out a gray book I called Jennifer's bible. It contained a condensed version of all the information I had collected. It was partitioned with labels; 'Tag Numbers from Las Crackers bar'. There were over 160 license plate numbers listed, followed by information I had collected on each one. I handed the book to him, and after glancing through a few pages he asked:

"How did you accumulate these numbers, and what do you do when you get a new one?"

"Tom, I have a theory regarding who abducted Jennifer; I follow those people wherever they go at night, collecting tag numbers from vehicles in the same place. Then I go to the License Bureau to find out their name and where they live."

"That is what I want to do the show on Kathy. You out there, investigating leads. What tag numbers haven't you done yet?"
"This one here, from Miami!"

"Okay, let's do it! How would you feel about me bringing our own private investigator?"

"That would be fine with me, I am bringing my Mom!"

"What time?"

"Let's meet here at 3 am Monday morning! Oh, and Tom, I don't want anyone knowing how I get those tag numbers, if you don't mind."

"Don't worry Kathy I understand. I will not show that part. We will see you Monday morning bright and early!"

It was Monday, April 9, 1984. We were all ready to go, but Tom hadn't just brought a private investigator. He brought an entire camera crew too! Mr. Paterson, the private investigator, was a perfect fit for his job standing 6'6", and weighing in somewhere around 350 lbs. Dark eyes stared at me from beneath his ball cap. In fact, he was just plain scary—dark hair, dark clothing, dark car and very tough looking. I was a little afraid of him and he was on my side!

Everyone introduced themselves and we loaded up for the ride to Miami. Tom, Mom and I traveled in my car; Mr. Paterson and the camera crew used a van. I was driving, Mom was riding shotgun and Tom was lying in the back seat, looking very comfortable with his pillow and blanket. I teased him about his blanket. It looked older than he did. He didn't fit the stereotype of a reporter; Tom wasn't abrasive in anyway; I found him to be a kind hearted gentleman, with ethics.

I didn't know if the Miami lead was any good, but Michael had taught me that every lead needed to be checked out. Then and only then, could it be crossed off the list. We didn't have a plan! We were just going to the address linked to the tag number, the Sanchez home. Show them a picture of Jennifer, and see what information they were willing to share. Mom and I were happy we had a private investigator along. We did not want a repeat of the Chicago lead. Whenever Michael had gone on leads with me, it seemed as though I was shown more respect than if I had asked the same questions myself.

We arrived after a long and exhausting drive. As we searched for the correct address, I noticed the homes were very close together, clean and in good condition. That is until we located the address we were searching for. The house was vacant and unkempt. Disappointed, I tried to lighten the mood saying:

"Maybe Captain Garcia called them with a warning."

Seeing their faces I quickly said,

"Just joking!"

It worked, the silence was broken and everyone laughed. Tom thought it would still be a good idea to question the neighbors on each side of the vacant house. We knocked on doors. Mrs. Tucker lived in the first home we stopped at.

"Hi, I am Tom Smith, a reporter for Channel 28. We are investigating the disappearance of Jennifer Marteliz. Our investigation has led us to your neighbors' home. Would you happen to know when and or where they moved to?"

Mrs. Tucker did indeed know of her neighbors; sharing with us that Mrs. Sanchez's husband had been arrested for drugs. He was sentenced to five years in prison. She added:

"A couple weeks ago Mrs. Sanchez moved her family, but I don't know where they moved to."

Tom requested her permission to film as he asked his questions and she agreed. Turning to the camera, Tom held up a picture of Jennifer next to his own face, and said:

"Good evening, I'm Tom Smith with Channel 28 news. I am here with Mrs. Tucker in Miami covering a story on missing 7 year old Jennifer Marteliz."

Turning to look at Mrs. Tucker, he asked:

"Mrs. Tucker, have you seen this girl?"

She took the picture, looked at it closely, and then said:

"Yes, I have seen her; she lived with the Sanchez family next door for a couple weeks. I remember her because she looked so much like the little girl who lived there."

I was standing in the back ground, but when I heard her answer, my heart stopped! When it started beating again, I moved, yelling:

"What? You have seen my baby?"

I ran up to her, threw my arms around her, hugging, and jumping at the same time. We both jumped when Tom yelled:

"CUT! Kathy, I am doing the interview, not you! What do you think you're doing?"

"Tom, I'm sorry, I didn't know she was going to say that. Do you realize what she said, 'she saw Jennifer', and I never dreamed she would say that!"

A look of understanding crossed Tom's face. He lowered his voice and said:

"No, Kathy, I am sorry! I wasn't thinking. You can ask her anything you want."

That was all that Mrs. Tucker could tell us, so after interviewing her, Tom suggested we continued going door to door. Silently, I asked God to please let the next person tell us they had seen Jennifer too. Each and every person who answered their door confirmed that they had seen my daughter!

'Yes, the little girl in that picture lived with the Sanchez family for a while.'

'No! I don't know where they went.'

'I heard the Sanchez girl calling her Jenny.'

'She lived with the Sanchez family. I heard her Mom just had a baby.'

'A heavy set woman brought her to the Sanchez home.'

'Yes, I remember her and the Sanchez girl running up and down the street pushing a baby in a stroller.'

'Jenny's mom just had a baby, so they were helping take care of her for a couple weeks. The Sanchez's daughter is around the same age. In fact, they looked like sisters.'

'I watched that young girl walking to school with the Sanchez girl. I believe it was Miami Elementary School.'

'No, I'm sorry; I don't know where they moved to!'

'Sorry, I didn't get their new address, but you could try the post office, surely they would know!'

Home after home they all said Jennifer had lived in their neighborhood with the Sanchez family. Not only that, but they were all filmed, as they were questioned. By the time we were done, Mom and I weren't the only ones excited. Tom had a huge smile on his face. The police and FBI couldn't deny this taped evidence! I could see they all believed Jennifer was really alive, and that we had come very close to finding her. The crew loaded their gear into the van and we drove to the Elementary School. It was 11:00 o'clock when we arrived. Tom asked the film crew to wait outside; he didn't want to upset anyone.

After introducing ourselves to the secretary, we had a short wait before the principal asked us to step into his office.

"Good afternoon Mr. Coleman, my name is Kathy Longo, this is my Mother, Frances Longo, and this is Tom Smith, a reporter for the Channel 28 News. My daughter was abducted on November 15, 1982. We heard she might have been a student here. She would have been living with the Sanchez family."

While we talked I handed him a picture of Jennifer. He studied her picture, and then said:

"I can't be positive; the young girl who looked similar to this picture wasn't here very long. Give me a few minutes to check with some of my teachers. Would you mind if I take this picture with me?"

"No by all means. We will be happy to wait."

He indicated we should take a seat in the outer office; he was gone for little over two hours. We quietly discussed how long he was taking. One of the camera crew members came in to check on us and Tom told him to take the rest of the crew and go get something to eat. He didn't know how much longer this would take. After waiting two more hours, Tom was half asleep on this little student chair, his hair messed up and his shirt half tucked out; he looked like he had been in combat. I know he is working on the story and I appreciate everything he is doing for me. My mother gets up and asks if she could see the principal but the girl at the front desk said he was working on something to please be patient with him. Two more hours went by this time and Tom was asleep. My mom and I just sat there we were so excited we were wide awake. The principal walked back and called us into the outer office.

"I am sorry I kept you waiting so long. I had to be sure so I checked with the teachers and lunchroom ladies. I know how important this is to you and I don't want to make any mistakes here. Mrs. Sanchez brings a lot of children here who have escaped from Cuba. The parents still live in Cuba; but the children have been sent here for a better life. The kids obtain school records and start learning English. My concern is for these children. Mrs. Sanchez brought your daughter to school here about 2 months ago. I thought she was from Cuba until you showed me her picture. Three different teachers and the lunchroom ladies all say they remember her; the other students called her Jenny. The Sanchez family was moving so they requested her records. I'm sorry, but those records will enable your daughter to begin a whole new life. One of the teachers said Jenny told her she used to live on a cock fighting farm, but her Mom had a baby. So she had to come here until her mom was feeling better."

I could not believe what he said. I just missed Jennifer again. They didn't plan on letting her come back! They had made it so she started all over as someone else. His words swirled around in my head as I tried to breathe normally! I needed to concentrate! Would I ever find a way out of this nightmare? Just please don't hurt my baby! I know it's going to get harder now. I wished I had a picture of Amber. Maybe someone here could have identified her as the heavy set woman. I needed to find the Sanchez family; she could still be living with them! I wasn't much use during the rest of the interview. I was involved in my own swirling, yet depressed thoughts!

Tom had requested the principal's permission to film as he conducted the interview. The principal had agreed.

The fog in my head seemed to lift as I heard Mom ask the principal:

"Did the Sanchez family use a local doctor or dentist?"

"Yes! Doctor Checkver! Most of the children here go to him. He is located on 7th Avenue."

We all helped load up the van and off to see Dr. Checkver. It only took about ten minutes at the most to get there. It was probably overwhelming to Dr. Checkver's receptionist when we all entered his waiting room together. Tom asked her:

"We would like to speak with Dr. Checkver please."

"May I tell him why you are here?"

"It's about a missing child"

"Okay, please wait here for a minute."

She retreated to a back office. We could hear their voices, but not make out what was being said. Dr. Checkver came out to the waiting room with her and said."

"Hello! I am Dr. Checkver! How can I help you? My receptionist tells me you are looking for a missing child?"

Tom's camera crew began filming but the doctor said:

"No camera's please! I would be happy to talk to you, but some of these people need to leave."

Tom asked the camera crew to go outside to clear the waiting room. We talked with the doctor after they left. He said:

"Hi Dr. Checkver, my name is Tom Smith. I am a reporter with Channel 28 News. This is Kathy Longo, the mother of the little girl we are looking for and Frances Longo, the grandmother. We were hoping you could shed a little light on the young girl in this picture. (He held up the picture of Jennifer)."

"Yes, I have seen that little girl. Mrs. Sanchez brought her to me. She was sick with the flu."

"Dr. Checkver, would you remember her name?"

"I believe her name was Jenny. I can't be positive though. Mrs. Sanchez requested all her children's records including this child's. She told us she was moving to Detroit to be closer to her family."

"Dr. Checkver, thank you very much. You have been very helpful!"

After we left Dr. Checkver's office, we decided to check into a motel. It had been a long day and none of us felt like driving all the way home. We were happy to know Jennifer was alive, yet sad when we realized it would now become that much harder to find her. It was a tough one today. First the excitement of everyone saying they had seen her. Now, the reality, that they can hide her forever.

I could hear my mother I thought she was asleep but she was crying. I am sure she was thinking the same thing I was thinking. I know she loves Jennifer so much but I know she hurts for me I am her daughter. Neither of us wanted to discuss how close we had come to finding Jennifer only to have had her snatched away again!

But never had I been so close, yet so far away in the same day. I now had proof that she was alive! As I prayed, I told God I would forgive anyone who had taken Jennifer! I just wanted her back home where she belonged.

When we all got up, we met at the restaurant. We started going thru our notes. We needed to find the location where the Sanchez family moved to in Detroit. We were done here; it was time to go back to Tampa.

Mr. Paterson, the private investigator, called Captain Garcia to notify him of our lead in Miami. He requested the Miami Police

Department to check out the principal's story. Two days later Mr. Paterson was notified that Mr. Coleman had changed his mind; he had made a mistake. Captain Garcia told Mr. Paterson they would not be following the lead any further.

I decided to call the principal myself. I was hurt. He had changed his story and I needed to know why? Once I got him on the phone, he explained:

"Kathy, everything I told you and your mother was the truth. But the officers said they would prosecute me if I didn't retract my story. My involvement with the illegal children from Cuba was a federal offense and I would go to jail. The Sanchez family used my concern for those children for their own gain. Your daughter was here Kathy! I'm sorry."

"Mr. Coleman, I want to thank you for telling me the truth. This isn't the first road block the police have put in my way."

I called Tom to tell him what Mr. Coleman had shared with me. He sounded extremely disappointed at this turn of events.

He asked me to meet him at the beach. I rushed to the beach as fast as I could. He was sitting there. His eyes were red, I knocked on his car window. He unlocked the door and I climbed in.

"Tom, please tell me what wrong"

"Kathy, I feel so helpless! My boss just told me I can't air the show! He said I wasn't fair in my report; supposedly I focused on your side of the story because I liked you! He called it one-sided story!"

"But Tom, those are real people you filmed. I didn't know them!"

"Kathy I know that and you know that, but it doesn't matter. If I run the film I will lose my job, plain and simple. If it was just me it wouldn't matter, I would run it anyway. I can't afford to lose this job! I'm responsible for my mother and brother's care too!"

"Tom, I understand! It's okay! At least I know Jennifer is still alive. That means a lot to me."

An astounding thought flitted through my mind; everyone who has helped me with my search gets hurt in some way. Is it so hard to understand I just want my baby back? That is all I want.

After getting out of his car and softly closing the door, I slowly walked down the beach. There was a cool breeze coming from the gulf. I watched the sea swallow the sun and for just a few minutes I didn't think about anything. I decided now was as good a time as any to tell Mom and Dad. Besides, I wanted to see Toni Lisa; hold her and tell her I loved her! After she went to bed, I told Mom I wanted to go home and catch up on some paper work. But I really wanted to go home and be by myself. When I opened the door at home, I could hear the phone ringing. I didn't want to talk to anyone; so I didn't answer. It would not stop ringing! Finally becoming frustrated with the ringing I picked it up. It was Mom!

"Kathy, Tom Smith just called from Channel 28, he said to call you; he wants us to watch the 10:00 o'clock news tonight."

"Do you know why Mom? Did he say anything else?"

"No honey, just for us to watch the news tonight." "Okay Mom, I will! Good night!"

At 10:00 I turned on the TV, and was shocked to see Carlos and Amber on the screen. They both said they couldn't understand how we could think they were involved in Jennifer's abduction. Carlos was crying, saying how much he missed his daughter. I felt like slapping his face on the TV. Next, Captain Garcia came on and said I was on a witch hunt to find my daughter. He said, on national television, that Carlos was as innocent as he was. Maybe Captain Garcia wasn't so innocent. Then a clip of me writing down a tag number came across the screen with a flashing note at the bottom which instructed the viewers to tune in tomorrow night. 'See what Ms. Longo has been through while looking for her daughter'. It was a 10 minute show, and I thought Tom had done a great job; the second half would be on tomorrow. I had Tom's home phone number so I called him.

"Tom, that was a great story! What changed your mind?"

"I got fired anyway Kathy, so I figured I might as well give them just cause. They have to air the second half tomorrow. There will be too many people watching."

"Oh Tom, I am so sorry! Didn't you tell them you weren't going to run it?"

"It didn't matter Kathy, they already had their minds made up. But it's okay, I called CNN, telling them what was going on. They hired me! I still have a job Kathy and I'm making more now than when I worked at Channel 28. We leave Wednesday for Texas; Mom and my brother are both excited about moving, so it has all worked out fine. CNN is a much better company. I hope the show helps you find Jennifer, I will miss you." "Thank you Tom, I will miss you too!"

CHAPTER FIFTY ONE—

MR. PATERSON

Three days later I received a phone call from Mr. Paterson, the private investigator. He asked me if I could come to his office, at his home in St. Petersburg. He wanted to talk with me. I tried to explain to him that I hadn't left the house, other than to go to work since Tom aired the interview. The highs and lows of looking for Jennifer had taken their toll and I was very depressed. I just wanted to be left alone. He insisted he needed to speak with me, now, but wasn't willing to discuss it further on the phone. As I drove to his office, I couldn't figure out what was on his mind and finally decided he must have discovered something after we left Miami. It was late when I left home, and it took me an hour to get there. He was standing outside smoking a cigarette.

He showed me into his office and offered me a seat. He didn't waste any time and told me he wanted $5,000.00.

"I worked for Channel 28 for free thinking we would find your daughter, only to be told they weren't going to follow the case any further. I have worked a lot of hours on this, and I want to get paid."

"I didn't hire you, the station did! I have my own investigator, Michael Mills."

He took a deep breath; leaned down to my level stared straight into my eyes and said:

"You will pay me $5,000.00 or I will make trouble for you and your family. I know things that will hurt your family!"

"So you're stooping to blackmail!"

I stared at him for a long minute speechless. I stood up and on wobbly legs, I walked to the door. When I turned back, he was watching me. He said:

"I expect to hear from you tomorrow!"

I retreated to my car and turned the music as loud as it would play. I didn't want to hear myself think! He had pushed me over the edge! Couldn't these people understand all I wanted was to find Jennifer! I hated everyone and everything especially people like Patterson who kept crawling out of a hole to put obstacles in my way. A feeling of hopelessness engulfed me. I just wanted to see Jennifer; hear her sweet voice. I arrived home and threw myself onto the couch. I stared at the black TV and it finally registered that underneath it were video tapes I had collected. I remembered that one of those tapes was my brother's wedding and Jennifer had been in the wedding party! I jerked forward, crawled to the TV and began searching through the videos, silently screaming at myself for not labeling. Systematically I put each tape into the player until I found Frank's wedding. Jennifer was the flower girl. My eyes were glued to the TV as she walked down the aisle. She was so tiny! Her beautiful little face sported a smile from ear to ear. A little further into the tape Jennifer pleaded with her Uncle Alfred to tape her while she danced. I played it over and over again! I kissed the TV where her little face appeared. I don't know if watching her made me weaker or stronger! I cried non-stop. I just replayed the tape until I fell asleep on the floor in front of the TV.

The next thing I knew, someone was pounding on my front door. I didn't even have the strength to get up, but I didn't need to; Mom opened the door screaming my name. Michael Mills was with her and they explained that no one had heard from me in two days! What had I done? I had gone to sleep crying and I was still crying.

While Michael made some phone calls, Mom pulled me into the bedroom. She helped me into my pajamas then into bed saying:

"Okay honey, everything will be okay now. I am here! I am going to make you hot tea and some chicken soup."

"I don't want anything! Can't everyone just leave me alone? I want to die!"

The shock on Mom's face as she walked out the door didn't even bother me. I laid there numb, caring about nothing! I could hear them as they talked.

'Frances, do you want to take her to the hospital'? 'No! She will be all right. I'm going to stay here with her. But I want you to take that video out of here'.

After Michael left, Mom brought me the tea, singing 'Somewhere over the rainbow'. She put the tea on my bedside table and said:

"I love you Kathy! More than you know, please come back to us. You are a very strong person. No one can keep you down for long! You're the tough one and Jennifer needs you. She needs you to find her! If you don't, no one will!"

I slept the rest of the day and Mom stayed by my side the entire time. That evening I was able to get out of bed without her help. It was a different house. Mom had homemade soup cooking on the stove and a beautifully set table for two. The curtains were open and the sun was shining in the windows. I felt like I hadn't really seen the sun for a very long time. Not just the sun in the sky, but the sun in my soul. After eating, Mom packed some clothes and moved me to her home. Toni Lisa was so sweet, hugging and kissing me! Toni Lisa hadn't just lost her sister; she had lost her mother too. Mom's words finally sunk in, I now understood what she had meant. That night when I slept in Toni Lisa's room, her continual chatter was music to my ears. Mom came in to tell us goodnight.

"My Kathy is back with us. Honey we were so worried! Don't ever forget that we love you!"

"I won't forget Mom. Thank you!"

Toni Lisa and Mom let me sleep late and I woke up tired and edgy. I needed to take care of the problem with Mr. Paterson. I got dressed and headed to the kitchen. She had all my favorites warm and ready to eat. She sounded so chipper saying:

"Good morning honey!"

I didn't say anything. I simply wrapped my arms around Mom and held tight. After eating, I called my boss to ask for a couple more days off. Then I called Michael Mills, explaining Mr. Paterson's demands. He told me not to pay him! I didn't want Paterson coming back into my life.

"No Michael, I am going to pay him the money. I want to be rid of that scum. Promise you won't say anything to my family. Michael, I only called so someone would know what I was doing."

"Kathy, I won't say anything to your parents, but I want you to take a tape recorder with you. Hide it in your purse and record everything!"

I thought that was a great idea: I put it in my purse right after hanging up the phone. I called Mr. Paterson, informing him I would be at his office at 7:00 pm. He was waiting outside smoking, when I put the car in park. He opened the door for me to get out, holding my arm as we entered the door to his office. He looked at my face with a horrible expression as if he knows about the tape recorder. As I stepped through the door, he swung me around slamming my forehead up against the wall. I couldn't move. For a second I thought I was back under Carlos control. Muscles frozen in terror, I just stared at the wall wondering what kind of mess I had gotten myself into now! I didn't know what this man was going to do to me. His voice was loud and angry as he said:

"Trying to set me up, uh?"

His hands began running all over my body. I felt violated and dirty, but anger was chasing the terror away, this wasn't my first experience with a bully. His voice invaded my thoughts again.

"I'm not stupid, you bitch! Where is the tape recorder?"

I don't know how he knew, but I had chickened out while driving to his office. I had taken the recorder from my purse and put it in the glove compartment.

"Are you insane? I don't know what you're talking about!"

"The tape recorder, I know you have one! I'm not letting you go until I get it. Do you hear me bitch?"

He jerked my purse off my shoulder and dumped it out on the desk. The money floated down around his feet.

"That is the only thing in there for you; not a recorder. I shouldn't even give it to you! There isn't anything you can do to me that hasn't already been done."

There wasn't any anger in his expression anymore, he just said:

"I am sorry."

"Just take your money and don't ever call me again!"

I felt lucky. My hands shook as I turned the steering wheel. That whole evening could have turned out a lot worst. I hated giving him the money, what a horrible man. I wondered how he had known about the tape recorder.

Dad was waiting for me when I got home. He wanted to talk to me.

"Honey, we are dealing with some very shady people. You need to be careful of the Paterson fellow, he called me wanting money. I told him if he called again, I would notify the police."

"Okay Dad, thanks for telling me."

What could I say? If only he had just told me a little sooner. . !

CHAPTER FIFTY TWO—
SANCHEZ FAMILY

Mom was very worried about me after we had checked the lead in Miami. I had gotten so sick that she had been afraid to say anything about Jennifer's case. She wanted to go to Detroit; she felt she needed to find the Sanchez family. I knew they weren't going to be there. I thought they wouldn't have been so stupid as to get Jennifer a new identity and then take her to Detroit with them.

Mom had been born in Detroit and still had family there. She had told Dad that she needed a break and wanted to visit her family. Dad would never have said 'no' to Mom about anything!

Once she made it to Detroit Mom didn't waste any time. She called an old friend who had become a Detroit cop and asked if she could meet him for lunch. During lunch, Mom told Darrel our story, and the reason she had come to Detroit. He quickly found the Sanchez family; Mom had been so excited she had to tell me.

"Kathy, I found them, the Sanchez family. I am going with my friend, Darrel, to see her tomorrow."

I was so proud of her and it made me happy to hear how excited she sounded.

"Okay Mom, call me right after you see them."

"I will honey."

The following day, Mom called to fill me in on the meeting. It didn't go well! Darrel told Mom she couldn't say anything while he conducted the interview. Apparently, he didn't remember Mom very well.

The neighborhood was very different from where they had lived in Miami. Mrs. Sanchez must have been having a hard time supporting herself and two children with her husband in jail.

Darrel and Mom had parked across the street in an unmarked car and waited for Mrs. Sanchez to get home with the kids. Darrel found out she picked them up from school every day at 3:00 and was usually home by 3:30. Adjusting his uniform as they walked across the street, Darrel explained to Mom one more time, to stand behind him and remain quiet. Darrel knocked on the door and Mrs. Sanchez had answered.

"Hello Mrs. Sanchez, my name is Darrel Squire and I am with the Detroit Police Department; this is Mrs. Longo. May we come in for a few minutes?"

"No! I am sorry, but we must talk out here."

Of course my mother could not handle that:

"Why can't we come in? What are you hiding?"

Darrel turned to Mom and gave her a sour look.

"Please Frances, I will handle this,"

"Okay!"

He held up a picture of Jennifer for the Sanchez woman to see and asked.

"Mrs. Sanchez, we are looking for this little girl."

Mrs. Sanchez looked very scared, but she said:

"I don't speak very good English. I don't know what you are talking about!"

Mom, again, jumped into the conversation. This time yelling:

"You don't know what we are talking about? I don't believe you, you're a liar! You have my Granddaughter give her back to me!"

Mrs. Sanchez backed away from Mom as far as her front door would let her, pleading with Darrel:

"I am sorry sir, but I do not know what she is talking about. I do not know that little girl. I have never seen her before!"

He again turned to look at Mom saying:

"Frances, can I talk to you for a moment. Mrs. Sanchez, would you excuse us for just a moment? We will be right back."

Taking Mom by the arm, he led her down the driveway, away from the door so Mrs. Sanchez wouldn't hear what he had to say.

"Frances you are not helping with these interruptions. You have her upset and on guard. I brought you along because you told me you would remain quiet. I can get into a lot of trouble, coming here off duty!"

"Darrel, I am sorry! I promise not to do it again."

"Okay, shall we try this again?"

"Yes, but Darrel ask to see the children. Maybe they can tell us something."

"Alright, but let me ask the questions."

Mrs. Sanchez said that her children could not speak English, refusing to allow any contact.

"We couldn't get anything out of her Kathy. She is a smart lady. I am sure she and her husband both know what to say when they see a cop. I'll be home in a couple days honey!"

"I'm sorry Mom! I know how hard it is to get excited about a lead only to have it fall through. It's hard getting geared back up."

Once again, another dead end!

CHAPTER FIFTY THREE—MAFIA

It had been two years since Jennifer's abduction. Desperation causes people to use poor judgment. When I was a young child, I spent a lot of time with my Grandmother, Nana. I remembered she would tell me stories of when she was a young girl living across from the head Mafia family. She actually played with their children and those children were now leaders of the Mafia in Tampa.

"Nana, do you think your friends still know you?"

She had looked upset that I even asked her that.

"Of course, when they see me they still come and give me respect."

"Respect Nana, what do you mean by that?"

"Respect! That is very important in Italian families. Respect is when you come here and you hug and kiss me, that's respect."

"So when you see them, they hug and kiss you hello?"

"Always!"

"Nana you love me, right?" "Why do you ask Kathy? Of course I love you!"

"Nana, could you ask one of your friends in the Mafia to help us find Jennifer?"

"Kathy, I have never asked for anything from them. When you ask a favor of the Mafia, they remember! You would owe them!"

"Nana, this is my daughter we are talking about! Please? I'm willing to owe them anything they want, if they help me find Jennifer."

"Okay, but don't tell your Dad."

I was so excited. I wished I had thought about this before. It would be just like the movies! Maybe we would hear about Carlos having a horse head found in his bed. I was just joking, but I thought the Mafia would have more effective resources than the police or the FBI. There are so many people in this town; someone would talk, or be forced to talk. So many ideas ran through my mind.

"Nana, what's next? How do we find your friends?"

My Grandmother was 75 years old, but she was a smart lady; nobody could get anything past her.

"You think I don't see what you are doing Kathy? Yes, I will take you with me to meet with them. There is an old Italian club in Ybor City. All the older Italian men play dominos there every Wednesday. That is when we will go; pick me up at 10:00 am!"

I had been amazed that my Grandmother knew when and where to find her Mafia friends. She had remained in contact with them throughout the years. I couldn't wait for Wednesday. I felt that now maybe something would surface about Jennifer. This was their town; they knew everything that went on here. I picked my Grandmother up, she was dressed very elegantly; her hair had been done and she wore makeup. I was dressed pretty nice myself because I wanted her to be proud of me.

Nana had directed me to a large, very old, but beautiful building with marble columns in the front. It looked like the old court house. We were escorted inside to a large room packed with twenty tables where ten men sat at each table. The room was filled with men only. We walked and they all stopped to watch us. I felt uneasy, but you would never have known if it bothered my Grandmother. She glided toward two older men who had gotten up from their seats to greet her with respect. (For purposes I'm sure you can understand, their names will not be mentioned) As my Grandmother introduced me, I hugged and kissed each man on their cheek. My Grandmother nodded her head; she seemed pleased that I had remembered to show the men respect. They escorted us to a private room in the back where my Grandmother sat down and pointed for me to sit next to her. After we were both seated the two men took their seats. My Grandmother started speaking Italian; a beautiful language, but I didn't understand a thing. During the thirty minutes of discussion I heard Jennifer's name mentioned several times. My Grandmother eventually arose from her chair and I tried to imitate her grace. I felt proud when I followed her lead as she hugged and kissed each man before we left the room. She held her head high, her back straight and her hand up for silence until we had exited the building entirely. Once we had reached the car, I had to ask:

"Nana, what did they say? Were they the leaders of the Mafia you told me about? Tell me everything."

"Only one gentleman leads the Mafia Kathy, the other man was his bodyguard. He told me he has gotten too old, he had to retire. His son just took over because the FBI had been watching him very closely. He told me I should have come to him sooner. Two years is a long time and the leads have gotten cold. He is going to talk to his son to see if there is anything he can do. He will call me next week."

I knew Grandmother wasn't in favor of asking her Mafia contacts for favors. In all her years, she had never needed their services. It meant a lot to me that she had requested their help to find Jennifer. I was so proud to have her for my grandmother.

"Thank you Nana, I love you very much."

When we got to her house, I walked her inside and gave her a big hug and kiss; telling her it was for BIG RESPECT. One week later to the day the man called my Grandmother. He told her she had come to him too late. Two years was just too long. The leads were cold and he was no longer in charge; he had stepped down. He apologized that the one time she had come to him; he wasn't able to help her. He said he would be watching and listening in case.

Jennifer With Her Great Grandmother

CHAPTER FIFTY FOUR—PICTURE OF HOPE

It had been four years and seventy-one days since Jennifer's abduction. The years passed, leads had been followed, and as yet, no Jennifer! There was still one lead that plagued me; the picture Susan Marteliz had seen of Jennifer holding Carlos' six month old baby.

My alarm had started blaring at 6:00am! I looked at the calendar in the corner and January 21, 1987 blinked. It was Toni Lisa's 16th birthday! I wanted to get to Mom's house before she woke up.

My car was filled with balloons and signs that I wanted to put up around the house before Toni Lisa walked out of her room. Tonight I had a big present for her, which I was very excited about. I parked in Mom and Dad's driveway and hurried into the house. No one was up, so I rushed around putting signs all around the house, including Toni Lisa's bedroom door. Then I started her a money trail from her bedroom door to the kitchen; quarters, dimes, pennies and even a few dollars. The trail stopped at her chair, covered in balloons where she would find her first present. I finished my preparations, took a deep breath and knocked on her door singing 'Happy Birthday to you.' I opened her door and saw this beautiful young lady grinning back at me from her bed. Throwing the covers off, she smiled from ear to ear, eyes brilliant with excitement. Looking down she saw her money trail; screaming (waking the entire house) she followed it, picking up the money as she went. Everyone came out of their rooms to sing to her, but she was too busy tearing the paper off her first gift. It was a new outfit for school. I told her:

"Hurry honey, get ready for school. I am taking you today!"

Mom stayed with me while I waited for Toni Lisa to get ready.

"Mom, I am having Toni Lisa's party at Gus's Restaurant. I know you haven't been feeling good and I don't want you to have to cook for everyone."

"Kathy, I don't mind. She is my granddaughter, and you spend all your free time here anyway."

"I know Mom! But I just don't want you cooking for everyone! Please? I already booked Gus's."

"Ok honey."

Everyone at school knew it was Toni Lisa's birthday. There was a bouquet of 16 red roses waiting in the office for her. She carried them from class to class because they wouldn't fit in her locker. She had a great day at school.

At 6:00 pm we left for her big party at Gus's Italian Restaurant. Our entire family and her friends all waited for her. As we walked through the door, they all greeted her by singing 'Happy Birthday'. The smile on her face was a happy sight. I suddenly found myself choked up. I wanted this night to be perfect for her. There was a table at the end of the room and she must have had fifty presents covering that table. Without exception, everyone commented on how delicious their meal was which also made me very happy. After opening her presents, Toni Lisa walked around and thanked everyone for their gifts, and for joining her on her 16th birthday. As the party wound down, she turned to look at me. I could see the love beaming from her eyes, it lit up the room.

"I love you Mom! Thank you for such a wonderful birthday party."

I handed her a set of keys and said:

"For my birthday girl! Sorry it isn't wrapped. It wouldn't fit on the table honey. I had to leave your present outside."

Everyone had been so excited for her; we all followed her outside to see a big red bow on a 1986 red Camero. She screamed, jumped up and down, tears poured down her beautiful face. I choked up and found myself crying too.

My parents weren't happy about the car. They were worried but they understood why I had bought it for her. I had told Mom many times how guilty I felt about Toni Lisa's life. She had not only been robbed of her little sister, but her mother too.

Toni Lisa was free to drive herself to school now. With that freedom, she exhibited some bad behavior. Skipping school was one of those mischievous things a young girl does with a new car. At least mine did. I decided I would have a talk with her; I didn't want her to end up like me, pregnant and married at sixteen. I was going to try and explain what had happened in my life so she wouldn't make the same mistakes. I called Toni Lisa and asked if we could have a mother-daughter night. I didn't tell her why, I told her I would come over and we could do hair and makeup. She loved the idea.

I should have been a little more specific with Toni Lisa; by the time she was done, my hair was dripping, my makeup smeared and my clothing was soaked. I wish I had said we were only doing her hair and makeup first. Mom's doorbell rang, and then we heard her say:

"Kathy, there is someone here to see you."

I couldn't have gone out looking like that; I would have scared them! Toni Lisa helped me wrap a towel around my hair and I wiped my face as best as I could. Toni Lisa grabbed something I could change into.

"I will be right there Mom."

I couldn't imagine who was out there. Mom had already let him in and he sat in the family room. As I walked in I could see Mom's face and she was upset.

"What were you girls doing in there?"

"Mom we were just having mother-daughter time."

"Kathy, this is Danny! He's our neighbor and he has something to tell you."

"Hello Danny, please excuse my appearance; my daughter and I were playing makeup."

He laughed and said:

"I can see that. You look like you were having a good time. Listen, I don't know if this is important or not. I had a so-called police officer come to my door asking me questions about you."

"What do you mean? He said he was a cop? What kind of questions?"

"He wanted to know what time you come home; who was living here with you. Stuff like that."

"Why would they be asking questions like that?

Well, Thank you, for letting me know. I will call the police station tomorrow."

"I just wanted to let you know what was going on. I am very sorry about Jennifer."

I thanked him and after he left I called the police station. No one with the name he gave me worked there. Mom started to get worried but I told her we had a lot worse happen. We could handle this one problem. I asked Toni Lisa if we could just clean the mess up and talk. I told her about her father and I, how we met and the mistakes I had made. She was well aware of how our marital relationship ended and was happy it had. She didn't want to talk about Carlos and I. She wanted to know what had been going on with Jennifer's case. In a very sincere voice Toni Lisa said;

"Sometimes I hear Grandma talking and when she sees me she gets quiet."

I know my mother did that so Toni Lisa would not get hurt I tried to explain;

"She just doesn't want you hurt honey. She loves you."

"I know Mom, but I'm old enough now. Can't I help?"

"Okay, let's get ready for bed and we will talk about Jennifer."

I had never seen her get ready for bed so fast. She was in her pajamas and in bed in 10 minutes flat.

"Toni Lisa, I am still watching your Dad and the bar he goes to. The most important lead I have right now is the picture of Jennifer that Susan told us about. I believed Susan when she said she saw Jennifer's picture. Without breaking the law, I haven't been able to figure a way into their house to find that picture."

"Mom, I want to help you find Jennifer. Can't I do anything?"

I was touched she had wanted to help look for her sister.

"I will take you with me this weekend. We can spy together. Would you like that?

"Sure Mom!"

We fell asleep laying there talking.

Saturday came fast and with it a call from Mom. Toni Lisa had not been home all day, and she didn't know where she was. I told Mom I was supposed to pick her up; she was going with me on my evening of spying. An anxious, uneasy feeling had formed in the pit of my stomach. My apprehension grew stronger as it got dark. I called Mom and told her I was coming over to wait with her. On the drive to Mom's house, I recalled her neighbor telling us we were being watched. I had blown that off at the time but, I realized I should have checked into it further. Toni Lisa's face haunted me as I made a U-turn and headed to Carlos' house. I couldn't lose another daughter! I wouldn't live through that! As I passed his driveway I made sure Toni Lisa's car wasn't there. What was I thinking? She hadn't seen her father in several years now, by her own choice.

As I drove into Mom's driveway, Toni Lisa's car was in her normal parking space. I could hear Mom and Toni Lisa screaming! I couldn't make out what was being said; alarmed, I hurried into the house. Mom was chasing Toni Lisa around the table. Toni Lisa screamed for me to help her; and Mom screamed at me that I better not. Toni Lisa deserved her punishment! I stopped them both, demanding that we sit down and talk about the problem. Dad was sitting in his chair watching TV and laughing at them.

"Your Grandmother is pretty fast isn't she Toni Lisa!"

I changed direction and led them to the kitchen, but on the way Toni Lisa said:

"Mom, Grandma, I have a surprise for you."

Mom was extremely angry with Toni Lisa and as we made our way to the kitchen she said:

"I bet! You're being punished! Do you hear me young lady; I am taking your keys away from you."

Toni Lisa, handed me an envelope, and in an exasperated, yet excited, voice said:

"Mom, look what I got for you. Look in the Envelope, Mom!"

I opened the envelope and peeked inside. There were three pictures. When I pulled them out I gasped aloud. Jennifer's picture, and she looked older, but sad. She was staring at me with those big warm eyes. I imagined I could hear her crying out to me, but I couldn't help her.

I had been to blame for Toni Lisa going to Carlos' house; she had done it for me.

"Where did you get these Toni Lisa?"

She was so proud of herself.

"I went to Dad's and got them. They were already in that envelope."

Fear engulfed me! Now, I was upset; what if he had caught her taking the pictures and done something to her? He had already lost one of my children.

"Toni Lisa, if you wanted to go there, why didn't you just tell me? What if something had happened to you? What would I do?"

"Mom it's okay. I'm okay! You talk about that picture all the time and I love you so much I wanted to do something special for you. I miss Jennifer too! I would give up my car to have her back!"

I couldn't believe what she had just said. I guess I just didn't know how much she had been hurting for her sister. Mom and I both got up at the same time to hug her.

I grabbed the pictures, spreading them across the table. Toni Lisa had three important pictures. One picture was Jennifer carrying her two white cats. Her hair was shorter but her bangs were long, almost as if she were trying to grow them out. She sat on a green velvet couch with a pattern of yellow flowers. Wood paneling covered the wall behind the couch which led me to believe she was in a trailer. The second picture was a closer view of Jennifer's face; her teeth looked more grown out. On the couch next to Jennifer was a picture of a baby. The third picture was of a man I didn't know working on my parent's house. That picture was a mystery to me, why was it included in the envelope with Jennifer's pictures? Why would they have a picture of someone working on my parents' house?

Now that I had the pictures Susan Marteliz had told us about, I didn't know who to take them to. I sure as hell wasn't taking them to Michael; he would have given them to Captain Garcia. He still believed in the legal system. I made a decision and dialed Detective George's phone number.

"Detective George, this is Kathy Longo, do you remember me?"

"Of course I do! What can I help you with?"

"I need to see you as soon as possible."

"Sure Kathy, I will be waiting for you."

By the time I got to his office it was very late. He looked strained, and had lost weight since the last time I had seen him. I asked him if something was wrong and he told me he was quitting the force to start his own business investigating fires. He told me he didn't want anyone to know yet, not until he had made some final arrangements.

"I think that is great, the force will miss you!"

I believed he was an honest cop, and I liked the way he worked. He didn't care who got in his way, he totally focused on getting the job done.

"What did you want to see me about Kathy?"

"I have three pictures my daughter found in her father's home. I need help. I don't know what to do now that I have them. I refuse to give them to Captain Garcia."

"Let me see them Kathy."

He looked at them for a while, and then said:

"Kathy, I believe Jennifer is older in these pictures, not much older, but older. We are going to have to verify that assumption!"

"What do you mean?"

"Kathy, we know this is Jennifer. We don't know the where or when. We need to check the film out. It's polarized and says Kodak, and if I remember right, Kodak got sued and had to stop making this film."

He had flipped the picture over to look at the back for a date or any other numbers which might have been stamped on it. The picture had been cropped so all the numbers had been cut off.

"Kathy, we don't have anything without these numbers."

I giggled. I was feeling good about my trash excursions now.

"Detective George, I have them!"

"What do you mean you have them?"

"I have the edges to those pictures. They were in Carlos garbage about four years ago. I saved everything!"

"Where is it? You kept their garbage for four years?"

The look on his face was worth all those dirty nights. I laughed and said:

"Yes, I did! I have them in my car; let me go get my suitcase."

I rummaged in the suitcase for a minute, pulled out the plastic bag with the picture pieces and handed them to him. He put them together like puzzle pieces; they fit perfectly!

"I am impressed Kathy, if this film was made after November 15, 1982 we have a clean and cut case against Carlos. He and his wife will go to jail for Jennifer's abduction."

So many thoughts ran through my mind. I could imagine the nightmare finally coming to an end. I would have Jennifer back soon! Detective George told me he would call Kodak in the morning, but he had a good feeling that the pictures would break the case wide open. I couldn't sleep that night because Mom and I spent hours on the phone.

Detective George called Kodak the next morning and they called him back an hour later, after referencing the numbers. They told him the film had been made in August 1982 but that there was a two year shelf life. When he drove out to tell us, I stared at him. He shook his head in apology, handing the pictures back to me. I was surprised by how calm I was; maybe it was getting easier, being disappointed!

"I don't care! The film was made in August but they still had to buy it! We have pictures of Jennifer in September; her hair was not that short."

"Kathy, I know a doctor who works at the Shriner's Hospital for Children. If you could get him to scientifically prove that, you may still have a good case!"

The news from Kodak meant that I would have to work a little harder. I didn't have a problem with hard work. It would have been nice to see some results though.

I made the phone call to the Shriner's Hospital and was pleasantly surprised by the reception I got. The doctor's assistant said:

"Ms. Longo I can't believe this is you! I was there helping search for Jennifer when she first went missing. My family still prays for you and your family. Don't worry, the doctor will help you, just bring the picture in and give me a week."

Like I said before, God always sends someone good to help me.

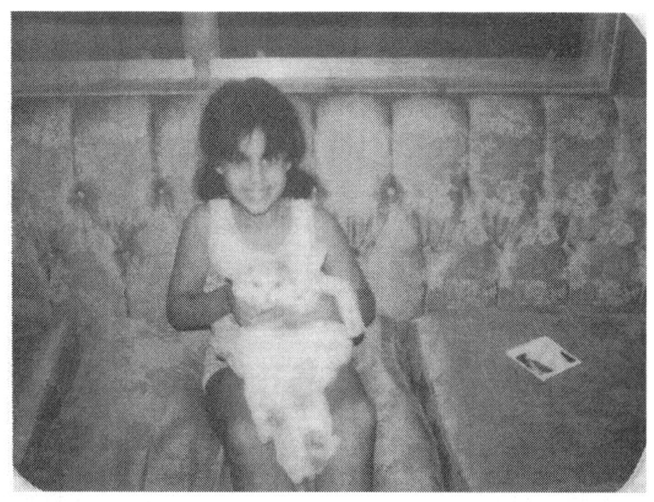

Jennifer With Her Cats The Picture On The Couch Is A Picture Of A Baby. It Could Be Carlos' And Amber's Baby Born After Jennifer Was Taken.

This is the letter Dr. Vegas wrote me:

Dear Kathy,

Thank you for asking me for assistance in trying to identify the approximate age of the little girl depicted in the photos on the yellow flower print sofa, holding the cats. This little girl certainly would appear to be one of Hispanic background in view of her facial features. She has a small gap between her two upper front teeth. She has a small indentation in the chin. Based upon her approximate size relative to the sofa and her overall features, her size relative to the cats, etc., I would estimate that this young lady is probably somewhere between 8 and 10 years of age.

I hope that this will help you in your efforts.

Sincerely,
John A. Vegas M.D.
Chief of Staff

I clutched Doctor Vegas's letter to my chest as I left his office. I was determined no one would take this piece of evidence from me.

I wanted one more official confirmation from Jennifer's dentist. His receptionist remembered me right away. She ushered me right into his office. I showed him the picture of Jennifer. After looking at it for a second, he took a magnifying glass from the center drawer of his desk. He examined the picture, and then compared it to her school picture. He assured me she was older in the small photograph. He told me he would be willing to testify in court that the picture had been taken after Jennifer's abduction. Thanking him, I left his office.

I had some great evidence, but was still stuck with the dilemma of who could or would help me with the pictures. I knew I couldn't take them to the Police Department.

CHAPTER FIFTY FIVE—MR. BURNS

It was Monday morning and I was back to work after a very long weekend. Mr. Burns was always so supportive of me in my search for Jennifer. He was a great boss and friend.

It was 10:00 and I had not heard from Mr. Burns. I tried to call him but there was no answer. I was getting worried, I decided to call Diana when he walked in. He was white as a ghost; he didn't say anything and just flopped down in his chair. I hurried over to his side and asked him what was wrong. He didn't answer me and stared blankly in front of him. I knew I had to do something so I called his doctor. Everyone knew me; I was like a daughter to him. The doctor instructed me to get Mr. Burns to the hospital as soon as possible. Thank goodness Diana showed up at work right then. I told her he needed to go to the hospital. Between the two of us we were able to get him into her car. He was in so much pain, I don't think he understood or remembered what had happened. Mr. Burns had never been sick, not in all the years I had worked for him. By the time we got him in the car we were both crying. Diana asked me to stay there at the office to keep the business going. I agreed but intended on going to the hospital as soon as it was closing time.

It was noon when Diana called me, she was an emotional wreck. She told me the hospital had admitted her Dad. I remember telling her not to worry; her dad was strong, never sick and everything would be okay. I told her I would be there as soon as I locked the doors at 5:00.

I hurried into Mr. Burns' hospital room only to find him looking bad, real bad. He didn't know I was there! He had been scheduled for surgery first thing the next morning. The doctors believed he had a blood clot in his intestines. They had put him on a high dosage of morphine for pain. It was shocking to see this man reduced to such a state. I could understand why Diana was so upset. It hurt me to see him hooked up to all those wires and tubes.

I didn't have to ask him. I knew Mr. Burns. If I didn't open the office in the morning because I was sitting in the hospital waiting for news of his surgery, he would have been very upset with me. With Mr. Burns, business was always first! I respected him for that. After work I couldn't wait to get to the hospital, but I wasn't greeted with good news. The doctors had to remove twenty eight feet of intestines, and they didn't know if the surgery was going to work.

Diana and I stood there hugging each other! She had been there for me when Jennifer had been abducted, and I wanted to comfort her. But I hurt too! Gary was like a second Dad to me. I spent as much time as I could in his hospital room every evening after work. I brought paper work in for him so he could keep up on everything going on in the office. But after his second week in the hospital he didn't care to look at any of the paperwork anymore. I knew he wasn't getting better. After three weeks of pure torture he died. What a sad day that had been for me; he was such a wonderful man. He had always been good to me and my daughters; respecting my absences while I searched for Jennifer. I was happy to have known him; he had given me a job at an important time in my life. It will never be the same without him.

CHAPTER FIFTY SIX—

JENNIFER'S SONG

It was June of 1987 and I worked at a place called Mail Boxes Etc. The job was totally different compared to what my job had been with Mr. Burns. It was a retail store that handled shipping, packing and a lot of other things. I loved working there; it was my own private social club. All the customers became my friends. I would listen to their problems and they would listen to mine.

Mom started coming into work to help me and we had a great time working together. You could tell we were mother and daughter because we did everything alike. When the store wasn't busy we would make flyers for Jennifer and mail them out to all the different schools. We were inseparable. I was so lucky to have had her for my Mom. She would bring lunch with her every day, and after work I would go to her house and she would have dinner for me. I never cooked. Why would I ever want to when I had Mom, the best cook in the world and my best friend!

Customers came in and we would fight over who would help them.

The investigation slowed down on Jennifer's case. There weren't any new leads to follow so we continued to follow up on the old leads. I still watched Carlos' house and Mom still worked with the

Missing Children's Center where we met and became good friends with John Walsh. Mom and John constantly discussed ways to help families with missing children. When John Walsh made a movie about the abduction of his son, John promoted Jennifer's case. He displayed a flyer regarding her disappearance on the front of his desk in the movie. He had been instrumental in bringing on-line the FBI's computer program which listed the cases of unsolved missing children. Jennifer's case was the first to be entered. She also had the first picture to appear on the milk cartons throughout the States. So it wasn't as if the search had stopped, it had just slowed down.

Time went by so quickly. During all the ups and downs in my life, the inconsistencies I had experienced chasing down leads in Jennifer's case, raising Toni Lisa, changing jobs and just living each day, there was always one unwavering factor constant in my life. Mom! She might have been small in stature, but her heart, wisdom, strength, constant presence, acceptance and love made up the rock I had always leaned on. She had always been there for me. It was Mom who helped me to my feet each time I stumbled or fell. There were times, if it hadn't been for Mom, I wouldn't have bothered getting out of bed. She had the most generous heart and I admired her for her constant, unselfish display of love. She always put her family's happiness before her own. I have been honored to claim her as my Mother.

She called me at work one morning to say we would be having a family meeting on Saturday at 2:00 o'clock. After everyone, including Dad had arrived; Mom had us sit at the dining room table. She started out by saying:

"Our family has been through a lot of tragedy. But we have always stuck together no matter what. Losing Jennifer has been very hard for our whole family, but we are getting through it together. Just as we will get through a new trial facing us. About a month ago I was feeling very weak and tired. I went to see Dr. Ford to get a B-12 shot. I thought that would get me going, that I was just run down. The shot didn't work. Dr. Ford insisted I come in for a checkup, which I did. After numerous tests it was determined that I am bleeding internally. Each week I have outpatient surgery where Dr. Ford cauterizes the bleeding veins in my abdomen. This stops the bleeding, but it isn't a permanent fix. There is so much pressure, another vein bursts and they have to go in and fix that one. I am losing blood faster than they can replace it. There isn't a cure for this condition and I've been told I have less than a year to live!"

There was an eternal second of total silence! It covered the entire room in a cloak of doom. Suddenly screams of denial erupted. None of us could stay in our chairs anymore, except Dad. Mom's confession had been comparable to finding out Jennifer was missing again. I felt as though I was being punished. How would any of us possibly make it without Mom? She was our foundation the very rock of our family.

I backed up against the wall, my hands splayed out for support; I watched my family fall apart as if I were watching from a great distance away. I felt a coldness wrap around my heart and it kept squeezing tighter. The erratic sound of my own breathing made me deaf to all other sounds. I was backed against that wall where I hugged myself in shock and disbelief! The question of why never entered my mind. I knew why! I was being punished! This was my fault! If I had been a better daughter . . .

How would we ever make it without Mom? Mom was everything to each one of us. She had always made each of us feel special. It didn't matter what anyone else thought, we had Mom.

Slowly, the realization sunk in that this wasn't going to go away. Mom was sick and we needed to find a cure. Nancy and I had looked at each other over Mom's shoulder and we didn't need to say anything, we both knew we weren't giving up! The doctors could say whatever they wanted, but we would keep searching for a doctor who was willing to fight.

A song Mom used to sing to Nancy and I filled my mind:

My Kathy, My Nancy how I love you.
My Kathy, My Nancy
I love you so true.
I can't believe you're really mine.
You make the sun the whole sky shine.
Your eyes, your ears, your nose, your toes are as pretty as can be.
My beautiful babies
I really can't believe you belong to meeeee.

I loved when she sang it to us. I loved everything about Mom. We did everything together and we just had to find a cure together. The shocking news had sunk in slowly and gradually we had all returned to the table. Nancy announced with conviction that we were going to do whatever it took to make Mom well:

"We will take her to the best doctors in the country, the Mayo Clinic."

I firmly stated I would stay with Mom no matter how long it took to find a cure. Mom sat next to Dad, holding his hands in both of her small hands and said:

"Girls, I have too many things wrong with me! I am bleeding internally! This condition is called 'watermelon stomach'. My liver is bad and I have breast cancer. The doctors want to perform a hysterectomy".

Her tone was that of simple acceptance to the inevitable diagnosis. Nancy and I had responded more to her tone than the news. It was as if she already was defeated. We declared:

"I don't care we are going (have) to try Mom, please."

At first, Mom was compliant:

"Okay, whatever you want."

Then she added in a strong, determined tone:

"I just don't want to see you all crying anymore. I love you all too much; you have given me so much happiness. I'm proud of each and every one of you."

I know the pain I felt was self-inflicted. I blamed myself for what our future held. All the stress I had brought to Mom caused her condition; the troubled childhood, marrying Carlos at 16, discovery of his abuse, Jennifer's disappearance, my arrest, an attempted kidnapping of me.

That night alone at the side of my bed, on my knees with my nose plastered to the floor, I begged God to take my eyes, my legs, my life; just let Mom live.

Nancy had contacted the Mayo Clinic, but was told they were booked tight. The only chance of obtaining an appointment would be to wait for a cancellation which would allow them to fit Mom into their schedule. We decided if that was the best they had for us, that's what we would do. I was the lucky one. I accompanied Mom to Minnesota and they Took her right in when we got there. When the testing process did begin there were many hours between tests and we made the most of our free time. Those were the best times Mom and I ever had. We shopped, visited museums, went to an art exhibit, and shopped some more. We weren't focused on Jennifer; we focused on each other and enjoyed our time together. One night, laying in our beds, Mom said she had a surprise for me, but she didn't intend on giving it to me until we left Minnesota. I told her the only surprise I wanted was the doctors making her better.

After completing their tests, the doctors called us in for the consultation appointment:

"Frances, we have good news and bad news, which do you want to hear first?"

We sat there side by side and we grabbed hands before she responded:

"Good news first!"

"Okay! You have a condition we call 'watermelon stomach'. We have a new surgery which can cure this condition. The tiny veins bleeding in your stomach are similar to varicose veins. These can be removed, thus putting a stop to your internal bleeding. Your liver condition can be treated with prescription medicine. The bad news is the cancer has spread to your lymph glands. This would normally be treated with chemo therapy; however, your stomach condition prohibits its use. We have other options, not as effective, but worthy of effort. The big offender in your case was the internal bleeding and we can correct that. I'm not saying you have any easy road ahead of you, just a hopeful one!"

Wow! From no hope to positive options. We were going to beat this. Relief spread across Mom's face like the sun coming out from behind rain clouds. I had been so wrapped up in my own feelings, it had never occurred to me what Mom must have been going through. Without hesitation I grabbed Mom up in a hug. A hug containing so much emotion, words would never do it justice, but Mom knew! We both did! Of course the tears ran excessively. Mom and I both prided ourselves on our appearances, but at that moment it just didn't matter. We left the doctors' office arm in arm, practically dancing our way out of the building, makeup smudges around our eyes. The phone lines buzzed with our happy voices until everyone we could think of, knew the news. Surgery was scheduled early for the next morning, yet it didn't dampen our spirits.

Surgery went well and we were on a flight home the very next day. During the flight home, Mom gave me my surprise. It affected me more than I let her know. It made me aware of just how devastated she had really felt about Jennifer's abduction. She admitted that her one wish prior to dying was to see Jennifer again. She needed to apologize. Mom felt that would help her to pass without any regret. She felt her actions toward Dad had caused the big blow up that night and if she had handled the situation differently, Jennifer wouldn't . . . The guilt had eaten at Mom all these years until it had made her sick. She blamed herself, and I know Dad felt his own guilt. Those emotions we each carried equally, however, in our own minds, it was our burden solely.

Handing me a piece of paper, Mom said:

"Here is your surprise! I hope you like it!"

It was a song! Lyrics and music. A song that cried out to Jennifer from Mom's broken heart. As I tried to read it through my tears, Mom quietly sang it for me. It was so beautiful:

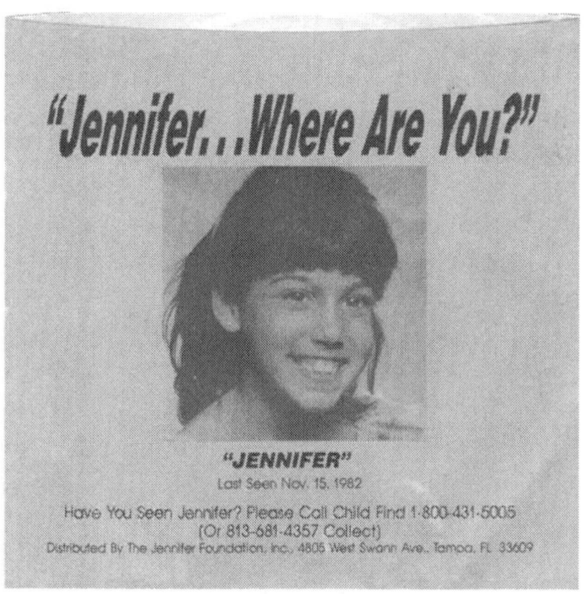

The Song My Mother Wrote For Jennifer

'Missing, missing, Jennifer where are you?
Jennifer, dear Jennifer where are you today
Jennifer sweet Jennifer who has taken you away
I think of you all day my darling and dream of you every night
Our hearts has been so very heavy
Since You disappear over night
Jennifer dear Jennifer where are you tonight
Jennifer dear Jennifer how I long to hold you tight

This wasn't just a surprise; it was a treasure I would hold onto for the rest of my life.

The flight attendants had my mother go out in a wheelchair. I know she hated it but she had just had surgery and it was a long walk out of that airport. But I was so proud of her. My dad, brothers, sister, all her grandchildren, were all there waiting for her when we got off the plane. The minute they saw her they couldn't run fast enough to get to her hugging and kissing her. They had flowers, balloons and candy. I am sure she felt like a queen which in my heart she is.

My decision to stay with mom had been made before we ever got on the flight to Minnesota. Once we got home, I helped Mom to bed. Everyone was still there with her, so I felt comfortable in leaving. Surely there was enough time to take care of my next chore without fearing I would be missed. Packing my clothes and the necessities for day to day living didn't take long. As I walked out, I took a last look at what was supposed to be home for the girls and I. It wasn't home, not without my girls. I locked the door and walked away without a backward glance.

I arrived back at Mom and Dad's house to find that everyone had already left. I'm sure someone had probably insisted on letting Mom rest. When I walked into the house from the car, my arms were loaded with stuff. Dad met me at the door and asked:

"Kathy, what are you doing?"

He knew exactly what I was doing, but I had to respond to his question.

"Dad, I am moving back into my old room!"

A little of the strain he was feeling drained out of his face as he gave me a hug and kiss.

"Thank you Kathy! Your Mom and I both need you!"

Here Dad thought I was being so unselfish, yet I knew I was being very selfish indeed. I wanted to spend as much time with them as I possibly could. Mom's health issues had brought into bright focus their mortality, which scared me straight into reality.

Dad grabbed a few things to help me move in and said:

"Kathy, your Mother is still up, shall we drop these off into your room and go tell her?"

I nodded my head and we headed upstairs. Mom was lying in bed watching TV.

"Honey, Kathy is moving back home with us!"

Surprise stopped us both in our tracks when we heard Mom say:

"No!" She isn't going to waste her life taking care of us!"

I knew she didn't mean what she said I knew they needed me.

"You are kicking me out of my home mom, is that what you are telling me. I can't live with you and dad"

Tears filled Mom's eyes

"Of course you can live here but I don't want you to waste your life taking care of your dad and me."

"Okay Mom, these are the rules! You can only ask me for help 325 times a day. That is about how many times you have helped me in the past 30 years. Don't take this from me Mom, I feel good for once in my life, I have a chance to help my parents for a change." That had pretty much settled any argument before it ever started.

CHAPTER FIFTY SEVEN—
STATE ATTORNEY

Back to work as normal the only thing Mom would not be coming with me. I would miss her but I could be there at night with her and she was getting better.

Wednesday morning, out of the blue, a Mrs. Bryan of the State Attorney's office called and requested a brief meeting. I told her sure anytime.

It was Friday and the store was packed when she walked in. I knew it was her by the way she dressed and carried herself. She waved to me as if I knew her and said:

"Hi Kathy, I am Julie Bryan with the State Attorney's Office. I can already see this wasn't the best time to drop in on you!"

"Hi Mrs. Bryan, please have a seat in my office. As soon I am done with this customer I will be right there!"

Smiling, she nodded that this was agreeable. The girls at work had given up asking me why she wanted to meet with me. I assumed it had something to do with Jennifer's abduction, so I was already on pins and needles and anxious about the meeting.

After my customer was gone, I hurried into the office and said:

"Sorry it took so long, but I am free now!" She came right to the point.

"Kathy thank you for meeting with me! I am investigating a company named Inter Eyes Inc.! Would they happen to be a box holder here?"

My hopes dropped like a rock. She wasn't here about Jennifer. She was investigating something else. Serves me right for assuming she was on Jennifer's case.

"Yes, they have a box here."

She requested to see their paper work. I walked to a filing cabinet in the corner and pulled their file. She spent around ten minutes looking through everything, and then asked:

"Kathy, would you be willing to appear in court as a witness for us?"

"I don't understand how I can help, but yes, I would be willing. What have they done wrong?"

"They are selling human organs to Arabian countries."

Standing up, she put her hand out to shake mine and said:

"Kathy, I really appreciate you doing this for us, if I can ever do anything for you just let me know!"

Having already told Mom I was being visited by the State Attorney's Office about Jennifer, how could I go home tonight and retract my words. Almost desperate, I said:

"Mrs. Bryan, there is something you could do for me. My daughter was kidnapped and I believe I know who did it! I just need someone like you to help me prove I'm right."

"Kathy, I am so sorry to hear that! Please, come to my office and bring everything you have. I am more than willing to look at your paper work.

"Thank you Mrs. Bryan!

I was excited, not only because a representative from the State Attorney's Office had agreed to look at Jennifer's case, but because a woman was going to become involved. Only another mother could know how I felt. When I got home that evening I told Mom about Mrs. Bryan. She had been looking very drawn lately and this brought a sparkle to her eyes.

Mom was shocked when I told her I was taking the pictures Toni Lisa found to Mrs. Bryan. She was surprised that I trusted this woman and said:

"Well, it's about time those pictures became part of the investigation. Now I'm really excited!"

I excused myself, got my suitcase and lay it on Mom's bed. "Let's do this together Mom."

I wanted to spend every moment I could with my Mom.

So if I wasn't sleeping or working I stayed by her side. I needed to organize my files for the meeting and had mom help me. We filed each suspect in a folder and labeled them. I was ready for Mrs. Bryan. It was getting late and I could see my mother was tired.

"Mom thank you for helping me I don't know what I would do without you. I am going to put the suitcase in my car and then I am going to bed. Is there anything I can get you."

"No honey I am fine. I am a little tired too.

I will see you in the morning. Love you."

I gave her a kiss and went to my room. As I passed the family room I saw my Dad sleeping in his favorite chair watching TV. I love them both very much.

As I laid in bed, all the memories of my life started to replay. What great parents I have, from the best birthday parties to always standing beside me in any decisions I made. I have been so lucky. But then I started to think about the dark side of my life being married to Carlos. Looking for Jennifer, all that I had tried to do and still no results. It's like my life had been put on pause. There wouldn't be a forward until Jennifer was found. I don't even really remember how my life was prior to her abduction. My brain only had Jennifer information; if you asked me about any lead I had followed, I could remember every word. Yet, if an old friend met me on the street I would have a hard time remembering their name. Dates are hard for me too! They have all run together into one continuous day. I'm sure when Jennifer comes home we can restart our life again, but until then, there is no life.

I woke up to the smell of Mom's cooking. I ran into the kitchen to find her making me a big breakfast. Eggs, bacon, grits and pancakes

I couldn't sit down fast enough. Mom was preparing me for my meeting. She said to me

"I know you have that meeting this morning are you ready for it?"

"Mom after this great breakfast I am ready for anything."

She just laughed. I could tell she was feeling better.
I think she's happy knowing someone is working on Jennifer's case.

Walking down that hallway, clutching a gray notebook (I called it Jennifer's bible) in my arms and pulling her flowered suitcase. I was definitely nervous! My relationship with the Police Department and FBI was a distrustful one to say the least. This would probably be my last chance to bring Jennifer's case to the attention of someone who could effectively help her, and me.

I walked into Mrs. Bryan's office and she greeted me with a big smile. I could tell she was an important woman, her office shouted her authority. I bypassed her hand held out to shake, and gave her a hug and said:

"Thank you Mrs. Bryan, you don't realize how important this meeting is to me."

"Kathy, I've done a little research on Jennifer's case, I am going to try my best to help you. Now tell me everything about the case, what you have been working on and if you have any ideas about who may have done this. I am all ears!"

She didn't sit behind her desk; she sat right next to me as I began to tell what I believed and why:

I told her I thought my ex-husband and his wife Amber had something to do with Jennifer's disappearance. I began listing the evidence as I saw it.

The night before Jennifer was abducted; Carlos and I were fighting about his method of correcting her. I threatened Carlos that Jennifer was coming home with me and he would have to pay child support.

A family emergency stopped me from picking Jennifer up that night. The next day she was abducted.

Jennifer had two beautiful white cats; they both disappeared the same day Jennifer was abducted.

When I asked Carlos to return Jennifer's belongings, he told me he had thrown everything away.

Amber, who supposedly was at home waiting for Jennifer, was actually two miles away, talking to a relative on a pay phone.

Both Carlos and Amber failed their lie detector tests.

Carlos claimed he was at work the day Jennifer was abducted, but he wasn't. His supervisor clocked him in illegally.

I found a letter from Jennifer in Carlos' trash months after her abduction. I had collected his trash every day since Jennifer was abducted.

Carlos demanded that my Father offer a reward for Jennifer's return.

Several leads have led me back to his wife's relatives.

A neighbor verified Darlene James, the bar owner where Amber used to work and Carlos still drank, was on 98th street around 3:00 o'clock. Smoking one cigarette after another, looking very nervous the day Jennifer was abducted.

A bus driver claimed he remembered Jennifer on his bus and gave a Detective information to create a composite drawing of the man she was with. Darlene James's boyfriend is the spitting image of that drawing.

"Kathy, I can see all of this upsets you, but do you have any real evidence that connects your ex-husband to Jennifer's abduction?"

"As a matter of fact I do! My oldest daughter, Toni Lisa, found a picture of Jennifer at Carlos' house four years after Jennifer was abducted. I had it examined by her dentist and he confirmed her teeth were more developed than in her school picture taken just prior to her abduction. I also have a letter from a specialist with the Shriners hospital stating she is approximately 8-10 years old in the picture."

"Wait a minute Kathy, wasn't Jennifer living with Carlos and his wife? Why would the bar owner have anything to do with this. Why don't you explain how you think they accomplished her abduction?"

"Okay, I'll try! Jennifer knew Darlene James and her boyfriend from Amber working at the bar and Carlos drinking there. Jennifer would have gotten into their car if she were told Amber wasn't picking her up, that they were supposed to pick her up. I believe Jennifer was taken to Amber's Mother's home and dropped off there. Carlos called the police at 3:15 that afternoon assuming they wouldn't do anything for twenty-four hours. He was wrong, the police began an investigation immediately. With all the searchers and press, they felt trapped and had to get Jennifer out of town somehow, so they used Darlene's boyfriend as an escort. The bus driver said he acted as though he didn't know her, but sat behind Jennifer on the bus. He took Jennifer to Miami, where they got her the necessary papers to be someone else. She was living with the Sanchez family."

I could see she was getting overwhelmed.

"Kathy, wait, I want you to stop there. I need to go over all this paper work you have. Then I will meet with the Police Department and see what they have in their file."

Driving home after the meeting, I hoped she knew how much I was trusting her. Her secretary made copies of all my information, she had it all. I liked Mrs. Bryan a lot; I just hoped I hadn't talked too much. This was so important to me; I no longer had any confidence in the Police Department or the FBI. They refused to discuss Jennifer's case with me, and had blocked every promising lead I had worked hard to get. I felt as though this was my last chance. Leaving at 5:00 o'clock had put me smack dab into rush hour traffic, so I had a lot to dwell on during my return home.

Six months passed since my meeting with Mrs. Bryan and I hadn't heard anything. My family and I were waiting for my niece's dance recital to begin when Frank broke the news to me.

"Kathy hurry! You need to come outside, I have to talk to you, and it's about Jennifer."

In the foyer, Frank told me that he had just seen Carlos and Amber being arrested! They finally did it. Carlos would break, I just knew it. Rushing back into the gym, I shared the news with the rest of the family.

Looking at Mom, I forgot about Carlos and Amber. Mom didn't look good; she was so pale it scared me.

"Mom, can we go home? No one will even notice we have left. I'm tired; if it's okay with you, I would like to go home."

"Sure honey, I'm tired too!"

I wasn't really tired, but I knew she would never have left for herself. She kept saying she felt fine, but I wasn't blind, something was wrong. I focused on Mom that weekend. We only watched the clip of Carlos and Amber being arrested; I left the case itself alone.

Monday morning I received a call from Mrs. Bryan. She wanted to meet with me on Tuesday to discuss Jennifer's case. We set the meeting for 11:00 o'clock.

Mrs. Bryan came to the point immediately:

"Kathy, I am sorry, I don't think Carlos or Amber were involved in Jennifer's abduction. I reviewed the Police Department's files and there is one person who proved to be a psychopath. I truly believe he is responsible."

I am sure Mrs. Bryan had become aware of my disappointment. I would just have to let this play out in the hopes I could change her mind. Her next words brought me back to the meeting:

"He is a drug addict named John Weeks. He lived in the duplex next door to Jennifer. He moved after Jennifer was abducted. Officers lost track of him until a psychic led them to his new location. Kathy I am going to keep working on this, I haven't given up."

CHAPTER FIFTY EIGHT—
FRANCES LONGO – BELOVED MOTHER AND FRIEND

I arrived home to lights flashing; an ambulance was parked in the driveway. I had to step back out of the way as two attendants wheeled Mom out of the house on a stretcher. I looked down into Mom's face, as they made their way to the ambulance, and I could see she wasn't doing well. I rushed alongside the stretcher and grabbed her hand, kissed her cheek and whispered in her ear that I was there with her. She didn't hear me! There wasn't any response!

Everyone rushed from the house like a swarm of bees, all headed to their cars. I hurried to Dad and asked what had happened:

"Your mother collapsed Kathy! I had to call the ambulance. Ride with me and I will tell you what I know on the way!"

Mom had been admitted into the hospital on February 30, 1990. We stayed the night, sitting in her room, talking quietly amongst ourselves. Sometimes there was just complete silence as we each contemplated our own thoughts. My thoughts weren't happy ones. I felt Mom had hung on as long as she could, she was tired and her small frail body could not hold on any longer. This was my Mother, my best friend, co-worker, searcher in arms! How could

God consider taking her when I needed her so badly? A sense of failure invaded my thoughts. Magically, mom woke up. She was so beautiful, even in that ugly hospital gown. Her heart of gold, shown from her eyes when she smiled. There were only two of us in the room at the time, Nancy and I. Mom reached out her small hand, once so strong; it shook as she patted my hand and gave it a gentle squeeze. She looked at me with her diamond bright eyes and said:

"Honey, when I die, somehow I will let you know what happened to Jennifer. I promise. Anything you want just ask for it and it will be yours. Thank you for being my daughter, I love you very much."

I was so choked up, I couldn't say a word. There were so many things I wanted to say, yet nothing could get past my closed throat. Tears and sniffles were my response to Mom. She then reached her hand for Nancy.

"Nancy, you are so beautiful, I love just looking at you my beautiful daughter. I love you with all my heart. You girls must hold our family together. Promise me!"

We both nodded; neither of us could speak because of our tears. She looked back at me and said:

"Kathy, you must stay strong. You are stronger than you realize. Never give up! Would you go get your father for me, please?"

Mom talked with Dad the longest, but she had given a loving message to each of her children. That was her way, always the strength to counter our weakness. Not thirty minutes later Mom became comatose. The last words Mom left with each of us was how much she loved us.

Mom's doctor had requested a meeting with us all in the waiting room, he said:

"Frances is a very strong woman! She has put up a very strenuous fight, but, I'm afraid the cancer in her body has metastasized. She doesn't have much time left."

Every time I had ever been sick, Mom had been at my side. Now it was my turn. I knew she was in a coma, but that didn't matter to me. In a coma or not I wanted mom as long as I could have her. She was still breathing so she still needed me. We all stayed there refusing to leave mom We decided we would take turns but none of us left her side. I even asked the nurse if my sister and I could take care of her. We wanted to be able to bathe her, change her gown and whatever she needed done. We wanted to be with her every second we could.

I did her hair and makeup. She had made me promise when we were at the Mayo Clinic to always make sure she looked nice. I kept that promise. I loved my mom more than life itself and if I could have changed places with her, I would have!

Mom never lacked for visitors. Family members from as far away as Detroit visited her. The room Mom stayed in no longer looked like a hospital room. Yes, the machines were still all there, but so were flowers, pictures, balloons and her family. The gathered family would have made Mom very happy. It was a testimony to how much we loved her! The impact she had on all our lives was immense.

Mom died on March 12, 1990. I found this poem in my mother's purse. I believe she meant it for her family to bring us comfort. I wanted to share it with you.

'Dearest loved ones, I am home in heaven.
Every restless tossing passed.
All the pain and grief over.
At peace forever in heaven, at last.
You must not grieve me, for I love you dearly.
There is work still awaiting you, so please do it fast.
When that work is completed, the Lord will call you home.
What joy to see you come at last.'

CHAPTER FIFTY NINE – FBI

I hadn't seen Mrs. Bryan in eight months and I excitedly prepared for a meeting with her. I arrived at her office and it touched me to see a picture of Jennifer on her desk. After a short wait, she walked into her office, pulled her chair close to mine and said:

"Kathy, it is so good to scc you again. First, let me tell you how sorry I am about your Mother."

The sorrow was still very fresh and I couldn't help but tear up. She handed me a tissue and asked me if she could get me a drink. I gratefully accepted. It gave me a little time to compose myself before she returned with some water. After a brief pause, she came to the reason for our meeting.

"Kathy, I met a gentleman at a seminar I attended in Orlando. He can analyze someone's statement and tell you what he is really saying. We hired him to analyze John Weeks' statement. Apparently, Weeks had worked at your parent's home and saw you with Jennifer. When he saw Jennifer that afternoon at your parents, something clicked in his mind. He recognized her as being his neighbor. It has been determined that he abducted Jennifer, raped her and in the process accidentally killed her. I would like you to meet with some representatives from the FBI. There is something they need you to do for us."

Mrs. Bryan was the only person I trusted and believed in. I know in my heart she did everything she could for me. She wanted to find Jennifer and end my pain. I know she believed this man John Weeks, took Jennifer. Mrs. Bryan was not afraid of anyone and she would have stepped on anyone's toes to get to the truth.

But I knew in that short speech, my hopes of resolving the case vanished. I didn't have a good relationship with the FBI. Dealing with the FBI when Jennifer had first been abducted had been less than satisfying.

Walking to her office door, she motioned for the agents to come into her office. They walked in looking very confident, dressed in black suits. I felt very intimidated by the three of them. I wished Mom had been there with me. Mrs. Bryan's office though large, felt claustrophobic. She introduced them as Agents Scott, Ned and Harry. Agent Scott sat in the chair Mrs. Bryan had vacated and said:

"Ms. Longo, I know this is going to be hard for you. We would never ask you to do this unless we were sure it would help this case. We can't tell you everything we have going on with this lead. If any information were to leak out, we could lose all possibilities of finding Jennifer. We would like you to visit John Weeks in jail. He is our prime suspect. We are hoping, since you are Jennifer's Mom, that you can convince him to tell you what happened to Jennifer by making him feel guilty. Do you think you could do that?"

"Let me get this straight. You want me to go into a jail cell with a man you believe abducted, raped and killed my daughter. Something I personally don't believe, and convince him to admit to it because my presence makes him feel guilty."

I paused for a moment then said; "I will do whatever you need me to do."

"Kathy, you need to believe he is guilty or this will never work. You must believe he abducted your daughter."

"Whatever you want me to do I will do it."

The strength of my beliefs were what had kept me going! These people had a lot of nerve! I sat there for the next six hours with the four of them teamed up against me. Just that little nudge of doubt. I wondered how anyone being questioned by the agents didn't eventually believe themselves guilty, even if they were innocent! I wiped weak tears away, and with my heart pounding I agreed to perform as their puppet. I couldn't afford to take the chance that I was wrong. I thought: This is what they do, they are professionals. Right? This could bring an end to my nightmare. I was ready to leave and had stood up with my arms folded in disgust except they weren't done yet! Now they told me I had to confront him and ask where he had buried my daughter. It made me sick to my stomach to think the possibility existed that he had killed her, much less believe it. How? Just how did they expect me to pull this off? I took a deep breath, and thought to myself. Okay, you can do this. If there was any chance Jennifer would be located with this scheme, I had to do whatever they asked. I wanted my daughter back home!

Agent Scott made it clear that he had been working on Jennifer's case a long time. He said it would be very rewarding for him to determine Jennifer's fate. He believed Jennifer was dead. He may have worked the case, but I LIVED IT, and I didn't believe Jennifer was dead! In my heart and soul I felt I would have known if my daughter had been killed!

Agent Scott interrupted my thoughts when he said:

"Ms. Longo, our first step is to have you visit with an FBI counselor. We would like for her to determine where you are mentally, just make sure you can handle this guy. We only have one chance at him, so we have to get this right the first time. Her name is Anna, she can help you with any confusion you may feel, I promise. Please keep an open mind to what she suggests, okay?"

He picked up the phone and requested that the counselor be notified we were ready for her in Mrs. Bryan's office.

"Ms. Longo, she is on her way!"

What could I have said? This presented me with an opportunity. As of yet, no one had listened to the entire story. It also seemed that each person who had helped me had been hurt in some manner. There had been beatings, threats of jail, divorce, loss of jobs, and even death.

The counselor walked into the office, with a warm friendly smile on her face, and introduced herself:

"Hello Ms. Longo, my name is Anna! May I call you Kathy? I am so happy to finally meet you Kathy; you are a very popular young lady!"

As Anna talked, Mrs. Bryan and the three agents exited the room. It was just as well because her friendliness broke through the wall I had built against them. Tears had started to pour down my cheeks. I had tried to be tough and strong, but it had all, just been an act. Anna had seen right through me; she saw the sadness and grief. She hadn't tried to console me, just handed me some tissue, and hugged me until my tears dried up on their own. Her shirt was wet with my tears: I tried to apologize but she wouldn't hear of it. When I finally looked at her, she had shed a few tears of her own!

"Kathy, I know this is hard to believe but I am going to help you, please have a seat. We have a lot of ground to cover before you're ready for this meeting. Are you fully aware of what they are expecting of you? They want you to confront the man who they believe killed Jennifer! In person, by yourself, in a jail holding cell. They need you to keep him in that holding cell as long as possible. Whatever it takes to convince him to talk with you. There will be a camera monitoring you, and the Agents will record your conversation as they listen. You won't be in any danger. They need a confession from him before they can move on with Jennifer's case."

"I think I do! How can I possibly act as if he did all this when I don't believe it myself? In fact I refuse to believe Jennifer is dead! Everything I have found out while chasing leads has led me to believe she is living, with a new identity."

"That may be a problem, but I think I can help you with that. First, let's start with you telling me about yourself."

Occasionally Anna scribbled something on her legal pad as we talked. The interview had been like a ping pong match. I eventually answered all of her questions, but she answered very few of mine. She was skilled in the art of subject changes and moving onto another question.

"One last question Kathy! Do you really believe Jennifer is alive?"

"There isn't a doubt in my mind Anna! Can you prove that she isn't?"

What a very long day! I had been in Mrs. Bryan's office for twelve hours. Anna walked me to my car and told me she wanted to see me one more time before the jail meeting was scheduled. I agreed, hugged her and drove home.

Just after midnight three days later, I received a phone call from Mrs. Bryan:

"Kathy, I apologize for contacting you so late. It has come to our attention that Bill Howard will likely lose this election. That means I won't have this job much longer. We need to set up this meeting as soon as possible. Have you come to terms with the part you will be playing?"

"I will do my best! Just tell me when, and I will be there!"

"How about this Friday, Kathy? Around 9:00 o'clock in the morning. Would that work for you?"

"That will be great, see you then. Oh, may I bring my sister with me?"

"That would be fine Kathy. I know we're asking a lot of you; any support you can get from your sister's presence is fine with me."

I'll admit, when I hung up the phone, my pulse was racing a little. I felt relieved; I wanted to get this ordeal over with and behind me. When I lay back down I knew trying to go back to sleep was useless. I remembered what Mom had said, that somehow she would let me know what had happened to Jennifer. I had questioned myself regularly after Mom's death and those questions returned with a vengeance. Is this Mom? Did this guy really abduct Jennifer? What about the pictures? I got out of bed and pulled out Jennifer's suitcase. I laid out the three pictures Toni Lisa had found and began talking to myself to work through my doubts.

"I know she looks older in this picture. I have proof from two specialists. Oh my God! This picture is of John Weeks."

Anna had shown me a picture of him during her interview with me. I started examining the picture closer; he was working on my parents' roof.

"This is crazy; the roof was done in 1981! A full year before Jennifer was abducted. How did Amber get this picture? Did she know Weeks before she met Carlos? Is that how they became neighbors?"

I sat on the edge of my bed and my head was spinning. I was so confused that I threw myself back flat on the bed in frustration. How I wished Mom had still been here. I missed her so much. No matter how crazy it sounded, she had always believed in me. I decided to wait before I said anything about the picture. I didn't want to mess anything up for Friday.

Nancy arrived early Friday morning. She had wanted to take me out for breakfast, but I was too nervous to eat. We were to meet Mrs. Bryan in her office at 9:00 o'clock. Mrs. Bryan had told me we had to drive several hours to get to the jail. It had been decided that everyone would ride together in one of the FBI vehicles. Nancy, Mrs. Bryan and I sat in the back while two agents sat in front. Nancy had remained silent the better part of the trip because the other three drilled me over and over again. I sat and nodded my head that I understood, but I was really reciting the Lord's prayer over and over to myself.

We pulled up to the guard gate and Agent Scott said:

"We are here ladies!"

The jail wasn't anything like I had imagined. It was a large one story building with very few windows. There was a fence around the entire complex at least twenty feet high. At the very top there was the razor wire and it looked like a long slinky being pulled around the building. The guards were intimidating as they questioned us! (Holding their guns) We walked through hallways from one barred door to the next. It felt as though we were walking through a tin can. The walls were painted an ugly gray while the floor was white with colored speckles. A guard escorted us to a small room where Agent Scott indicated that I was to sit in the chair facing the other door. The other door Weeks was to use to enter the room. He told me they had positioned a camera, inside a briefcase sitting on top of the filing cabinet, so they would be able to monitor him while we talked. He told me there were three microphones in the room, but he wasn't going to tell me where they were for fear my body language would alert Weeks. My sister and the others were to observe the interview from a closet sized room next door. I felt bad for Nancy; she hadn't really been involved in any of this before, in fact this was her first time in a jail. Thanks to the Tampa Police Department, this was my second. I wondered if anyone could see how nervous I was! I couldn't help but grimace, when my stomach tightened. I sat and stared at the door Weeks would come through; there had been a lot riding on this meeting between Weeks and I. The others had coached me, but actually doing the interview was a different story. I heard Mrs. Bryan just outside the door and she said:

"Kathy, we are right outside this door! Just try your best to get him to confess. I have faith in you! Here he comes, Kathy, good luck!"

As the door across from me opened, I was shaking inside; I was not afraid of Weeks, but I wanted to do this right. He came through the door with a very cocky attitude; as if he owned the place. He didn't look anything like I remembered him and he didn't look like his picture. He was a little huskier and cleaned up. With a hostile tone, he demanded:

"Who are you and what do you want"?

"Hello Mr. Weeks, I guess you don't remember me! I'm Kathy Longo! Jennifer Marteliz's mother!"

"Oh, yeah! I remember you! Are you wearing a wire?"

"No!"

"I am not saying another word until you bring me my attorney."

He had known just what to say! Nothing he said from that point on would have been admissible in court. The agents had coached me enough to know that but I didn't care. I thought I could still get him to talk about Jennifer.

"Please, I need you to tell me what happened to my daughter!"

"I don't know what happened to your daughter! What I do know is I am getting tired of people constantly questioning me!"

He had gotten up from his chair and had started walking toward the door.

"No wait! Please stay, I'm begging you, please stay and talk with me!"

He had turned around in mid-stride and looked at me with a bizarre expression on his face. He looked almost as if it had excited him for me to beg him to stay. I didn't care! If I had to beg him to stay, to get his attention, well, I wasn't afraid to beg. I had done worse! He sat down, slouched in his seat and let his hands dangle between his legs.

"My mother just died, I would like to bury Jennifer next to her. If you know where Jennifer's body is, please tell me. I need closure, please can't you help me?"

"Lady, I'm sorry to hear about your mother, I liked her. She was decent to me, but I don't know anything. I was buying drugs when that happened. Those cops scared the crap out of me and I thought they were there for me when I drove into my drive and saw them all around. That's all I know!"

"They allowed me to read your interview. You said Jennifer brought you your mail sometimes. Did she bring you your mail that day?"

"I am telling you the truth. I've told the cops a hundred times that I didn't have anything to do with her missing! Jennifer did bring me my mail sometimes, but not that day. I was out buying drugs like I told you! Look, I felt bad for you and your family! I even went to the Police and told them what I thought might have happened. They haven't stopped questioning me since. I just want to be left alone, serve my time and get out of here. I'm sorry, but I don't know where your daughter is!"

I got angry at his calm denial. I felt the tension in my shoulders and my head was throbbing so hard I was sure everyone in the next room could see it. He had acted like none of this mattered to him. I tried again!

"Please have a heart, give me peace. Let me bury my daughter the right way!"

"I only said those things because I liked the attention I was getting. I didn't have any idea they were going to try and pin her abduction on me. I didn't have anything to do with it. Jennifer was a nice girl, she made me laugh. I liked her!"

He abruptly stood up and walked to the door he had entered and slammed his hand against it. He yelled:

"Get me out of here!"

He turned back to look at me briefly as he walked away, and there appeared to be pure relief on his face. I lost it! I jumped to my feet, leaned as far across the table as I could and started screaming at him:

"You need to tell me the truth! Please don't go! How can you sleep at night?"

I screamed at him until he couldn't be seen anymore, finally collapsing back into my chair. I laid my head on the table. Tears streamed down my face, my shoulders shook with the intensity of my grief. The others came out of the closet, Nancy ran to me wrapping her arms around me, crying too. Behind me I heard Mrs. Bryan and she said:

"Kathy, you did a good job, you kept him talking for thirty minutes. As you know though, when he requested his attorney, anything he said afterward could not be used. I hate to say this Kathy, but you're not done yet. You have one more job ahead of you. You have to go on TV and discuss this interview. You have to inform the public that you believe John Weeks took your daughter."

Emotionally I was drained. The thought of appearing on TV depressed me. Agent Scott said:

"Kathy, you did good, real good! I want you to know that we have an undercover agent in the cell with Weeks. Sometimes after an interview like this, they get cocky. They start getting loose lips and talk. That's what we are hoping for anyway. The interview you do for TV will be aired in the prison. Guys like him like to brag about their actions."

"Is there any way to tape this interview and not show it on live TV. Everything I believe will be thrown out the window if I do as you ask. I would be telling the world to stop looking for Jennifer because you want me to say she is dead. I don't think I can do that."

Mom always knew the right thing to do, but she was gone. She had been my strength! She would give me pep talks that acted like an energy drink. She could pump me up and get me going. I felt so disoriented I didn't know what to think anymore.

Mrs. Bryan said:

"I don't think the studio would agree to that Kathy. Your story is an audience catcher and that is what they are after. Can we count on you Kathy, will you do the interview?"

"Yes, I'll do the interview!"

"Good, tomorrow at noon, we will meet you at the Kathy Fountain Show studio. I'll have my secretary arrange your visitor's pass and get directions. She should have that ready by the time we arrive back at my office."

The ride back to Mrs. Bryan's office was quiet. It seemed as though everyone had been busy with their own thoughts. I know I had been. I had decided I would appear on the show, give an interview, but I would not say I believed Jennifer was dead. There was just so far they could push me.

"Welcome everyone! Today we have Kathy Longo, mother of missing Tampa girl Jennifer Marteliz, with us! Hi Kathy, it is nice to have you on the show again. I hear you have some new information on Jennifer's case that you would like to share!"

I started to cry! God knows I hate myself when I show I am weak, but my emotions had been stretched to their limit.

"Yes, I met with John Weeks, the man the FBI believes took my daughter Jennifer. I met with him at the jail yesterday."

"Kathy did he admit to taking Jennifer?"

"No, but by the way he answered my questions, I know he did!" God would punish me for that lie! I was on national television lying to everyone. I had dug my own grave, and all that was left was to crawl into it. Basically that is just what I did after the show. I was so depressed I refused to talk with anyone. I went home, locked the door and felt sorry for myself. It didn't work for long; I awoke to the phone ringing. Before I had time to think, I had picked up the receiver. I was compelled to answer. It was Mrs. Bryan and she said:

"Hi Kathy! I wanted to thank you for everything you did. I have some bad news to tell you though. Yesterday after the show aired in the Jail, other inmates who had watched attacked Weeks. They beat him up pretty badly; he had to be confined in a cell by himself for his own safety. I'm sorry it didn't work out like we planned Kathy."

What could I do? I thanked her and hung up the phone.

CHAPTER SIXTY—KATHY LONGO

First let me say, I don't, nor have I ever believed John Weeks abducted or killed Jennifer. To me he is an open lead, just as Michael Mills taught me. His picture being in the envelope Toni Lisa found leaves me with unanswered questions, but it certainly does not confirm he abducted Jennifer.

I have had so many wonderful people try to help me find my daughter. It just hasn't been in God's time to bring her back yet. Maybe 'now' works with his schedule.

I will NEVER GIVE UP!

She is my precious baby no matter her age. I will continue to look for her until the day I die. I pray every night that she is happy and living a wonderful life. I would love to hear her voice, but a greater present would be to see her. Be able to hug her, touch her beautiful face.

To tell her how much I love her.

Jennifer if you are reading this, I love you more than you can imagine. I would give my life to see you once more!

There isn't an ending to this story! I could continue telling you about my life; How Dad died a year later from a broken heart because he missed Mom. It has been said that his ghost still waits in the house they lived in.

I could tell you about the births of my nephews, nieces, and my grandchildren. Or that I'm finally seeing a man I care for deeply. But none of that has to do with Jennifer.

My search for Jennifer was the reason for this book. It can't end until I've found Jennifer or I die. In which case I believe her sister will continue looking for her.

There have been recent stories which have renewed my faith in seeing Jennifer again. Not as a seven year old child, but as a grown woman. The age progression photo done of Jennifer portrays her as a beautiful, vibrant young lady who I greatly desire to know. Maybe a reader of my story can help me find my daughter. No better present could I receive than just to see my baby.

What Jennifer Would Look Like Today

Any Information Please Email katherinelongo@aol.com

Synopsis

Based On A True Story

A mother's world is torn apart when her seven year old daughter, Jennifer, disappears. After her disappearance her mother, Kathy, spearheads a multifaceted search that uncovers an intricate web of deceit, lies, and corruption. Numerous sightings of her daughter by multiple eye-witness' after the disappearance convinced Kathy that Jennifer may still be alive. Promising leads, close calls, and disappointment pave the road of their journey.

The family crusaded to get Jennifer's name and picture published and distributed in any conceivable form. Frances even wrote a song titled "Jennifer Where Are You?" that was distributed to radio stations around the country. Jennifer's face was on semi-trucks, billboards, magazines, and was one of the first missing children to appear on a milk carton.

This is a true story of a family's fight to find answers in a twisted world. Their goal is to bring Jennifer home, no matter what it takes.

Made in the USA
Columbia, SC
21 July 2017